Deathless Light Body Deathless Consciousness

The Future Evolution of Humankind

ThiruR.Kuppusamy

Leela publishers,

No: 9, seventh cross

Brindavan Road

Fairlands

Salem - 636004

Tamilnadu, INDIA

Cell: 9842751510, 9943045023

E.mail: r.kuppusamy@gmail.com

This book is dedicated to

ThiruArutPrakasaVallalar

எல்லா உயிர்களும் இன்புற்று வாழ்க!

PREFACE

Originally this book formed part of a bigger volume entitled "Globalization: Culture, Spirituality and Human Evolution". The manuscript has been with me for quite some time. The life and durability of anything depend perhaps upon the degree of strength with which it is marketed.

This covers only the 'the evolutionary dimension' of my book on Globalization, only about one-fifth of the book.

I believe that this book contains significant messages for mankind. The idea of writing on this theme evolved when I was asked to deliver a lecture on 'Globalization and Culture' at Sree Narayana Gurukula at Varkala in Kerala in 2000. It is my habit to explore a problem from all possible perspectives. So, when I viewed the global process of globalization from the perspectives of evolution, I gained many insights. Two books came my way. One was a compilation of the works of Sri Aurobindo called 'The Future Evolution of Man', published by the Sri Aurobindo Ashram in Pondicherry. The second was 'The Future of Man' by the French Jesuit scientist Teilhard de Chardin. I had already gone through his previous work, the immortal classic 'The Phenomenon of Man'. Hence, I started thinking on the lines shown to me by Sri Aurobindo and deChardin. Somehow, they did not serve my purpose. I found the real yoga or technology of the future evolution of humankind in Tamil literature specifically in the Thirukkural, in the Siddha literature, and in Swami Ramalinga's books. 'From whom does it come?' This question has never troubled me. Is it the truth? That is my only concern as a seeker after truth.

I consider it my duty as a human being to advance humanity to the next stage in evolution. I am eager and ready to listen to any message from any tradition, big or small, well known, or hidden. I am the proud possessor of all traditions irrespective of creed, caste, color, or time. I am a citizen of the world. This world has given me so much and I am thankful for it. When I leave this world, I wish to leave behind a better and more peaceful place for future generations, if I were to leave it.

The ideas expressed and the solutions forwarded in this small volume may not be acceptable to all. No idea will be. Atleast give your attention to the problems; humankind may not progress to the next level in evolution without solving these problems.

ACKNOWLEDGEMENTS

This book has benefited from the professional copy-editing services of Ms Shoba Rajeev.

My heartfelt thanks to her.

Leela my wife, my anchor – how can I thank her – has always been more than a better half. She has always been by my side through all life's ups and downs.

I thank Mrs. Priya for her excellent jacket design.

Without the Financial aid of Mr. and Mrs. Murugan of Sydney and Dr. Selvamatharasi @Jothy B.sc, M.B.B.S, of Malaysia, this book would not have seen the light of day.My heart felt thanks and blessings to them.

I thank Ms. Padma for typing the manuscript.

TABLE OF CONTENTS

INTRODUCTION

All the spiritual disciplines of the world can be classified into three categories viz., i] the way of the word or breath, ii] the way of consciousness or mind and iii] the way of the body.

The way of the word was upheld and extolled by almost all religions. God's word, it was asserted, was revealed to some chosen prophets such as Moses, Jesus or some Vedic rishis. To receive that divine scripture, the chosen vehicle must have the qualification of having a pure, uncorrupt body and a pure being. So, a small boy of three or five years was chosen even before the formation of the ego consciousness in him and groomed by gurus in a special, pure atmosphere of spiritual satsung. Then on the day when the process of purification of the child's body and mind was complete, the revelation of God would descend upon his body. A Dalai Lama is chosen in Tibet in this manner. J Krishnamurthy was chosen when he was fourteen by Bishop Leadbeater of the Theosophical Society for such a purpose. After the descent of the Holy Spirit upon that person, whatever is uttered by such a person is called revelation or Vedas, Agamas, Bibles or Scriptures.

What is the relationship between word and breath? Word and breath are inseparable. They are like the two sides of a coin. One determines the other. Mind is determined and created by breath and vice versa. The Siddhas say "wherever there is mind, there is breath{prana} and wherever there is breath, there is mind".[1]

The quality or level of breath determines the quality and level of mind and vice versa. When the breath goes through the left nostril called *Idaikala* a certain type of thinking takes place. When it functions through the right called *Pingala,* a different type of thinking takes place. When it operates through both the nostrils called *Sushumna,* it brings in a totally different way of mind or a silent mind or a non-mind state.

But all these three types of breathing belong to the realm of death. All three are types of human level called *SaagumKalai*[breath of death].*Kala*in Tamil means breath, [it also means light]. There is an absolutely different type of breathing, unlike human breathing. It is called undying breath [*SaagakKalai*] by Saint Ramalinga. It does not make use of the ordinary, known respiratory system like nostrils and lungs. It does not go downward to the lungs from the nostrils. It circulates inside the brain itself. It is not air. It is

----

* *Manmanamengundovaasianguundu*

Vaasiengu undo manmanamanguundu

pure prana energy having the aspects of sky, light and sound. It has all the qualities of the five senses and mind, but it is divine in quality. It is the power of creation of God himself.

It is God's breath. According to the Old Testament, when God created Adam, he made him out of clay and breathed into him His own divine breath or Holy Spirit. Thus, Adam came alive. Such a divine breath or spirit is already there in the human brain inside the pineal gland. Every human is born with it, but it is not in operation. To make it function, to bring it into operation is the way of the Siddhas. It is the 'Chit' of Satchitananda of God- truth, consciousness power and bliss. It is the second aspect of power or kinetic knowledge, the power of creation, the power of all-compassion of the absolute. It is the 'Psi' of Taoists, the 'Rhua' of the Old Testament, and the 'Holy Ghost' of the New Testament.

It is inseparable from God. That is the real meaning of the opening sentences of John's Gospel: 'In the beginning was the word; the word was with God; and the word was God'. In Hinduism it is called the Divine Shakthi or the inseparable consort of Lord Nataraja, Sivakami.

Again, in the New Testament, we find that Jesus is called 'The word made flesh', meaning the Holy Spirit clothed itself with the human form. Therefore, whatever Jesus Christ uttered was the word of God. 'I and my father in heaven are one'. Only a Jesus, a fully God-realised being, could say that. Or a Saint Ramalinga another of recent history, also a God-realised being could say that. He uttered: 'All the words I proclaim are the words of God'. *

So, a being who has contact with this Divine Breath and is blessed with the power of handling it – the only qualification being total abolition of individual ego-consciousness and attaining the absolute consciousness – by God's grace gives humanity a new Revelation, a new Veda, a new Aagama, a new Bible, a new Scripture.

Any single human being has the qualification to aspire toward it. It is his birthright given by God or nature. No person or authority can take away this right from him. Human history is a record of fights for this right also as with all the fundamental rights. This right was declared as reserved only for some chosen beings called prophets by authoritarian religions and all human beings were debarred from this right. It is recorded in the annals of Sufi literature that a female Sufi saint was killed for declaring that she had become God. It was made the sole privilege and power of churches of all religions. Only the priestly class could have access to the real import and meaning of such revealed scriptures. Kabala was supposed to be such a secret, esoteric interpretation of the Old Testament. These esoteric

---

* *Naan uraikkumvaarthaiellam*

Naayagan than vaarthai – ThiruArutpa

interpretations were kept secret by the priestly class. The power it gave and the privileges that it ensured were solely enjoyed by them. Such a class of power was born from this way of the word. When this power tried to compete with and engulf the power of kings, wars erupted between kingly powers and the priestly powers. When democracy prevailed upon the world, humankind heard the war cry of an Emerson in America: 'Let us write our own Bibles'.

It was echoed in India by Swami Vivekananda: 'Let us write our own Vedas'. Revelation {Arutpa] arose in all dialects and vernaculars. For example, in Tamil, the 12 scriptures of Nayanmars and 4000 sacred songs of Alwars were born.

Once the revelation that is the Veda became a centre of power, all sorts of corruptions entered into it and through it, into society. The powerful class or the privileged class wanted to subdue and enslave other classes permanently by wielding this ultimate weapon of the word of God. In the name of God and His word, in the name of the very truth, it was declared that only a few were chosen people of God and others were to obey them and serve them. In India, the caste system was inserted into the text of the Rig Veda and the Bhagwad Gita. According to the Hebrew Bible, only the Jews are declared as the chosen race. What followed is known history with all its ugliness and indescribable sufferings. Innumerable human lives were legally slaughtered by slavery and the caste hierarchy.

To fight this evil that masked itself as the revelation of God, the way of consciousness, the psychological method, or the way of yoga was born in ancient India.

The system of yoga covers the entire spectrum of consciousness, from the level of consciousness of a stone to the absolute consciousness of God. The purpose of yoga is to refine and expand one's consciousness to the subtle and broad levels of the consciousness of God. In short, how to purify and expand or empty human consciousness and attain the pure, absolute, divine consciousness is the way of yoga.

This psychological method was refined and perfected by the Buddha. Even before the Buddha, during the period of Indus Valley Civilization, yoga was known and practised in India. The idols of Lord Siva, the inventor of yoga technology, were discovered in Harappa and Mohenjadaro. Lord Siva is seen in advanced postures of kundalini yoga in these idols. All the meditation techniques of the Buddha and the modern New Age gurus are only modifications of the ancient yogic system of Siva and Saivism.

The Saivaite Agama literature had millions of verses written about yoga and gnana (wisdom). In fact, the Agama literature was much vaster in quantity as well as quality than the four Vedas. There were 28 major Saivite Agamas and 205 minor Agamas. Theywere divided into four sections called, Sariya, Kriya, Yoga and Gnana. Every Agama contained all the four sections and many thousands of verses in each section. In Tamil wisdom teachings, we have the exact equivalents for these four stages of yoga, namely, *purapuram* or the outermost level of man – the five outer organs or senses, the human body and the outer world; *puram*or the outer – inner equipments comprising mind; *akapuram*or the inner – individual soul or psyche with its hereditary and eternal blemishes of 'I and Mine' consciousness; and finally *akam*the innermost – the Self, the Atman representing God, the pure consciousness shorn of all stains of individuality.

*Sariya*means service done to God and humanity with the body. *Kriya* means puja or worship to God done with the mind. *Yoga* means the yearning of the individual psyche for the union with the absolute. *Gnana* means clarity of consciousness the pure state of all-consciousness. With gnana, one has reached one's destination. Life is a struggle against vegetable, animal and human levels of consciousness with their limitations, the target being the absolute consciousness. Life is a journey from limited consciousness with all its representative sufferings and sorrows born of its interaction with nature or *prakriti* to the liberated state beyond nature, and control over it. Science conquers outer nature by first understanding its laws and then conquering them by manipulation. Yoga conquers nature in the human body and mind and learns to control it from the inside. It is in a way better and more durable. One need not depend upon gadgets such as microscope or telescope but develops and refines one's own consciousness to their levels and efficiency. This is greater science, the next logical development of science. When religion loses its grip upon mankind, when the scientific community is no longer afraid of religion and its oppressive powers and superstitious beliefs, when most of humankind has turned away from religions and become secular, this step will be taken by the scientists. Until then science will be very cautious and adopt its objective stance, a stance born of fear arising out of the haunting image of burning stakes and the flames that consumed innumerable rational thinkers and scientists such as Giordano Bruno.

Saiva Agama literature is available now in the Indological society in Pondicherry. Thirumantram, the Tamil scripture contains most of Agamic lore on yoga in an exhaustive and encyclopaedic manner. This was translated into English by the noted Indian economist Dr Natarajan. Now it is published by Sri Ramakrishna Mission and by Marshall Govindan of Kriya Baba Siddha Tradition of Bangalore.

Now in the so-called 'New Age' this second way of consciousness or the psychological method is adopted and practiced all over the world. This way has been ruling humankind for the past thirty centuries or so. Secular spiritualists such as Buddha, Jain Mahavir Vardhamana, Lao Tse, Confucius, and Thiruvalluvar; the rational philosophers such as Socrates, Plato, Aristotle, Russell, Emerson, Gandhi, J Krishnamurthy, Sri Aurobindo and Vallalar are following and refining it. This is the age of psychological method.

Instead of starting at the apex with God's breath or word this psychological method starts with the intermediate level of consciousness – thought – and tries to ascend to no mind and to the pure and absolute truth-consciousness. The gradations between the two have been variously calibrated according to the times and gurus. Thiruvalluvar divides it into ten stages. Sri Aurobindo and Ken Wilber of late have been very keen on mapping out the spectrum of consciousness and labeling it in very minute details.

The third way, the way of the body was adopted by the Siddhas of Tamilnadu, the Taoists of China and the alchemists all over the world. It is not that they were not aware of the former two ways of the word and consciousness. They had known the significance as well as the limitations and evils of both ways. Then why did they choose the third way, a different, more difficult way? Because, first they were evolutionists and considered themselves as instruments, vehicles, carriers and servants of the evolutionary force based on body and organic evolution. Second, they had discovered the secrets of the human body and matter. The human body is a microcosm, a miniature universe. Humans can see God only inside the body. And 'matter shall reveal the spirit's face', as Sri Aurobindo, the latter-day evolutionary philosopher said. They wanted a more endurable, more permanent victory. They not only wanted to realize their selves and God, but also wanted to become like God with his five powers to transform the physical matter and phenomenal reality of this world into a divine, spiritual reality. They did not want to go to Heaven after death. They wanted to conquer death and live forever here and transform this world into a spiritual world or heaven. For like Sri Aurobindo, they wanted to bring down the supramental consciousness or truth consciousness of God into this world. Sri Ramalinga had very clearly formulated this ideal of 'greater life of deathlessness' and transforming this world into a spiritual heaven by making all humans attain the level of compassionate consciousness. For only compassion toward all beings can attract the power of God's grace toward this world and nothing else can do that. No power over other beings could transform a human into a superman as Nietsche and Hitler wrongly supposed.

1. GLOBALISATION AND EVOLUTION

Until the idea of evolution emerged on the world scene in 1859 by the advent of Charles Darwin's "The Origin of Species', the physical body of science lay like the inert clay-body of Adam on the mud. Then like God, Sir Charles Darwin breathed the spirit and life of evolution into its nostrils and Adam came into life. After that there was no turning back at all. Now we know that the theory of evolution was not an act of infamy against God but through the person of Darwin, it was God who instigated into the minds of humans his true religion, the religion of pure science and pure knowledge, shorn of all dogmas, rituals, the privileged priestcraft and worn-out institutions who came in between Him and His children. In his eyes, there was no division among his children, no chosen people or the slave races. He belonged and belongs to all, even to animals and plants equally. This fact, he revealed to the world through the advent of the evolutionary theory. When all the religions partitioned mankind it was science, the science of evolution that brought it together into one fold, into one family – even the inorganic and inert nature was not left out. Science voices true humanism, the real religion. If some scientists sell their souls for thirty silver coins or thirty million dollars to create weapons of destruction, we cannot blame science itself, the loving mother of mankind, who wants to give her milk of comfort to every son and daughter of hers.

~~~ ~~~ ~~~

2. BERGSON AND EVOLUTION

Bergson was perhaps the first philosopher of the west to understand the dimensional difference between thought and intuition. He rightly compared life to a running river. Thought is like a map of that river showing us only its landmarks, static points on its course. By looking at the map one cannot understand what a river is. On the contrary, if one is immersed in the river and is taken along the course of it by its drift, then he could understand the full meaning of it by directly experiencing it. Bergson calls it duration. The exact amount of experience and its full implications cannot be measured or shown by the clock, only heart or intuition by being a part of the experience can know it.

Bergson was right in his argument but only partially right. There are two differences between his point of view and that of Vedanta. First, intuition can be of two centres, of thought as well as pure intelligence. For one true intuition of truth, there are millions of false intuitions given by thought. Following these false leads, thousands of lives of scientists have been wasted; all minor poets and minor philosophers have followed these false leads to their graves.

Even with true intuition, there is a danger. A lot of energy is consumed by a single flash of intuition and man cannot withstand too many. The human body is too fine a filament of copper not to be fused and go burst against such a torrent of current.

As long as the subject, the ego, the experiencer is there, this defect and danger will be there. Vedanta says, "Become the river experience without the experiencer". This is the state of *Samadhi, Sahaja Samadhi.*

Then what happens? You become not only the river but you also go beyond it. You are at the same time the river and the witnessing consciousness as though from above with an aerial view. For you become the absolute consciousness.

The river is a part of the cosmos. You become the cosmos. You stay forever in the state of Krishna the consciousness of *Vishwa roopadharshan.* Arjuna got frightened of that state and wanted to come back to his everyday consciousness because, the experiencer, the subject, was not extinguished in him. To attain the level of Krishna is meant by the absolute consciousness. Then there is only the self always witnessing as well as taking part in the functioning of the cosmos.

Reality is a perpetual flow; Bergson understood rightly. Unless you are a participant in it, you can never understand it. This is experiencing of duration. This is also okay. However, there is something more which Bergson and all the other western philosophers were not able to understand. The participant at the same time can also be a witnessing consciousness or self beyond reality. For man is both *prakriti* and *atman.* Reality is only the *prakriti.* Upanishad says, there are two birds on the tree. One is always eating the fruits. The other is always witnessing. The first is *prakriti.* The second is the witnessing consciousness. Both together constitute man.

Life [élan vital of Bergson] is also in the flow changeable, having birth and death. Only spirit is unchanging, eternal. Bergson was right in stating that life is motion in time that can be understood only by intuition. On the other hand, spirit is beyond time and intuition. Intuition acts only as a flash, a lightning and then it is gone. Perhaps one can say that the highest level of thought or its purity is intuition. However, spirit is beyond intuition. It is a changeless condition. It has nothing to do with factors of change, with instruments of change like body and time, for both are of *prakriti.* Self is pure consciousness untainted by any changing, decaying factor of *prakriti.*

Every experience or level of experience can be understood only by its corresponding centre of consciousness. Intuition is only one centre like thought of a divided consciousness. Self is total consciousness, pervading not only the physical body but also the whole of cosmos, the Brahman-consciousness. This centre in us must be activated. For that to happen, all centers of analysis and fragmentation like thought, body, and individual sense of ego must go. Then total being with its whole energy can come into operation. Self is total energy, total consciousness. Anything that divides it even by an iota will deter us from attaining the state of *advaita,* the oneness with creation.

Evolution

When Nataraja Guru told Narayana Guru about the evolutionary theory guru asked him: what is it that evolves, matter or spirit? At that time there was no answer for that question from the west. Later, in the 1920s two philosophers, Teilhard de Chardin from France and Sri Aurobindo from India have tried to answer it.

With the advent of thinking man evolution has taken a new turn. It has become spiritual. It has become conscious. It is no longer in the hands of nature. It is in the hands of individual men. By their own conscious effort, they have to evolve themselves. When a certain number of the world's population or the critical mass reaches a stage, mutation might occur.

Who was right, Darwin or Bergson? Both, I would say. Darwin emphasized the role played by nature. Bergson pointed out the importance of the inner urge or élan vital of beings, the individual effort of the species. Both are true. Both are needed. Nature is the raw material stone. The evolutionary force is the artist, the sculptor, who creates whatever he desires to create. One thing must not be forgotten. Nature is not only the outside world but also the very body of the being.

The whole of the western culture, including all their greats, have been making a mistake here. This error is the cause of the rift between Darwin and Bergson. This error would never arise here in India. What is this error? Body is nature in miniature form. Body is microcosm. Body is world, body is the outside here. That is why it is called 'the outermost' [*purapuram*] here.

Western science says nature can be conquered only outside with advanced instruments devised by technology. Yoga says nature is your body-mind machine. Nature [*prakriti*] is you, a part of you, and your own body. Conquer nature here. It is as good as conquering it outside. It will give the same results. You will have telepathy instead of telephone or television. You will travel to the stars with a refined consciousness like a rishi, instead of in a rocket. For your consciousness is not only the maker of all your gadgets and instruments but also the ultimate instrument, both a microscope and a telescope. It can see atman, the subtlest of the subtle as well as the cosmos the biggest of the big like Arjuna.

This fact of the omnipotent power of consciousness was fully realised by the Indians-like Christ. Therefore, development took place in the inner technology of consciousness, instead of the outer technology of material science.

Nevertheless, this is obviously a more difficult job. Everyone must work very hard forthemselves. With science and technology, one need not work and can lazily ride on the back of others. One can exploit the efforts of others especially the brain of scientists and technocrats. A Marconi will give one the pleasures of a radio for a price, an Edison the enjoyment of a movie for a sum. Therefore, if one can make money somehow, by hook or crook, one can barter that for any convenience or comfort of life. Money became the all-powerful weapon of mankind, the literal ruler. Economics and its ally politics occupied the seats of wisdom.

The basic flaw is in the westerner's mind – his sense of exploitation of others born out of laziness and a desire for comfort. Unless these two *asuras* – the laziness and craving for comfort without working for it – are eradicated from every single individual of humankind, no reform, economic or political can bring about any good. This is the one truth not to be evaded or ignored. This tendency in man erected the tradition of 'hereditary kings' in all societies having power and comforts without working for them. Today, in our kingless society, it has produced the two deadliest evils – the lottery and the stock market.

Just pay ten rupees and buy a ticket. You can get a crore. You can have all the comforts of a king without working. The whole population is corrupted by this mental pollution. The raffle ticket is a modern evil, deadlier than the atom bomb. The atom bomb kills only your body, in an instant.

This goes deeper and kills your very effort, will and with it your whole life. This is mass character assassination.

Another poison gas is the stock market, the pinnacle of greed. One Mr.X is one of the richest men of India. He reached that position in a decade, through the bullish trend of it. This is just manipulation, meaningless manipulation of some forces. It does not need any hard work, physical or mental, on your part. For many centuries in the old Roman Empire and for seventy years in the Soviet Republic there was no stock exchange.

I read a dialogue from a western drama: 'what is business? It is OPM and OPW. What is it? Other people's money and other people's work.

Billions of people are labouring arduously just for winning their daily bread. Industrial houses that have been giving jobs to millions of people for centuries are pushed backward. Suddenly overnight you find one man rich beyond anyone's imagination. The government recommends this trend and upholds it with all its laws. This is madness, sheer madness. There is something terribly wrong with our civilization and its education. Greed, cunning, corruption, and manipulation – these are the only virtues extolled by government, press, and the intelligentsia. Is there any hope for man? I doubt it very much.

To pluck out these two thorns, eternal thorns from the flesh of man, the Indian *rishi* devised renunciation and tapas – renunciation of comforts and extraordinary effort to counter and destroy sloth. Every renunciate is a scientist literally, a scientist of the inner technology of consciousness, a conqueror of nature in his own body and mind.

Instinct

What is an instinct? How does it arise? These questions were not answered by Darwin or Bergson, convincingly. However Indian spirituality gives the right answer. It says, instincts are the invisible laws of nature. Only through these subtle chains, nature rules over the slaves of men. At the same time, if you are wise enough, you can make use of these same instincts for your own development.

The same instincts are also the channels, the riverbeds flowing with cosmic energy. Every instinct is a river of enormous amounts of energy. Dam it and canalise upward. You can reach the spiritual domains. When you know how to understand it and master it, every instinct is a boon to you; an unruly bull tamed and turned into a kamadhenu the legendary cow of 'give-all'. The task is really difficult but not impossible. People such as Buddha, Christ, Narayana Guru and Saint Ramalinga have already done it in their lives.

For example, when the sexual energy is sublimated it opens the faculties of intuition – highly recommended by Bergson as an alternative for thought – insight, inspiration and revelation. Freud calls this process 'sublimation'.

~~~ ~~~ ~~~

3.THE TAMIL SIDDHA TRADITION

Sri Aurobindo started his life as a yogin and a vedantin well versed in the foundations of Sanskrit tradition. Unfortunately, like everyone, he too was blissfully unaware of the most ancient but fully developed Siddha tradition in Tamil which was in most ways antagonistic to the goals and methods of Sanskrit tradition and in some ways complemented them. That was why when he wrote about 'the foundations of Indian culture', he wrongly identified it only with the Sanskrit and north Indian tradition. The history of India from the advent of Aryans has always been a dialectical conflict between the Sanskrit tradition and the Tamil Dravidian, Siddha tradition. For example, the Tamil tradition does not accept the three negations of the north Indian traditions of Vedanta, Buddhism, and Jainism, namely the negation of the body, world and life.

The Siddhas being, basically Alchemists based their theories upon matter and fully explored its science in the outer world as well as in the human body. Atomic science was known to them. The evolutionary concept of Darwin that only matter [when purified] is converted into life in the right atmosphere of water, heat and gases was known to them. The right process of such purification was also known to them. This process when completed in the outer world, in the laboratory, was called as *ema siddhi* [the power of converting any form of matter into live, philosophical gold], when completed next in the human body was known as *sagakkalvi*[the science of physical immortality]. Sri Aurobindo called these two processes as 'the transformation of the physical' and 'the transformation of the vital'. Even then in his system, the way or process of transformation is given only in yogic and philosophical terminology and methods. However, the Siddhas were real scientists competent in the advanced physical, chemical, biological and cosmological sciences. They gave the process in scientific details starting from matter first, converting it into gold and diamond, then into physical light and finally into light of consciousness or life and spirit and divine substance through total compassion.

Sri Aurobindo's concept of 'supramental consciousness' or 'mind of light' was known to Thiruvalluvar some two thousand years ago. He had named it as '*vaalarivu*'. *Vaal* in Tamil means light. Arivu means knowledge. Swami Ramalinga in the nineteenth century called it *Suddha Siva Turiyatheetham*. In the Vedas, Sri Aurobindo says, one finds that the Vedic rishis had reached only upto the level of *Guru Turiyam*.The same thought was expressed in the same words by Swami Ramalinga before Sri Aurobindo.

The aim of Sri Aurobindo's integral yoga is not individual salvation but the transformation of this material, phenomenal world into a heavenly, divine world. Again, this was uttered by Sri Ramalinga in similar words in Tamil.

He called it *Ikathai param aakkuthal* [to transform this world into the other or kingdom of God]. To make this transformation possible, Sri Aurobindo asserts, we humans must pray and work yogically 'to bring down the Supramental consciousness into this physical world from above or beyond the universe'. The method of the Siddhas differs from his. God or supramental consciousness is already here in the world in plenty. In fact, every human being is born with it. Every human's being or life force is the real temple of Chidambaram, inside which the Lord, with his supramental consciousness or truth consciousness, is eternally dancing. To consciously enter into this living temple in one's own head, through the pathway of the third eye or sacred square inch of immortality in the words of the Chinese Taoists, and see the Lord of divine light and consciousness was the entire yogic science of the Siddhas and saivites of Tamilnadu. This yogic education was called 'the education of *Thiruchitrambalam*' 'the education of God-knowledge or supramental consciousness'.[2]

The place of the third eye in the human forehead is called *Thiruchitrambalam*, meaning 'Eternal, Small [as well as chit, the divine power] Temple of God'. This complete system of education of Siva Vidya that takes place only inside the human head was the unique and ultimate discovery of the Siddhas. To explain this doctrine of immortality and eternity they built the Siva temple at Chidambaram more than two thousand years ago. The yogic knowledge was given to the common masses in the understandable form of architecture as well as in puranic stories. 'The dance of Siva' represents the complete yogic and wisdom knowledge of Tamil Siddhas. It is a scientific formula containing in itself the whole system of the Siddhas rendered in more than five thousand manuscripts, most of them still remaining unprinted, in palm leaves.

The fourth concept of 'not bifurcating and fragmenting life into two as life and yoga', which is beautifully explained in all its aspects by Sri Aurobindo in the first chapter of his immortal classic, 'The synthesis of yoga' was also known to the Tamils. Sri Aurobindo condemns the Vedantic and Buddhist concept of emphasizing only the other world at the cost of this worldly life. In the Tamil tradition, the very word, 'I' [Naan] means four extending into four divisions of man, namely i) Akam the innermost self, ii) Akappuram the inner or individual psyche, iii) Puram the outer, the mind in all its four divisions of manas, chittam, buddhi and ahankara and iv) Purapuram, the outermost or the five senses and the body along with the outer world, meaning simply all things of matter, made up of five elements.

So, man's life is one lived simultaneously in all the four levels and dimensions. This is the whole, integral life. Swami Ramalinga in his book on 'everyday regimen' called Nithya Ozhukkam, gives us four disciplines and prescriptions of behavior for each level:i) IndriyaOzhukkam pertains to the ordering of behavior of the body and the five senses or sensory living at the spiritual or divine level. That is why he condemns even shedding tears which act is meant only for expressing the anguish of a bhakta for not seeing the Lord. In "Karana Ozhukkam', he elaborates on the various techniques of disciplining the mind, the most important one admonishing everyone to always keep his attention inside the forehead, in the third eye waiting at the gate of the Lord's temple for its opening. All the senses should be focused only on this spot. All activities physical, mental, vital, and spiritual must be done only centred at this spot. One's consciousness should never leave this place.

'Jeeva Ozhukkam' aims mainly to cleanse away the ancient hereditary stain of karma or aanavamalaa or individuality. It admonishes us to love and sympathize with all human beings irrespective of caste, creed, color and all divisions in mankind. In short, "love thy neighbor as thyself". It covers almost all aspects of eradicating the disease of 'I and Mine' – consciousness. All acts of compassion or jeevakarunya like poor-feeding are stressed emphatically. Not even yoga, meditation, tapas or austerity is given as much emphasis as acts of compassion to other beings.

'AanmaOzhukkam' is something unique about the Tamil tradition, SuddhaSanmargam in particular. It goes beyond 'humanistic tendencies' of the western humanist tradition as well as most of the world's religions.

It says love thy neighbor as thyself. But do not stop here. Love all beings as thyself, not only humans but also all sentient beings, vegetable, animal etc. There is one more dimension to it. Love all beings not only as thyself but as the dancing God. Therefore, when you see and approach any being, approach it with the reverence, worship and prayer you would normally give to the Lord in a temple or church. For the being is the real dwelling house of the Lord, not the structure ofbrick, mortar or stone. Moreover, life means only the interaction between two live beings, not between man and inert matter. That is a dead and inert relationship. Every moment, have a relationship of love and compassion with any being animal, vegetable or human. Your body, mind, soul and psyche should be stripped of all thoughts, feelings, emotions, and actions. All that remains should be compassion for all beings in a reverential and worshipful manner. Thus, every being is God. Every moment you are in prayer. Every act is an act of meditation upon and interaction with God himself. What are the consequences of such a doctrine of compassion toward all beings? Killing any human, animal or tree for any reason whatsoever is prohibited. Eating flesh is totally forbidden. Not only war, but also all sorts of violence like fishing, whaling and the like are condemned as sin. The first article of Truth or test of it is non- killing.

Onraaganalladhukollaamaiathan pin saara

Poyyaamainanru – [Kural]

[The number one value in morality is non-killing. Even truth ornon-lying comes second], says Thirukkural whose spiritual commentary and interpretation was the teaching of SuddhaSanmarga of Ramalinga Vallalar.

Sri Aurobindo was born a poet. A poet by nature cannot remain in renunciation of the world either of Vedanta or Buddhism. His temperament is after beauty that is sensual, intellectual, spiritual, divine. So, by compulsion of his temperament, every poet transcends Vedanta and enters into Neo-Vedanta and starts enjoying the aesthetic splendour of this world, this life and this body also. This was the story of the birth of Neo-Vedanta first in Bengal. This new stream of Vedanta had its source in the poetic genius and temperament of Rabindranath Tagore, the world-renowned Bengali poet. This new school of Vedanta was further developed by Swami Vivekananda who wanted to mix science with religion and found a universal religion.

Swami Vivekananda was also well versed in the scientific literature of his time. He was constantly updating his knowledge both scientific and spiritual. He also understood the vital fact of his day that without accepting the theory of evolution one cannot get admitted into the scientific community. Without being known as a scientist or at least as a man with a scientific point of view of life, one could not get recognition in the western world. Moreover, he was a master yogi. Yoga is the scientific way of transforming the raw materials of nature into pure, artistic, whole products of beauty either of body, mind or spirit. Science condenses, compresses and miniaturizes all natural products and processes in the world, say, for example, the billion years long process of trees being transformed first into carbon and finally into diamonds, is being done in the laboratories in a few minutes by artificially applying the same amount of enormous heat and pressure. Similarly, yoga compresses and miniaturizes the 400 billion year long past evolution and the unknown future evolution of man into a short span of a man's lifetime or even in a few years or as Swami Vivekananda emphatically asserts in six months. He was in correspondence with the English evolutionary thinker, Herbert Spencer. He also met him in London.All these western influences forced him to go beyond academic or pure Vedanta and update it to include scientific theories like evolution into forming Neo-Vedanta.

In my humble opinion, Sri Aurobindo was an extension of Swami Vivekananda and his teachings in all its aspects and more. Sri Aurobindo was a greater personality, more gifted in faculties, training, preparation and achievements. He was also blessed by God with longer and fuller life. His attainments and achievements as a yogi, philosopher, poet, religious thinker and so on were far greater than and superior not only to Swami Vivekananda but also to any man in the nineteenth century, except perhaps Swami Ramalinga. These two were the greatest synthesizers of all knowledge both human and divine. They were not only spiritualists, but they had also understood the truth of science as the only way to truth.

The only snag or limitation in the case of Sri Aurobindo was the fact that he had to labourvery hard to discover the laws of the transformation of the physical, the vital and the psychic into the Divine substance by bringing down the light mind or supramental consciousness. He arrived at his conclusions originally and ingeniously by his own effort and in his own way and expressed them in noble and beautiful English, philosophically in his 'Life Divine' and in practical yogic terminology in his 'Synthesis of Yoga' and in his 'Letters on yoga'. It was unfortunate that he was not able to tap the enormous amount of knowledge of the Siddha tradition fully available as a complete science in Tamil. Perhaps he came to know about the basic and rudimentary principles of it through his Tamil friends such as Subramania Bharathi, V. V.SubramaniaIyer, Chidambaranar and so on. He also started learning the Tamil language and translated some of the sacred poems of Nammalvar from Tamil into English. He also mentions later in one place in his vast literature that some of the Vaishnava saints of the Tamil land had attained the level of supramental consciousness.

For an English reader, it would be a better plan to first get acquainted with the teachings of Sri Aurobindo in English and later to compliment and complete it with the teachings of the Tamil Siddhas and of Swami Ramalinga in particular. Some of them are available inEnglish but mostly still in Tamil untranslated into English, which laudable task is being done by a modern-day Siddha yogi, Marshall Govindan of Canada. Not only the Tamil world but the whole of humanity is indebted to him for making these vital, scientific, spiritual ideas available to the whole world whose impact, I believe, will manifest in the future as a third Renaissance of the world. Most of the questions posed by the so-called pure vedantins as well as scientists such as 'can matter become life?' and so on are already answered by Sri Aurobindo, the Spiritual Master, beautifully and convincingly. The Tamil people should also thank him for rendering their tradition and its major principles into beautiful, philosophical and yogic masterpieces in chaste and grand English, and made known to the whole world.

In short, if one wants to know about all the vital knowledge about human evolution and its next mutation and advancement, he is advised to go to the writings of Sri Aurobindo and the Mother and then to the teachings of Siddhas and finally to the culminating and crowning achievements of Swami Ramalinga both in his writings as well as in his life-events, his gospel of deed and word. The greatest act was his conscious transformation of the physical into a body of wisdom-light by total compassion for all beings.

~~~ ~~~~~ ~~~

4. TEILHARD DE CHARDIN, SWAMI RAMALINGA AND HUMAN EVOLUTION

Teilhard de Chardin [1881-1955], the French scientist cum Christian theologian occupies a unique place among thinkers on human evolution such as Sir Charles Darwin, Samuel Butler, Nietsche, Bernard Shaw, Henri Bergson, Sri Aurobindo, Tholkappiar and Swami Ramalinga of Tamilnadu. The west may not be aware of the last two names; but as usual, the hidden traditions like the Tamil have also produced some of the intellectual and spiritual giants. By forgetting or ignoring them, it is humankind that stands to lose by way of essential knowledge or experience.

To be precise Tholkappiar was the first grammarian of the Tamil language who had discovered and announced to the world in his immortal classic *Tholkappiam*, the law of evolution by sensory organs – the first sense to develop was touch [e.g plants], the second, the tongue or taste [e.g mollusks such as conch], the third,the nose or smell [e.g ants], the fourth, the eye or sight[e.g insects], the fifth, the ear or hearing [e.g. animals] and the sixth, the mind or the reflective consciousness [e.g. man alone]. Without the reflective or self-consciousness, most men remain animalistic with five senses [maakkal]. Exactly when did this turning point in human evolution with the reflective consciousness happen? It was Teilhard who gave the exact time. He says that this 'frightening power suddenly emerged in a Pliocene primate, to change the whole face of the earth in the course of a million years'. It was Tholkappiar who showed the world the only difference between man and animal – self-consciousness. Man is called by him 'the higher species, UyarThinai', meaning the species whose consciousness keeps on developing and enlarging till it reaches the absolute consciousness of Godhead. All other beings are called by him as 'the lower species, Akrinai' because their consciousness keeps narrowing down. Man's consciousness is not bound by his body whereas the consciousness of lower species is bound by their bodies. Man alone is conscious of his own consciousness. This point was well understood and elaborated by Teilhard throughout his book, 'The Phenomenon of Man'.

The further implication of the discovery shows humankind the direction in which his strength lies, in the inner consciousness. The culmination of the development of consciousness is 'love energy' which alone can lead man to the Omega point or Christ –consciousness. The great sage Thiruvalluvar equates life energy with love and also declares that the immortality of man is possible only with the development of love. In short, Christ-consciousness was nothing but total compassion.

The nature of life is love,

The immortality of life is love.

[Anbinvazhiathuuyirnilai]

Spiritual intelligence is born only of love, says Swami Ramalinga.

Intelligence is the light emanating from love.

[Anbenumuyirolir arrive]

Saint Thiruvalluvar and Swami Ramalinga go further and equate love with God himself, the power that created God, the power that created and sustains the universe.

Only fools say love and Siva are two

Only love becomes Siva, nobody knows this – Thirumoolar

The form of Sivam is love – Swami Ramalinga

This, in short, is the summing up of Teilhard's unique discovery in the theory of evolution – that of bringing into its scientific fold, the role of 'love energy' and defining supermanhood as Christ-consciousness unlike Nietsche's superman of mental power. Both these points he might have taken from the tenets of Christianity or he might have come into contact with the Tamil wisdom either through his reading of Sri Aurobindo's workson evolution in French or hemight have got this information directly during his travels in India between 1928 – 1938. However, the similarities between the evolutionary philosophy of Teilhard and the spiritual evolution of the Tamil Siddhas particularly Swami Ramalinga of the nineteenth century [1821-1874 the year of transformation of his body into a wisdom-light-body] must be kept in mind.

Cosmogenesis must precede human genesis, says Teilhard. The creation of matter is the background for the evolution of man. The purpose of matter is to give a push to life as well as negative restriction. Life comes out of matter. That was why he called matter 'pre-life'. Matter itself contains the seed or tendency toward life. That was the reason why Sri Aurobindo declared, "Matter shall reveal the face of the spirit", and the Mother said 'salvation is physical'. And these ideas of Cosmogenesis and life-properties of matter were well documented by Tholkappiar and the Siddhas of the Tamil land. Perhaps Sri Aurobindo and the Mother were influenced by them or by Darwin and Henri Bergson's 'Matter and Memory'.

The Siddhas like the Alchemists of the west had known about the secret of matter, about the first matter or universal matter or universal solvent that could dissolve any object in the world. Again they dreamt of and talked about creating "homunculus' or artificial human beings in the test tube from matter. From matter to life to mind to spirit to divinity – the formula of evolution was well known to them and it is amply documented in their innumerable books. The westerner could sample their knowledge by reading a few pages from 'Poets of Power' by Mr. Kamil Zvelabil, the Tamil scholar fromCzechoslovakia.

For them physics of matter entered into biology of life, then into thought of metaphysics and finally into the religion of spirit, there is no division in knowledge. And this total knowledge is available in the human body – from matter to God. Here is what Claude Sumner says of Teilhard:

Already he was conceiving a generalized physics, which would not be metaphysics, and which, without rejecting the transcendental principles of classical metaphysics, would satisfy the craving for totality which, underneath all the compartmentalizing and all the difference in techniques, is the hidden impulse of the scientific spirit: 'I should be happy to see you do what I am trying to do, that penetrates still further into spiritual and human questions by the use of the methods of science, substituting for the metaphysics of which we are dying an ultraphysics [the real phusike of the Greeks, I imagine] where matter and spirit would be embraced as one single coherent and homogeneous explanation of the world. [pp192. Volume II 'Philosophy of Man'outline of his philosophy: integral evolution]. "Teilhard's great discovery was the recognition of a cosmic focus in evolution, with all the consequences implied in the notion of cosmic convergence; the law of complexity-consciousness; the confluence of human branches, the existence at the summit of noogenesis of an Omega point, the rebound of evolution through the energy released by the conjunction of cosmic and Christic." These conclusions are derived from Teilhard's attempt to build a total science of the planet Earth in the terms of Julian Huxley, from his essential achievement of linking science and religion across the bridge of evolution.

Teilhard's endeavour was to sketch a unified science of the globe. Where physics ordinary accounted one thing and biology another, Teilhard was struggling to create a generalized physics, one which would embrace such forces as are found in life-consciousness, spontaneity, even probability. For he saw life as part of a universal process, terrestrial life being a function of the sidereal evolution of the globe [a function in its turn of total cosmic evolution]. It is true that one of the branches of biology is called anthropology; but it later, as Teilhard knew it, was the study of the flesh and bones of man, excluding, as not relevant to positive science, man's incredible power to think, so that man, precisely in his most human aspect, remains a kind of embarrassing leftover.Teilhard, in contrast, envisaged a generalized biology, insisting on the totality of human phenomena as an integral part of nature, of Earth and of cosmic evolution. Thus, Teilhard not only created a generalized biology, in which the noosphere the thinking envelope of the earth, is the natural crowning of the biosphere, but also integrated such a biology with a generalized physics, in which the biosphere, as the legitimate issue of the hydrosphere, is the normal consequence [given favorable conditions] of cosmic evolution.

The consequences of this realisation of the wealth of the cosmos as concentrated in the single phenomenon of man are tremendous. In the first place, matter – Sacred matter – is conceived as the medium of spiritualization, the spirit is born in the heart of the matter and as a function of matter'. [op. cit pp 196-197]

Teilhard's phenomenology is total. He sees man as a total; comprising of nature, beings and god. According to the Siddhas man is four in one, nature, life, spirit, and God. Their division of man is four fold;

i] (Aham inner) = spirit and God

ii] (ahappuram) inner outer = life

iii] (puram) outer = mind

iv] (purappuram) outer outer = five senses and the world

The inseparable character of man with the world is emphasized by them. Whatever happens in the outer world, pollution and the likes is bound to reflect in the body-mind machine of man and vice versa. Thus, ecology is not a separate something belonging to outside nature as the westerner thinks. Man is not the boss to lord over nature.

He is nature incarnate. His body and mind are built up by materials from nature. Ecology as far as the Tamils were concerned was not physical but spiritual. That was why Tholkappiar when he designed his psychology of man's mind, called it 'the inner landscape' reflecting five types of land.

The Tamil word Thinai means classification. The world is classified as i] lower nature [Akrinai] comprising of all nature, mineral, vegetable and animal and ii] higher nature of man endowed with self-consciousness [uyarthinai].

The physical land, as well as the inner space of man, is classified into five lands reflecting five types of moods:

1. Mountains – Kurinchi
2. Forest – Mullai
3. Farmland – Marudham
4. Seashore – Neithal
5. Desert - Palai

The poets were asked to sing their songs according to this classification. A mood of depression can have only a desert as the right background. Ecology was for them poetic and spiritual. The ancient Tamil community had developed their sensitivity to a highly advanced stage. This material world itself had been transformed into a world of spiritual experience. The whole sangam literature is an evidence for the fact. How they declined to the present pitiable material condition of poverty and illiteracy, lethargy and inertia is a million-dollar question before sociologists and anthropologists.

Teilhard had somehow captured their vision of life's totality and man as a total phenomenon. To quote from the same book:

'Phenomenology – in the most general and the deepest sense of the term, his philosophy is phenomenology. The word itself is used only in the phenomenon of man, as a synonym of generalized physics. Referring to the quarrel between materialists and the upholders of a spiritual interpretation, he writes, 'I am convinced that the two points of view require to be brought into union, and that they soon will unite in a kind of phenomenology of generalized physics in which the internal aspect of things as well as the external aspect of the world will be taken into account.(Vallalar had already done it in his suddhasanmargha).

The phenomenology of Hegel had attempted to constitute a total logic of reality, a rational dialectical development of history and the categories of spirit.

In agreement with Hegel on the inseparable character of man and the world, it is on several points in opposition to him.

Like Husserl and Merleau – Ponty and against the abstract separation of materialism and spiritualism, Teilhard renounces the dualism of matter – spirit, body andsoul.

But he objects to their type of phenomenology because it does not include conscience on the objective reality of the universal movement of reality'.

Integral Evolution

The science Teilhard has in mind will present man in afully integrated way.

First integration: within man himself. The radical dualism of matter and spirit, of body and soul, dissolved before his eyes, like fog before the rising sun. Matter and spirit seemed no longer two things, the latter reducible to the former, but two states, two aspects of one and the same cosmic stuff. Spirit which slowly emerges from matter takes precedence over the physical and chemical, and it is in spirit, in the highly complex, that all substantiality, all consistencyresides, so that we must not look backward to matter but forward to spirit. [pp 200]

How is a spiritual dimension born in man? Listen to Teilhard: 'it is in spirit, in the highly complex, that all substantiality, all consistency resides'.

Substantiality, consistency– these two words are the key words in the transformation process – from matter to life, from life to mind, from mind to spirit. Density is the way. Carbon of the body or mind, or life must be turned into diamond under enormous artificial and yogic pressure and heat generated by penance. Consciousness solidifies, becomes dense and a magnetic centre and objective consciousness of man number 7 – in the words of Gurdjieff – are born. Love is the magnet that draws towards it all consciousness and gets larger and denser and finally with compassion arrives at Christ consciousness or Omega point. Thought-energy or noosphere is transformed into spiritual energy or Omega point. Saint Thirumoolar saw this process and declared it to the world in the following verse:

If the body goes, life goes

One cannot get solidified consciousness of enlightenment

I knew the secret of longevity

I lived long by developing my spirit [love energy]

Let us continue with the summing up by Claude Sumner of Teilhard's philosophy.

Second Integration: Teilhard had a strong sense of Earth, a sense which although congenial, was developed by his experience as a research scholar working with international scientific teams and societies. His idea of human convergences, his hope that mankind would find through socialization, the self-realisation which it seeks increased his distrust of the literatures. By literatures he meant those who see man as a kingdom within a kingdom and are blind to his roots in the cosmos and to the fact that socialization is by nature biological since its roots go back to animal socialization. For a long time, like everybody else, I nearly choked in the old habit of considering man in nature as an anomaly. But now that my eyes are open, now can I say that in the justified awareness of being one with the whole world, I have found myself anew, and that I breathe at ease.

As far back as 1926, he contemplated a kind of book of earthwherein he says, 'I should let myself speak not as a Frenchman or as belonging to any separate category but as man or simply as planetarian. I should undertake to express the confidence the ambitions the fruition and the disappointments too the insecurities and the feeling of dizziness of one who has realised what destiny awaits the earth: mankind as one complete whole. I should not be concerned to reach agreement with any of the accepted currents of thought only with expressing endeavour and in human unity and my impatience with all the petty barriers that divide and isolate minds whose true future lies in coming together. I should like too to picture the frustration we feel at finding ourselves imprisoned on one little sphere which will soon have nothing more to offer us and our desolation when we realise that we are all of us equally alone in starry space'.

Socialization is the way of salvation, says Teilhard echoing Christ's faith without works [service] is useless and 'love thy neighbor as thyself' and 'love thy enemy'.

Wisdom is the key to the house of moksha [freedom], says an ancient Indian proverb. This unfortunately made people renounce society and go to lonely mountain spots to do penance and attain gnana or wisdom. Society was ditched by these greats. Teilhard, the Christian and Saint Ramalinga, the compassionate do not agree. The saint declares:

Compassion is the key to the house of freedom.[3] Integration not separation is the way. More and more of expansion of consciousness is the way of Zen and yoga, leading finally to cosmic consciousness of viswarupa of Krishna.

Third integration: With the Christic – in a letter of October 8, 1947, to G Barbour he writes, I devoted myself more and more to the study of what I am calling the phenomenon of man i.e. the study of humanization in its present phase, something which naturally leads me to search deeper for the relationship and necessary connection between Christianization and humanization.

How was this connection and integration achieved? The notion of the universal Christ achieves the synthesis between the cosmic and the Christic and so by a stroke of genius what might have been pantheist becomes a pan-christicism that preserves human personality while drawing all to converge upona universal person –Christ omega. This synthesis between the god above [the classical transcendent god] and the god of the future [the immanent god] whoseface has been revealed in evolution as a phenomenologist and in particular by disclosing the Christic function of the universe. Thus, the human is the necessary unit between the cosmic and the Christic; for the noosphere is an essential stage between the biosphere and the ultra-human. And so, cosmogenesis proceeding through anthropogenesis culminates in a christogenesis.

The first integration takes place in man. Divisions in the mind and body go. C.G. Jung's individuation process stops here. Swami Ramalinga calls this Discipline of senses and mind.

The second integration takes place between man and humanity. Religions speak about this brotherhood of man. Even atheists like Marx accept this level. Swami Ramalinga calls this level of discipline as the discipline of the individual life force of Jiva. Treat all men irrespective of caste or creed race or religion as yourself.

The third integration is the most difficult. It is the integration of man with all beings as well as all matter in cosmos. This is the ultimate stage in the evolution of compassion. When Buddha offered to sacrifice his body in order to save a lamb, when Christ died on the cross for the sins of humanity, when Swami Ramalinga wept at the breakdown of a piece of mud clot under his foot, they were demonstrating this. To see allbeings and even matter as your spirit is the final integration.

Human Energetics

At a time when science was already progressing towards a synthesis of the laws of matter and of life, Teilhard was going still further. He envisaged a unification of the laws of physical chemistry with the laws of physical psychology; as a part of the latter he was elaborating a human energetics and spiritualized energy seemed to him the flowering of cosmic energy. This human energetic is one of the most original points in Teilhard's thought and gives further testimony to his inclination for synthesis – synthesis of matter, life and reflective intelligence and synthesis [leading to a panenergetics] of physical energy and psychic energy.

The discovery of the noosphere as the last of the scientific series [barysphere, pyrosphere, lithosphere, hydrosphere, biosphere] to which he was to add the christosphere – was a step towards the integration of man with the cosmos, entailing as well a cosmic view of man's situation.

The revolution introduced by Teilhard into the thought of his day through the definitive substitution of Cosmogenesis for the notion of a static cosmos, may therefore be outlined in two successive and complementary synthesis; first the noosphere as synthesis of the cosmic and the human; second the christosphere as synthesis of the cosmological and the Christological[pp 65'].

Human energetics is the new branch of science that can transform man's body and mind into those of a spiritual

Christ. Gurdjief and Ouspensky talk of an elaboratesystem of hydrogens and how to produce and store them in the human body. Perhaps they got the system from Madam Blavatsky's 'The secret doctrine'. She might have got it from the Indian rishi who wrote Taitriya Upanishad or from a Siddha.

Swami Ramalinga was an adept in this science. He says there are four things which lead man to death: food, sex, sleep and fear. All these four must be gradually eliminated. Alternative sources of energy like inner breathing, transforming and sublimating sexual energy into ambrosia and love, bhakthi and compassion must be developed. His very life was an example of what could be accomplished with the science of bioenergetics about which Teilhard touched only the lid.

~~~ ~~~~~ ~~~

5. MIND AND NO MIND

Mind is represented by the westerner's psyche. The typical example was Socrates, Man-thinking, as Emerson used to say. The poet, the scholar, the scientist, the technocrat – all are only variations of the thinking man. The basic unit of mind is image. And its various denominations are the sign, symbol, word, sound, thought, ambition, imagination, intuition and so on. The thinking man is a stage in evolution. This stage has to be consciously transcended. This learning to think is essential before remaining thoughtless. Man must first learn to think through any subject and correctly. This habit is fully represented by a scientist and technologist. It must precede before learning yoga, the art of stopping to think like an Indian. In this aspect, the westerner is going on the right path perhaps and the Indian, by avoiding thinking totally is mistaken. The root cause of all the miseries of the Indians is that they donot know how to think properly. This is unfortunately not taught in schools or colleges. That is why the average Indian relies upon any cheap, selfish politician who promises to think for the public. One fact is forgotten in India that democracy needs two qualities for its survival, tolerance and individual discriminative thinking. Only the former is kept to some extent in India but cannot go on for long. The cause of ills accruing from politicians, bureaucrats, goondas, robber barons of industry is this neglect of thinking on the part of the voting public. This was not so in ancient India when philosophical systems flourished everywhere, and philosophical debate and discussion in the marketplace was an everyday common sight. This fact is ignored by modern Indian mystics and seers. They want their illiterate public to leap into mystical states without going through the right channels. All the textbooks of Vedanta advocate argumentative thinking as the initial way for the student before going to the final stage of experiencing non-dual science. Sankara's books are ample proof of this fact.

Self-consciousness is an essential stage in the evolution of consciousness. From herd-instinct, through self-consciousness to cosmic-consciousness, from man to a Buddha – this is the right form of conscious evolution. A Buddhist or a vedantin must be a scientist first and the scientist must learn silence. Only then will the world have complete men and be free from the dangers of fragmented minds.

In the western intellectual tradition, this process can be seen in the lives and works of literature of Jung, Goethe, Dante and Homer.Jung and Goethe represent fully the second stage of self-conscious human. The first, the animal stage is unfortunately represented by the common consumer of the west. This reversing of the natural original evolutionary process is the dangerous aspect of consumerism. It is a threat to man's survival. If this consumerism continues and succeeds all over the world -

the man turned into an animal again -he shall be left behind by the élan Vital as it has done in the past with dinosaurs and other innumerable species. It is the foremost duty of the leaders of the western intellectual tradition to warn the public and stop them from the second fall of man. With this second fall perhaps, there would be no redeemer. The species could be extinguished once for all from the face of the earth.

The I T revolution and computer education are the right signals given by the evolutionary process. They are making even people from the rural areas of India to think. For the first time, man is becoming a man, self-conscious animal in the process of thinking. Learning mathematics is the right way to become a thinker – an objective, scientific thinker free from prejudices and idiosyncrasies. When more than 50 percent of the world's population achieves computer literacy, mankind will enter into its next phase of evolution that is the spiritual phase. Not before. A Buddha, a Christ, a Sankara, and a Thiruvalluvar – these few individuals are not the whole ofmankind however great and illumined they were. All the cells in the body go to make a human body. The loss of one cell is also the loss of the body. Which cell in the body is me? Every cell. Thus, every cell is important and must become fully conscious, fully alive to make the body totally awake. The meditative technique of vipassana discovered by Buddha teaches only this wisdom. The east must learn the art of thinking and computer literacy from the west, not its base consumerism. The west must learn the yoga of silence from the east. Only then the human species has a chance for survival.

In 1924 Jung travelled to America. There he met OchwiayBiano [Mountain Lake], the chief of Taos Pueblo Indians. He revealed a truth about the white man's psyche to Jung and he agreed with him. Jung writes: He struck a vulnerable spot and unveiled a truth to which I was blind.

'See', OchwiayBiano said, 'how cruel the whites look. Their lips are thin, their noses sharp, their faces furrowed and distorted by folds. Their eyes have staring expressions; they are always seeking something. What are they seeking? The whites always want something; they are always uneasy and restless. We do not know what they want. We do not understand them. We think that they are mad. They say they think with their heads not with their hearts as we do. [Head – thinking is an act of self-consciousness, a fragmented consciousness and heart thinking here is nothing but herd instinct of animals, man–animal one can say, not compassion of a Buddha.]

Jung reflects: I fell into a long meditation. For the first time in my life, so it seemed to me, someone had drawn for me a picture of the real white man'. Here started the mid–life crisis of Jung and he discovered the remedy in his own brand of yoga, 'the process of individuation'. Every white man must follow the footsteps of this sage of Switzerland, not the voice of the advertising media which will take him and his culture to the grave and not to any real substance or immortality.

Even this sage was mistaken in one aspect. He said that it was dangerous for a white man to learn yoga from the east. Perhaps it was mere professional jealousy. Millions of white people have learnt yoga and have proved him wrong. His predecessor Goethe was right when he said:

> East and west
>
> Can no longer be kept apart
>
> For the human species is one.

Goethe's creation of Faust was the exact portrayal of a modern man of the west. Goethe, the true poet was the right voice of the evolutionary force. In 1826, he writes about Faust.

He is a man who feels impatient and ill at ease in the limitations of earthly existence, regarding even the possession of the highest wisdom, the enjoyment of the best that life can offer, as incapable of satisfying his aspirations in the least, so that he comes back from any experience he essays unhappy than before.

This monster without aim or peace he calls himself in the Urfaust. Faust and Goethe long for the fullest experience of life, even though he is convinced that nothing will satisfy him.

Now contrast this, 'longing for the fullest experience of life on this earth' with a Buddha's, a Sankara's or a Christ's longing for total renunciation of this life and entry into the other world.

Faust and Goethe will feel satisfied only with this spiritual culture of the east, not with his professed self-culture of the physical of the artistic, the intellectual, and the emotional centres. For total integrity, one more centre of consciousness has to be tapped and experienced: the spirit.

The level of consciousness of a Faust or the modern man of the west is well illustrated with a parable in Vedanta. A dog bites into a bone. The blood oozes. It sucks the blood and enjoys the taste. But the truth is, there is no blood in the food, in the bone. The bone pierced the upper roof of its mouth and blood comes out of the wound. The dog is sucking and tasting only its own blood, mistaking it to be coming from the food. No, the taste comes from within, from the spirit. Bone or food or the external object is only a switch, an instrument that brings on the light of the taste. When all the taste the bliss is inside, in one's own spirit, one's own consciousness, why rely, unnecessarily on the outside world? asks Vedanta.

Again, this exclusiveness on the experience of the spiritual at the cost of the physical is one-sided. The right answer perhaps was provided by Homer's Ulysses. The tradition was followed later by Virgil's Aeneus and Dante in his Divine Comedy. It is to learn and master the secrets of both the physical world and the spiritual world and enjoy both from this station, the earth. Ulysses learns to enter into Hades and comes back, Aeneus does the same. Ulysses is not deceived by the words of Circeand wants only one thing, to go back to his wife Penelope and to his homeland. Dante went one step further. In his reverie or meditation, he travels like Ulysses and Aeneus not only into hell, but he also goes to purgatory and the very heaven, the spiritual world where God lives and comes back to this world. Now the development of consciousness is almost complete. I say almost because he has not mastered death and conquered nature – both physical and spiritual. This was done and the cycle completed by the Tamil Siddhas, particularly in the life of Saint Ramalinga [1823-] of Vadalur in Tamilnadu. A Siddha is one who sees the spiritual world from his seat here on earth.

Siddharsivayogamingeyetharisithaor

---Saint Thirumoolar

Saint Ramalinga consciously converted his body of flesh into a body of light, which he claims, can never be destroyed. With this body of spiritual light given to him by God he could travel in an instant to all the galaxies. The Siddha becomes a complete astronaut capable of travelling in both physical and spiritual worlds like God. His spaceship is his own immortal fully conscious spiritual body of light. The first man of light body was Saint Ramalinga of Tamilnadu, the pioneer of the next phase in human evolution.

The scientific process is detailed step by step in his elaborate works. His message was the conquest of physical death and the life of immortality for everybody.

The right model for the west to follow now is the middle path of the ancient Tamil tradition, particularly, the way of Thiruvalluvar, a thoroughly practical saint. He says emphatically, 'for one who has no money, this world is not. Therefore, make money first. Make money out of efficiency and also with ethics. Money is made of creating ideas [iyatral] a very modern concept. And for one without compassion, there is no other world of bliss.

He writes about 780 couplets on living in this world and 250 couplets on sexual life, a total of 1030 out of 1330 couplets.

~~~ ~~~~~~ ~~~

6. CQ – CONSCIOUSNESS QUOTIENT OF A PEOPLE

IQ [intelligence quotient] and EQ [emotional quotient] are only half-measures. The real measure of a man or a people or a tradition is the CQ [consciousness quotient]. CQ is the numerical point or a degree of awakening of a man or a people.

Total awakening of pure consciousness is the absolute consciousness as manifested in a Buddha or Christ or a Saint Ramalinga. *PragnanamBrahmam*. Lesser degrees of awakening of consciousness are manifested in great poets, scholars, scientists, and all creative people. The common man or woman is only partially awake. He or she does not awake fully in life ever. As the Koran says, man is born in sleep, lives in sleep and dies in sleep. Our wakeful state is only partial sleep. Total permanent conquest of this inertia, this spiritual sloth, accidie, laziness and perennial sleep is called awakening or enlightenment. Even a great scientist like Einstein wakes up perhaps for a few moments and receives a flash of intuition about the theory of relativity and falls back into normal sleep once again. Man is by nature a somnambulist; all of us are, to some extent sleep-walkers. Creativity is a peep into the outside, real, sleepless reality for some time. Thus the more there are creative people in a society, there is renaissance, renewal of life, upsurge, prosperity and success. All problems are seen in new perspectives and solved in new ways. Nationwide movements are indications of such mass upheavals in consciousness. War is the natural but negative mechanism of this phenomenon. Cultural renaissance born out of cross-pollination of minds and ideas is the greatest thing that could happen to a society. It is something like falling love with the life of a man or woman. Both are invigorated. Life becomes meaningful once again. Every sight, smell and sense is new. Life is joy once again. The only snag is one of the two could become the culprit and want to exploit the other for material purpose. Then the whole experience for both could turn into a hell. Everything newly gained will be lost once again. Scientists say that normal man uses only 3 percent of his brain and a creative man may use 15 percent. What about the remaining 85 percent of the unused brainpower? How to bring out this slumbering potential? No human potential movement has given the right answer so far. Before the answer must come the right analysis. The right analysis is the right picture of consciousness.

A creative life was rightly defined by Emerson as 'soul in action'. The Hasidic Masters defined it as 'souls on fire'. Both mean the same thing. But now the soul is asleep in the normal condition of man. Only his body is in action, only his thought or emotion is in action. Both thought and emotion are parts of mind, the lower, material level of consciousness. Therefore, it is useless to talk about or learn only IQ or EQ. Awaken the sleeping soul, that is, the sleeping giant within. When he wakes up, unlimited power is unleashed. Man becomes a God in power. Just to reach the inner cave beyond mind where this giant sleeps for ages needs a lot of concentration and energy. A normal individual has no such energy or training. However, in amass upheaval initiated by an awakened Master such as Christ, Gandhi or a group of creative people, he gets a glimpse of it by joining them and working with them. Only in such movements, the CQ of people goes up. Something concrete could be accomplished only then. Cultural renaissance is such a creative period. Now we are witnessing such a world renaissance for the first time, some people say. No, it is only a fiction created by the media, say the opponents of globalisation. Both the groups offer convincing evidence. But gaining in the degree of consciousness, the increase in the CQ of movements usually translated into its material and financial equivalents are stolen by a small class of cunning, scheming exploiters. The tremendous energy unleashed by the Gandhian movement was absorbed by the capitalists of India after independence. The masses never tasted the fruits of their labors. The same result was witnessed after the French revolution. Not the whole society but a small enclave is the beneficiary of this rise in CQ. Will history repeat itself once again and only the cunning privileged classes will become richer, or will the whole of mankind get the benefits of globalisation? This is the crux of the problem. Will man ever learn the lesson of history? In the fairy tale, the hero, innocent and valiant will be forced to undergo all sorts of risks, risking even his life, to go to a far-off region and seek the Golden Fleece. Once the prize is got, the evil magician will capture it by his designs and schemes. This is what has happened all through history. Justice has never been restored in real life as in the fairy tale. Even now justice remains only a faulty tale as far as the common man of the world is concerned. Let us hope for the best, this time.

Can CQ be measured as in the case of IQ? Yes. Roughly a unit of thinking is worth about 30,000 units of physical labor. A unit of emotion is worth about 30,000 units of thinking. A unit of intuition is worth about 30,000 units of emotion. A unit of insight, the operation of the whole consciousness, is worth the whole world. A Buddha is born then. Mankind is shown the next step in its evolution.

This psychological fact of hierarchy of CQ was known in the ancient past in India and exploited fully in the system of the caste by the past masters. A man's *swadharma* or level of CQ can be discerned from his temperament. A man with low CQ naturally opts for physical labor, but by accident or by the company of a great man, he might want to break out of his shell and try to develop his CQ. This freedom must be given to him by the society. When this free atmosphere is not there, the system becomes a closed one. Kant in his essay on 'what is enlightenment?' stresses only this point. By subjugating a man to physical labor for life you deny him the opportunity to develop his CQ. He is doomed forever. Spirituality is only a dream in fiction for him, not a real thing. How many millions of lives and their potentialities were lost in the name of tradition? The English man was a godsend indeed with his English education and science and technology, the true liberator of the masses from the prison house of caste system. When the Vedas were denied to the masses, the Bible and the Koran came to their aid.

The purpose of history is to make available for the last man the word of God, in one form or another. If the Hindu Vedas cannot reach him, God will see to it that the Christian Bible or the Islamic Koran reaches him. The means may even be invasion. Invasion is only the outer shell, the mask of God. The truth behind the invasion is the spreading of God's word to every human being. It is a natural phenomenon like the cyclone. Where the vacuum is created, the cyclone is bound to follow. This is the real interpretation of history. Real scientific knowledge is God's word. Real science is the modern religion of God.

Now even if we consider globalisation as a form of the westerner's invasion of the east, let us find out the inner meaning of it. What is the word of God here? What does He intend us to learn? It may be the latest scientific and technological knowledge and the global wisdom offered by the internet for the last citizen of the world in a mere village. The access is opened to him for the first time in world history to all the inherited knowledge of humankind, knowledge accumulated by every culture and race of all periods. This is the real Alladin's lamp by rubbing which the genie of technology might offer him the long dreamt for but ever denied freedom and knowledge and comfort. Globalisation is a real boon from God or a curse from the wizards of western capitalism. At present, the common man or woman of the east is not able to judge.

~~~ ~~~~~ ~~~

7. DISCOVERY AS A WAY OF LIFE

Only an inventor or a discoverer is a man, in the true sense of the word. He alone has fully blossomed. Other people are only vegetating, mere consumers and parasites upon the tree of the world. One man invents television, millions enjoy its benefits. One man discovers a sea route to India and Europe and its millions enjoy the benefits.

Every tree by instinct knows its purpose and destiny in life – why it was born on earth. It finds its joy and pleasure only in fulfilling that destiny. Even a tamarind tree knows its genius. It finds its joy in bringing out tamarind fruits. It does not want to produce apples. There may be difference of values in the human imagination but no such difference exists in nature. The tamarind tree and the apple tree are equally joyous in producing their respective creative works. And the tree is supposed to be endowed with only one sense.

Unfortunately, man with his six senses, does not know by instinct what his purpose in life is or why he was born on earth. He has to find it out for himself from the outside world. He needs somebody such as the Buddha, Christ, Saint Ramalinga or a book like the Bible to tell him his mission in life. The bible says that he is in fact the tree of light.

It says God has given him free will instead of the unconscious instinct and he must learn to use it properly with discrimination. There is only one tree in him, the tree of light or life. But he may, by his perverted sense, see the shadow of this tree of being which is called the tree of knowledge and identify himself as that tree producing only shadows, never touching the real reality of his being. Shadow, the counterfeit, the copy is mistaken for the original. Matter and the apparent physical world are the shadows. All knowledge born of science, arts, and humanities is only superficial shadow fruit by eating which man's real hunger of being cannot be pacified.

The Upanishad says there are two birds in the tree of man. One is mind. It wants to enjoy the physical world of dreams. Its enjoyment or suffering is nothing but the enjoyment and suffering in a dream, only more illusory. The other bird is the being. It merely watches the play or the dream. It does not want to participate. By participating it might lose its identity of the absolute character and identify itself with the changing roles offered by the manager of the troupe that is the conditioning of the society.

The Koran says, man is born in sleep, lives in sleep and dies in sleep. Even wakefulness of man is only partial sleep. Man must first understand this fact and then try to wake up by constantly remembering his true nature of being. George IvanovichI Gurdjieff, the Russian mage made this war against sleep his central teaching. He says he got this message from both Buddhism and Sufism. For this reason, the Buddha was called 'the awakened one', the permanently awakened one, never to fall back into sleep. Sleep was eradicated from his consciousness once for all. Even during sleep, he retained his consciousness. The consciousness of such an enlightened one becomes like one unbroken waterfall of oil [*thailatharai*] through ages and aeons, through eternity. There is no sleep or death for this consciousness. There is no time, place or limitations for it. It is 'I am that I am' – it reaches that level of godhead.

This concept of sleep, we are able to understand and follow today. But it is only a psychological name. Its philosophical name was 'illusion' in Buddhism, 'Maya' in Vedanta. Its scientific term is matter or the constantly changing aspect of reality.

Every age and every place combine together to produce in man a certain temperament. Vedanta catered to the argumentative temperament. Ours is the age of psychology and our temperament is a psychological one. We cannot understand otherwise. Therefore, all the terms and concepts of reality must be reinterpreted and given in psychological terms. Sleep is the word or concept understandable for man. Perhaps the psychological age of man started with the Buddha. His very title 'the awakened one' bears ample evidence of that. Long before Gurdjieff, the great Thiruvalluvar equates sleep with death. He says,

The sleepy are the dead [*thunjinarsetharinverallar*]

In another couplet, he says,

(*Uranguvathupolumsakkaduurangivizippathupolumperappu*)

Death is like sleep; birth is like awakening.

Thiruvalluvar offers a better system than that of Gurdjieff and Ouspensky. The latter go only half-way. It does not touch the root-cause of sleep. Unless the root cause is discovered and rooted out, there is no permanent remedy.

Find out the disease. Find out the root cause of the disease. Find out the remedy. Apply the rightremedy according to the needs, time and other conditions of the patient.

(*Noeynaadinoeymudhalnaadiadhuthanikkum*

Vainaadivaippaseyal. – *Kural*)

This one couplet contains in it the whole methodology of Buddhism. It also points out where Buddhism went wrong in offering, say, one remedy for all, like surgery for all types of patients.

The degree or intensity of the disease, the condition of the patient, the climate and other factors were not considered.

It offered only one remedy for all: renunciation. The whole country was turned into a vast monastery after Ashoka. Maybe the ideal was right. Maybe the attitude of compromise or gradation may not work out in the field of spirituality. Only total concentration of all of one's forces on a single point could do the job, as Napoleon used to say in the art of war in vanquishing the enemy. The enemy within is the most powerful one in creation. Perhaps that is why Jesus said, seek ye first the kingdom of God and J Krishnamurti said, there is one step and the first step is the last step.

Maybe Gurdjieff did not want to frighten away the westerner with his penchant for material enjoyment. He pushed the westerner first into the esoteric field and then he qualified as an initiate, that is, who had developed a magnetic centre, who had come to the conviction that to attain the spirit was the top priority in life. He did not perhaps want to waste his energies on the merely curious. Therefore, he offered good food, even great dinners and wine. He even allowed normal sex for his disciples. He stressed only one thing, constant self-remembering of one's imprisonment in the lazy, sleepy normal consciousness. His only purpose inlife was to wake up permanently from this spiritual sloth and accidie.

But this is to evade the real issue. This is to ignore the root cause of the malady. Food only causes sleep. Wine makes man sleepier. By taking food into the body, man takes into his system the habit of unconsciousness and sleep and the instinct of death of the plants and animals. By eating three meals a day, right from his birth man goes on keeping sleep, death and habits of inert matter into his body. This is like spending ten rupees to earn one rupee. This tends to constant pauperism. Man lives like a pauper and dies like a pauper. It was the poet Milton who rightly said, food only causes sleep. Unfortunately, Milton was not known as an enlightened master by his own people. Even the scholarly Samuel Johnson could not understand the heights in consciousness Milton had touched in his masterpiece, the Paradise Lost. Milton to my knowledge was one of a rare handful of master poets who had touched the real reality through the medium of real imagination not through fancy.

There are three steps offered by the Tamil Siddhas, including Thiruvalluvar for attaining total awakening, which is possible only with a pure body. That does not produce any waste matter whatsoever. This stage of the physical body is known as pure body [*suthadheham*]. The instinct of hunger for food will be totally extinguished in a pure body says Thirumoolar.

Top gear as the BBC serial showed, means the best engine as well as the normal meaning in the dictionary, the highest gear of the car when it attains its maximum speed. In the case of man though he has been blessed with top gear the best of all possible machines, 'it is always running like a tortoise, in the lowest gear or mostly in neutral, that is running on the spot'.

The Tamil Siddhas and Ramalinga Vallalar in particular have revealed the full potentialities, possibilities, powers attainable by man with his body, mind and spirit, specifically the best potentiality of the human body. In their eyes, the ancient dictum, 'as above, so below', the microcosm is the macrocosm, was a scientifically realizable fact. And they showed the world in deed and word, how it could be done. Unfortunately, this hidden treasure of a hidden tradition has not been shown to the world by the media or Indian spiritual gurus. It has to be brought into the open to the notice of every human born on the earth. Man is a self-sufficient being, really the master of his reality, the captain of his ship. Everyone can realize this truth in his or her own life by becoming a Siddha. The western human potential movement opened not even a fraction of what is possible for man. The fortune of mankind needs and awaits for such a new movement, a new renaissance.

~~~ ~~~~~ ~~~

8. THE METHODOLOGY OF CONVERTING SPIRITUALITY INTO SCIENCE

Science is the understanding of the laws of outer nature and technology is the conquest of it. Spirituality is the understanding of laws of inner nature and siddhis are the fruits of the conquest of it. Both are sciences. Both are based on understanding the basic laws of nature. The purpose of both is to go beyond nature and control it. The very word 'man' [aal] in Tamil means only this: to manage and to rule over nature; to rule over both the outer and the inner. The laws of the outer nature may differ from those of the inner as we find in physics and quantum physics. Spirituality is like quantum physics of consciousness. The task of the scientist today is to discover the exact laws of the quantum consciousness. The ancient scientists of consciousness or seers sharpened, developed and intensified their consciousness in order to increase the powers of their only instrument – consciousness. The future scientists of consciousness may even invent instruments and gadgets to measure exactly the units of consciousness. Already we have a taste of such instruments in the biofeedback machines.

How to survive without food, water and air for breathing without losing energy? What is the alternative source of bio-energy? Can information replace food, water and air as the source of energy? These are some of the questions before man at the juncture of his next mutation in evolution. The food for the astronauts in the form of pills, direct oxygen breathing for patients in critical conditions are some of the indications of the ways in which the future scientists must pay their attention.

Gurdjieff was only partly right when he said that man needs only three types of food namely, solid food and water, air and impressions. Perhaps he got this idea from the *Taitriya Upanishad* where it is said that man has got five bodies, the food body, the air body, the thought body, the intelligence body and the bliss body. Beyond the five bodies lies the Atman. Thus,two types of food and two denominations of it are missing in Gurdjieff's system. Intelligence [*vignana*] and bliss [*ananda*] are also the needed foods of the body of man. How to get them? Intelligence can be had by four ways namely, earnestness, truth, yoga and greatness [*mahas*]. Bliss or *ananda* can be had by love.

The *Taitriya Upanishad* also lays out the truth behind the five bodies. These bodies are as it were one behind the other. The food-body is influenced and controlled by the air-body. The air-body is influenced and controlled by the thought-body. The thought-body or mind is controlled by the intelligence-body. The intelligence-body is influenced and controlled by the bliss-body or love-body. Love is the last or highest denomination of energy in the body not only in the man-body but also in the god-body or world-body. A well-developed love-body will start producing energy necessary for the assumption behind the injunction of saints such as Christ 'to love even thy neighbor as thyself'. When a man is always in love, he is constantly producing the positive and the highest kind of food in the world. Even true knowledge or intelligence is only a lower denomination of energy, say the rishis.

Intelligence-body is the aim of a yogi. Earnestness, discrimination, alertness and watchfulness, light in the mind are some of the qualities of this body. A modern scientist like Einstein with his unprejudiced and objective knowledge is a good example of a well-developed intelligence-body. Nevertheless, without a well developed love-body or bliss-body a scientist-body or intelligence-body can become dangerous. He can become a veritable *Asura*. Thus, starting at the highest level, with the love-body is not only the most profitable economy of humankind but also the safest. Love is the only saviour of humankind, the only truth both of physical body as well as the spiritual body. The science of love alone can liberate humankind, no other religion or technology. What are the various gradations of love? What are the exact relationships between various denominations of love? These questions must be answered by future scientists in mathematical formulae.

P D Ouspensky gives a formula in his book: 'Emotion is 30000 times faster than thought, and intuition 30000 times faster than emotion'. Gurdjieff's table of hydrogens is another marker; also,Vallalar's measurement by carat value of gold in a body: 24 in a pure body, 108 in a pranava body and infinite in a compassionate-light body. Thought belongs to the mental body, emotion to both the mental and vital bodies and intuition to the intelligence-body. Love is called by him as the higher emotional body, and he forgot to add it to the formula. But it has to be scientifically true. But as a starting point this will do. future scientists must proceed further. They must discover the true relationship and denominations of energy. For there is only one energy in nature as Einstein said in his unified field theory. And that energy is solidified into six levels of matter namely i] inorganic matter, ii] organic matter, iii] mental matter, iv] psychic matter, v] spiritual matter and vi] divine matter. The more consciousness it has the higher denomination it attains. That is the law of evolution. By giving this hierarchy of matter, Swami Ramalinga Vallalar, with one stroke cuts the Gordian knot of the Cartesian dualities of soul and body, macrocosm and microcosm, life and matter, conscious and the unconscious, free will and destiny and so on. Now there is no dichotomy between science and spirituality, between the common life and the monastic.

~~~ ~~~~~~ ~~~

9. CONSCIOUS EVOLUTION

In the light of evolutionary biology, man can now see himself as the sole agent of further evolutionary advancement on this planet. He finds himself in the unexpected position of business manager for the cosmic process of evolution. He no longer ought to feel separated from the rest of nature, for he is part of it – that part which has become conscious, capable of love, understanding and aspiration. He need no longer regard himself as insignificant in relation to the cosmos. – [Evolution in action – Julian Huxley, 1953, p.132]

Birth and death are automatic natural processes. They are not under the control of man. Except for a few yogis and saints, no one knows what happens in between death and rebirth. Books, such as 'The Tibetian book of the dead {Bardo Thodal}' and 'Garuda Puranam' have been written by ancient seers about this intermediary life; but one is unable to brush aside the doubt of their veracity since they give different versions.

Anyway, the point of conscious evolution is: man should learn to have control over both the processes of birth and death. The key word here is control. Who or what controls your life? Destiny, nature or you? You must control your destiny.

The control should change hands. Now it is in the hands of nature. Man should take it in his own hands. Then he becomes immortal. He retains his consciousness forever. That is the aim of conscious evolution. At least you should be always alert and conscious, even at the time of birth and death and in between. In short, one must be fully conscious, conscious of all that goes on in the outer world as well as the inner. Buddha and J Krishnamurti want one to be totally conscious at every moment of one's life and death. Every moment life takes place. You are being born every moment. Every moment you are dying. A part of your body cells and a portion of your mind and life force are dying. Be ever alert and watchful and see all this change every moment of your living, here and hereafter. See how death terminates every second of your life. Learn to live with death. Die to every second. Be born every moment afresh. This is the way of conquering the processes of life and death. Life and death are there only for vital, pranic life force. When you awaken your intelligence fully and develop it consciously all through the 24 hours of a day, never letting it sleep even for a moment, the life force gets consolidated, and a new magnetic centre is born in you. This is called, 'the birth of being or spirit'. Once this spirit is born, there is no break of sleep or death in your consciousness. Then you become an immortal life, a god.

Gods are beings of light. Gods have bodies of spiritual light. They are believed to grow younger as they accumulate the love-energy in their bodies. However, even with them, the process of death is unconscious. According to tradition and the law of Karma, if one does extraordinarily good and charitable deeds, he would be born as an angel in the land of the angels though it is not decided by him. One fine morning he finds himself in *devaloka*(world of Gods) and then start living as a god or angel.

The aim of a Siddha is entirely different. With full awareness and total consciousness, he wants to transform his physical body into a body of light like that of an angel and wants to live here upon earth, taking care of his human brethren and sisters and all sentient beings and not to live in a far-off land of heaven however blissful it might be. He wants to wrench the control of his life from the hands of nature and to keep it for himself.

The former may be a myth or religious dogma. It may even be a fiction of the human mind. It cannot be verified scientifically nor proved. There is no such problem with the latter process. It is quite scientific. Every stage of the process happens here before the eyes of people as evidenced at the time of resurrection of the body of Jesus Christ and by the transformation of the physical body first into a pure-body, next into a sound-body and finally into a spiritual and divine-body of light in the case of swami Ramalinga of Vadalur in Tamilnadu.

The basic process of this transformation according to both Christ and Swami is twofold; non-eating and love. Food corrupts the body and finally this corruption leads to its death. Therefore, reduce the quantity of intake of food slowly and gradually and finally stop it absolutely. Even this minimum quantity of food should consist only of foods that do not change their character or physical properties even after their digestion by the body such as honey, raw sugar, calcined iron and copper and minerals and so on. This emphasis on food is given great importance in the teachings of swami Ramalinga whereas Jesus only touches upon it when he says in one place, 'I have another kind of food which you don't know'. What is it exactly, no one knows. [Only scientists of the future should discover these secrets of biology and reveal to the world]. And in another place, he says, 'I will give you living waters which will stay in your body and be a fountain giving eternal life'. It is not clear what he means by this. Swami Ramalinga also talks about 'amirta' the Indian version of 'manna' and also about 'water that does not run'. Both were Master Siddhas. They are adepts in the art of transforming matter into divine matter. In my humble opinion, Jesus must have come to Tamilnadu during his life between the age of twelve and thirty which period is not documented in any of the synoptic gospels. Some people agree to a theory that he came to Tibet, stayed there in a lamasery, and learnt the secrets of love-energy and the science of resurrection from Tibetian Buddhist Lamas. They may be right as far as their theory on love energy is concerned; but they are wrong about the theory of his learning the secret science of resurrection. This science of immortality is available intact only in the literature of Tamil Siddhas such as Thirumoolar and Thiruvalluvar. Thiruvalluvar talks in detail about both the aspects of non-eating and the development of love-energy into compassion. Both are needed for attaining immortality.

Avoidance of food helps the process in a negative sort of way by stopping the poisoning of the life-energy. For all food is poison. How to convert this poison into nectar or manna is a secret process known only to Siddhas. They had learnt to live on pure water, calcined metals and pure air by practicing *Vaasi yoga*, advanced form of kriya yoga as taught by ParamahamsaYogananda in recent times. He says Lord Krishna teaches it in the *Gita*.

Man's life principle is residing in his body, in the region of the third eye like an atom. Its power is felt like that of a magnet all over the body. The very nature of life is love, according to Thiruvalluvar. He says,

Anbinvazhiathuuyirnilai

Love is the nature of life

Love is also the way to immortality.

The word *'uyirnilai'* means both the 'nature of love' as well as immortality.

This atom-like life energy or love-energy must be developed by feeding it with more and more love, slowly it starts growing. It should be developed to such a stage that one day it covers the whole physical body and even goes beyond like a field. Life is the protector of the body from decaying and dying. This is evidenced in the fact that the moment life force leaves the body at the time of death, the body starts decaying. Therefore, develop your life force through love-energy and encompass your physical body. This will protect the body from disease and decay. For the first time, the body becomes immune from wound, unless one wills it as in the case of Christ. Earlier when a woman touched his garment from behind, he turned back and asked, 'who touched my garment?'. It shows that he was covered with a field of bio-electricity or love-energy.

Now life is inside the body. You should place your body inside life. You should develop your field of life-energy to such a high level. They say Buddha's life-field covered some two hundred miles. All the sentient beings, even inorganic things within that field felt the bliss with Buddha being nearby, it is reported.

Non-eating stops the poison from food being accumulated in the atom of life force and the former effects of karma are cleansed from it. The atom of life-energy is made as pure as possible. That is why Thiruvalluvar says,

Unnamaiullathuuyirnilai

Non-eating leads to immortality.

Like the physical sun, such a Siddha-body does not need energy or food from outside. It creates its own food and even donates it to others. That is why swami Ramalinga says in one of his prose works, 'I asked of God to give me a self-luminous body like that of the sun and he immediately granted my wish'.

Thiruvalluvar classifies people into three categories; 1] those who eat meat will go to hell's perpetual darkness. Hell will not allow them to get out easily; 2] those who eat vegetarian food will enter into the cycle of birth and death; and 3] those who take no food will become immortals and escape the wheel of *samsara* of life and death. Therefore, food is all-important for the Siddhas.

Here is Thiruvalluvar's immortal couplet:

Unnamaiullathuuyirnilaioonunna

Annathalseyyathualaru

Non-eating leads to immortality

Meat eaters cannot get out of hell.

Here a question of common sense arises. Does not one die without food? Yes, absolutely. If you do not take food, you will die perhaps in thirty or forty days of starvation. If you eat food, you will again die perhaps after fifty or hundred years. Food only postpones your death but makes it certain. Though it sounds like a paradox, the solution has been found by the Siddhas and Chinese Taoists who were also Siddhas. They had communication between them. The great Tamil Siddha, Bhogar is reported to have come from China.

The economy of energy of the body is reduced to a minimum. Do not move your body around too much. Stop all activities and sit in meditation. Save all your physical and mental energies. Save your semen. Save your breath. Stop thinking and save your thought. Fast and save your gastric juices. This saving of all energies will enable you to take less of food. Eventually, you would have accumulated so much of your energy in your body you would not need energy from outside through food. When the body becomes pure, a spoonful of honey and a cup of water will be enough for you for a whole day. Unlike now, the whole matter of food will be totally transformed into energy. Now more than 99.99% of what we eat is turned into waste matter and excreted out of the body. Now the process of digestion is a mechanical and chemical one. Then it will be an atomic one. Later when the body is turned into a pure body, it will, like a plant, start producing its own food. Nectar would be secreted from the brain.

The process is twofold; first, understand how food conditions your body and secondly release yourself from that conditioning. Attain freedom from food.

To attain immortality man needs to obtain freedom from four things that lead him to death: food, sex, sleep and fear.

This is a dictum of swami Ramalinga. According to Thiruvalluvar man willingly boards four ships that take him to the land of death:Procrastination, forgetfulness, laziness and sleep – these four ships of death are willingly boarded by men. Free yourself from these four and you will be free from the clutches of death.

~~~ ~~~~~ ~~~

10. THE TEN SENSES OR DEGREES OF KNOWLEDGE OF MAN

Throughout history, knowledge has been variously calibrated and denominated. Sanskrit literature has broadly divided it into two categories, namely *para* [divine] and *apara* [human]. The school of Tamil Saiva Siddhanta has broadened this division adding one more; *pasaarivu*[material and scientific knowledge], *pasuarivu* [human knowledge] and *pathiarivu* [divine knowledge]. In the west it has been commonly classified into four as 1] sensory knowledge 2] thought 3] universal reason or inspiration and finally as 4] revelation. The second and third categories of human knowledge were the contributions to philosophy and subsequently to romantic literary criticism respectively by the German transcendentalist philosophers such as Immanuel Kant, Shelling, and so on and S T Coleridge in English through his classic 'Biographia Literaria'. This division between thought and universal reason, between fancy and imagination was carried to its extreme and explored in all of their dimensions by Ralph Waldo Emerson, the transcendentalist of America and J.Krishnamurti of Indian origin. J Krishnamurti went so far as to declare that thought is man's number one enemy and that almost all of man's ills along with the gifts and achievements in arts and humanities are due to thought. Only by transcending the level of thought, which is the source of all evil and polarity of good and bad, high and low, the beautiful and the ugly, man can reach the special energy of love or pure intelligence.

What J.Krishnamurti labeled as single energy of love or intelligence, was divided into two higher forms of knowledge by Gurdjieff and P D Ouspensky as 'higher emotional' and 'higher intellectual'.

Sir Francis Bacon the father of science, had in his 'Advancement of Learning', divided it like the Sanskrit tradition: all knowledge as human and divine.

JacquesMaritain, the catholic existential philosopher has written a whole book on 'Degrees of Knowledge'.

Sri Aurobindo in his monumental "Life Divine' has tried to be very exact and detailed in calibrating and classifying all the degrees of knowledge. Beyond thought or mind, he discovers and labels about half a dozen states of special and superior kinds of knowledge like – higher mind, intuitive mind, over mind, super mind, supramental consciousness and the like. In his last days, he used to call the supramental consciousness as 'mind of light'.

This mind of light was not something new to the Tamil tradition. Even the great Thiruvalluvar some two thousand years ago pointed out in his second couplet that the ultimate purpose of all education and learning was to reach this level of light-knowledge of God:

What is the purpose of learning but to attain the divine feet of God with light knowledge?

Katradhanaalaayapayanenkolvaalarivannatralthozharenin

This light knowledge is named as *Vaalarivu*by him. Vaal means light in Tamil.

According to the Tamil tradition, everything concerning God or the Divine level of existence is of light. His food is of light. His breath is of light, his knowledge is of light.

This food of divine light is called by Ramalinga as *pogaappunal* unmoving inexhaustible water; this is also called *arulamudham*, nectar of the innermost or divine grace.

This is something similar to Christ's water of life. The Siddhas claim that man's brain can secrete such immortal ambrosia and that onedrop of it from the pineal gland through the pituitary into the mouth via the uvula is enough food and water for man for some twelve years. They assert that this drop of divine nectar is so concentrated that unlike ordinary water or food, it does not leave the body and stays forever in it and keeps on providing it with an inexhaustible supply of energy.

Similarly, the breath of light was called by the Siddhas and Ramalinga as *Vegaak Kaal* unburnable air or *SaagaakKalai* undying breath. This is different from the ordinary human breath of atmospheric air which is always in short supply and gets exhausted at one stage and man dies. Unlike the atmospheric air, this breath of light is at once of air, of space, of fire, of water, of sound, of smell, of touch, and the like. It is again inexhaustible. Once a man comes into contact with this unburnable gas, he attains immortality. Furthermore, Ramalinga reveals that thereafter he can perform real miracles. Not before that. This breath of light is the miracle – producing stuff, like the Christian Holy Spirit.

In Tamil Siddha-yoga terminology ordinary breath is vaguely denoted and veiled as *Asura* the dark demon. In Saivite and Vaishnavite literature, this yogic phenomenon is carried over into innumerable forms of demons to be assailed by Gods Siva and Krishna, Subramania and Rama. The conquest of this *Asura*, the dark demon of atmospheric air as respiration by taking in the divine breath of life and light is the final and climactic achievement of man. This is given in story form and that too in divine stories as God slaying the demons.

With every breath, the Siddhas say man is losing four units of life energy. With inspiration, one is inhaling eight units of prana contained in the air. With expiration, one is exhaling twelve units of prana out of the body. According to entropy, the second law of thermodynamics, the atmospheric air sucks in the pranic energy or life force or body heat. To defy this law of nature is the sadhana of man. This law is the cause of man's sickness, old age and death. This law is man's number one enemy. This scientific law was known to swami Ramalinga. That is why he admonishes us to cover our bodies from head to toe; otherwise we would lose our body heat. He also advises us to bathe only in warm water and drink only hot water.

Buddha was a philosopher and a mystic only. So, he said that desire is the cause of old age and death. Once you are born, you have to bear with all these. You cannot escape them. You can only try to stop being born again. But swami Ramalinga was not only a philosopher and a mystic but also a Siddha that is a scientist. So, he discovers the law of entropy long before modern science and applies it to the human body. Even in this birth, even with this body, you can do away with old age and death if you know how to fight with and overcome the law of entropy.

Prana is different from oxygen. Oxygen is only a carrier or container. Oxygen sustains body. Prana sustains life. Prana is everywhere in the universe. Oxygen is only in the atmosphere. That is why an astronaut has to carry oxygen cylinders. Whereas a Siddha has direct contact with prana. He can travel anywhere in the universe and live. According to the second law of thermodynamics, the law of entropy, atmospheric air is sucking man's energy and heat.

All demons are dark and arise as phantoms from the thought level of mind as the Buddha long ago showed to the world. Once the boundary of matter and mind is crossed by a noble yogi, he has no more dreams or nightmares. That is the reason enlightened masters like J Krishnamurti claim 'I have no dreams'. They have subdued and conquered their minds. There are no waves in their minds. Their seas are always silent and calm and under their control. Like their hands and legs, their minds are also under their control and they act only when ordered and activated by the master. In ordinary human minds, the wandering, the wool-gathering, the constant inner chattering is never stopped even during sleep. It manifests itself as a dream.

As for the knowledge of light of God, very clear-cut delineations are given by Ramalinga. It is deep inside the Chidambaram of man's brain. It is the ultimate source of all light. In fact, it is known and worshipped by him as vast grace light [*Arutperumjothi*]. He says that all human learning is too slow like a bullock cart and dark as the mind of a computer because it is of matter born of thought whereas this knowledge of light is born of love and compassion and understands all in one moment.

This is a very important and subtle discovery of Vallalar. He says there are two kinds of learning, born of thinking and love. The former is mechanical and born of matter like that of a computer, which thinks only in computations one by one. With its electronic speed, it can count very fast, but it is only counting mechanically. It is dead counting. Thought is matter though subtle, says J Krishnamurti. He is absolutely right. In Tamil, the word for thought is *ennam* which also means number and count. So a man like a computer is only counting or compounding when he thinks.

What Ramalinga calls knowledge of light is totally different, [*Anbuenumuyirolir arrive*], it is born of love that is an indication and manifestation of life. It is living knowledge, knowledge that is alive. Here is an example given by the saint himself.

Our mind is like the tungsten filament in an electric bulb. The electricity is the love. Unless this electric current is passed through the filament, it cannot get activated, heated or illuminated. Once it is illuminated, the light coming out of it is knowledge of light. When instead of love its final fruition, compassion is passed through the filament, everlasting, eternal light is born out of it. This superior light is called by Vallalar as *Arul Arivu*, it is nothing but divine wisdom. That is why it is stressed in SuddhaSanmarga that 'not thinking' is not the answer even if it is correct or incorrect, logical or contemplative – because all are varieties of thinking which is only of matter, and hence dark like that of a computer. Love and compassion towards all beings is the only gateway to knowledge and wisdom and finally to release and liberty called *Moksha*.

The knowledge derived out of thinking or mind is mechanical because mind consisting of four divisions of *manas, chittam, buddhi*, and *ahankar* is only an instrument, dead and inorganic. The human soul, the jiva that is alive, like a magnet sends its power of aliveness to the instruments of mind and body and activates them. So, the mind and body are only partially alive and activated by the psyche. Again, the limbs of the body and mind vary among themselves in degrees of life. For example, nails and hair are almost inert and lifeless whereas the eyes, the reproductive organs and the like, are very sensitive. According to Siddhas, the very purpose and function of humans in the course of evolution is to totally convert these partially dead and partially alive organs of the body and mind into total life and then into spirit. This transformation is known in Siddha and Saiva Siddhanta literature as 'transformation of human limbs and equipments into divine limbs and instruments'.

Pasukarangalpathikarangalaagamaarum

Until such time they remain only partially alive and partially awakened. In fact, according to Siddhas, total awakening of a Buddha is not total. The Siddhas were scientists. Every effect must be measured exactly. Total awakening for them is measured by the total transformation of the dark matter of body and mind into spiritual and divine substance or resurrected body like that of a Christ, and all the instincts and sufferings of the body and mind called *avastha* must be totally conquered. For example, natural instincts like hunger and sleep are attributes and limitations of the body. So called So-called masters of the path of consciousness like the Buddhists, Vedantins and their counterparts of modern new-age gurus are not bothered about these limitations of the body. They eat while they are hungry. They sleep while sleep comes. This is not accepted by the Siddhas. According to them, sleep must be totally conquered in all its dimensions. There is the sleep of the body, sleep of the mind, sleep of the soul/ psyche/ being. It is deep-rooted in all the layers of the body, mind and psyche. It should be totally exterminated from the roots. And the roots are in the cells of the body, in their DNA. Conquest not only of mind and its sleep, conquest not only of the self and its sleep, but the conquest and control over all the cells of the body and their DNAs are also emphasized by them. Unless the body and its limitations are conquered once for all, it is not total awakening for them. That is why saint Ramalinga repeatedly sings in various places in his Arutpa,

Sleep is lost, sun appeared

Thookamtholainthathu, Surianthonrinan

Not even an iota or vestige of sleep must be allowed to linger in the body.

This is possible only when hunger and respiration are conquered permanently. For only food and respiration cause sleep in the body. This is another great discovery of the Siddhas. Practicing 'vaasi yogi' and the right way of pranayama are the right cures for sleep, not overworking of the body as Gurdjieff thought and taught. It will only make the body more tired. Tiredness and fatigue will bring in two bad effects like more hunger for more food and the need for more rest and sleep. Gurdjieff was known as an overeater. This point that food only causes sleep in man, unfortunately eluded Gurdjieff. Food the Siddhas scientifically argue, whether vegetative or animal is already full of sleep, for the plants and animals are all beings of sleep. They all are born in sleep, live in sleep and die in sleep. Therefore, when food containing sleep is added into the human body that has a tendency to sleep, only more sleep will result. This was understood by the Siddha Thirumoolar and so he writes;

Idakkaivalakkaiirandiyummatri

Thudikkaiyalunnavallarkusoravumvendaam

Urakkathaineekkiunaravallarku

Irakkavumvendamirukkalumaame - **Thirumantram**

If one instead of taking food,[of air] by left hand [meaning left nostril] and by the right hand [the right nostril] takes food [of air] by proboscis, the central column of *sushamnanaadi,* he will not suffer from sleep or dullness. And once sleep is conquered, he need not die and can live everlastingly.

Gurdjieff's misjudgment of pranayama was very dear and costly. Not by overworking of the body and overeating but only by the conquest of hunger and breathing can sleep be conquered permanently. Saint Ramalinga and the teachings of SuddhaSanmarga show us the better road to the conquest of sleep and death. It is a complete science, nowhereelse available in the world.

Coming back to the knowledge of light, saint Ramalinga gives out the exact recipe for attaining it:

Othathuunarthidaolialithuenakke

AathaaramaagiyaArutperum Jothi

When he entered into the inner sanctum sanctorum of Chidambaram in his heart, the Lord dancing there blessed him with a light of grace. And with that light of grace, he attained the knowledge of light. He claims: 'now my consciousness has the capacity to reach everywhere even beyond the galaxies'.

[Ippozhuthuennudiaarivuandaandangalukkuappalumvirinduirukkira thu]

-    Prose works of ThiruArutpa

One more claim by him of the power of this light of grace is astounding and awe-inspiring but it reveals the ultimate secret of God-science. He says,

'When I saw a corpse with my eyes blessed with this God-given light of grace, it came to life'.

One can ask: is there any other evidence or proof of his having attained this miraculous knowledge of light by the light of grace? Yes. The scientific knowledge found in his masterpiece "ArutPerum Jothi Agaval" is truly remarkable. Even in 1860s, he had known about the sub-atomic world and its particles and activities, some half a century before the birth and development of modern atomic science. He talks of cosmology and various dimensions of space, and various beings living in fire and space. Only now science has discovered that even in very high temperatures like 5000°c some beings might be alive. He labels sub-atomic particles as kurundavies, asalais, amalais, and friendly atoms and so on, long before our atomic physicists and he also gives descriptions of them. Truth about his scientific discoveries of the subatomic world and cosmology is yet to be verified by scientists. The stupendous and encyclopedic knowledge he displays about Sanskrit literature, Vedas, Upanishads, agamas, tantras, about the Siddhas,saivasiddhanta literature, the grammars of both Tholkappiar and Panini, the vast works of literature, of Tamil and Sanskrit, his yogic philosophical knowledge and vast poetic powers are unthinkable of attainment in a short span of human life of about 50 years.

If there is any single book that contains in a nutshell, almost all of mankind's knowledge both secular and spiritual, it is Vallalar'sThiruArutpa. It is my humble opinion born out of some four decades of reading, studying and thinking about the world's great books like the series of 'great books of the western world' edited by Mortimer J Adler and published by Britannica Inc, and the series, 'sacred books of the east' edited by Maxmuller and published by Messrs Motilal Banarsidas of India.

Of course, Thirukkural is there in comparison with it. But it is written in sutra form, in a highly condensed and concentrated form and it has to be interpreted by the right commentators without distortions. In a way,ThiruArutpa of Vallalar is the right commentary on it and more.

My answer to the question 'who is a scholar or well-read man?' will be: it is only one who has studied ThiruArutpa thoroughly. It is a conviction arrived at after roaming around the world of knowledge into all exoteric and esoteric systems of knowledge as a seeker after truth.

Let us go back to the beginning of our topic of ten senses of man. The most ancient Tamil text of Tholkappiam affirms the organic evolution of man. The material, phenomenal world appeared out of a combination that was right of the five elements of space, air, fire, water and earth. Life wasborn then, first as a single sensed being like amoeba and later developed into the vegetable kingdom [Thaavaram]. The first sense was touch, the tactile. It evolved next into two sensed beings like molluscs like snails with touch and taste. Along with skin, the tongue was born. The urge for a new sense developed into a new organ. Likewise, three sensed beings with the added sense of smell and the respective organ nose, four sensed beings with added sense of sight and eyes, and five sensed beings with hearing and ears were evolved. Furthermore, in man the sixth sense called mind was added, says Tholkappiar.

Is mind a sense only or an organ or both? Where is it located in the body? These details are not given in the verse. Perhaps they were lost as thousands of ancient Tamil works were lost. However, he gives one strangely scientific   definition   of   mind. *AaruArivuathuveavatrudanmaname*. Note the word 'avatrudan' - with them, meaning all the five prior senses. Thus, what is the sixth sense of mind? Mind is like the maestro with a baton in his hand, of an orchestra of five senses and their functions through their organs. It can turn our outgoing attention, for the first time, inward and watch the performance of all the five senses. It can also watch itself. In short, mind is given to man not only as a coordinator of all the five senses but also when it is fully developed by love and compassion and shorn of all negative aspects, might replace all the functions of the five senses as well as movements and motion of the body. This idea is a bit difficult to grasp for it enters into paranormal powers. But it is possible, says Siddha Ramalinga in his work on compassion called Jeevakaarunyam.

When compassion becomes the way of life of one, by being seated in one place, his hands can give in a far-off place removed, say, by a thousand miles, his legs might go and reach it without moving from his seat.

Two important conclusions about mind are arrived at by the Siddhas. Mind is a very important event, a turning point in the course of evolution. Mind is the uniqueness of man. The first truth about the mind is that it is the place where matter is converted into life. Although, even the first sense of knowledge is the manifestation of this conversion, it took place mechanically, was done by nature, in a state of sleep. Here with the advent of mind in man, nature departs and hands over its reins to man. This is the real free will given to man. He has been entrusted with total freedom either to keep his mental apparatus [and subsequently his physical body also] as inert material equipments like the animals do by allowing free play to his negative aspects of mind or he can transform them into live, undying organs like the limbs of a Siddha or those of a resurrected body of a Christ where no part of the body or mind is made of inert matter but alive like that of God himself.

The second truth is that when once this transformation of the material mind into live mind takes place, its powers will vary phenomenally. It will be endowed with paranormal powers after that. The limitations of the ordinary mind of matter with its limited powers of shadow life or moonlight-like space and time will be transcended. In short, the conversion or evolution of matter first into life, then into mind, from mind to spirit and finally into divine substance [param] takes place consciously first with the mental equipment and then with the body. The transformation of dark matter takes place first into unconscious, physical light matter and then into conscious light of wisdom. *[gnana]*.

This conscious transformation of matter into divine substance is the topic of study of all evolutionists such as Darwin, Nietsche, Bergson, Alexander, Lamarck, GB Shaw, Sri Aurobindo, and Teilhard de Chardin and before all these stalwarts, the ancient Alchemists, Taoists and Siddhas. The advent of Sri Ramalinga is the crowning achievement of this evolutionary process, literally or real enlightening of the human body and finally the outside material world.

This process of transformation has been variously shown by the above scholars in all its stages. Sri Aurobindo first divides it into three stages called the triple transformations of the psyche, of the vital and of the physical. This rough division is further denominated into minor subdivisions like the higher mind, the intuitive mind, the illuminated mind, the overmind and the super mind or supramental consciousness. With the bringing down of the energies of these minds particularly super mind, the lower strata of thought, vital body and the physical body are transformed.

Such a finer classification was already done by the sage Thiruvalluvar long ago. He divides all knowledge into ten levels or stages.

1. The sense or knowledge of touch or skin

2. The sense or knowledge of taste or tongue

3. The sense or knowledge of smell or nose

4. The sense or knowledge of sight or eyes

5. The sense or knowledge of hearing or ears.

[Please make a note of the fact that these sensory organs are evolved and placed in the face in an ascending order and also that from the third organ, nose onward, they are divided into two and have two functions.]

6. The sense or knowledge of mind or Self-knowledge or the capacity to be conscious of one's own consciousness. [Arivuarithal]

Though the sixth sense, mind itself is evolved with this capacity, in most of the humans, it is only in the budding stage. It remains only a potential power yet to be realized consciously. When it is fully developed and becomes a constant habit of mind it evolves into a seventh sense.

7. Intuitive Mind [KurippuArithal] or symbolic mind, or knowledge by allusion [Iraichipporul, it is called by Tholkappiar, in the section on similes]. Actually, it goes beyond the direct symbol and is only hinted at. Here the tradition or/ and a special code [kuzhooukkuri] plays an important role in exploring and elucidating the meaning of the given text. For example, the inner meaning of the symbol 'lingam' [vulgarly called phallus] one finds in a Siva temple means only number ten, denoting the conjoining of A or 8 and U or 2 which has a special exact and unique

meaning according to the Tamil Siddha tradition. It goes beyond the meaning of devotion or bhakthi as in Sanskrit tradition. It is something unique among all the esoteric traditions of the world. One, who knows the meaning of the number 10, becomes eligible for siddhahood, not before.

8. Insight Mind can be defined as the inner knowledge derived from a fact. When the fact of gravitational force is mentioned, all of the essential knowledge concerning it, will simply flow into the mind of one having insight from the storehouse of cosmic intelligence or Tao.

As an example, I can cite the dialogue between J Krishnamurti and David Bohm the world-renowned physicist on 'The ending of Time'. David Bohm is a very able, competent and practising scientist, fully versed with the knowledge of the concept of time as it is explained by Albert Einstein in his 'relativity theory' in all its aspects. J Krishnamurti was not a physicist but only an esoteric spiritual philosopher. He had experienced all the dimensions of time not only as a concept but also as a living experience. He had also developed the Insight mind. That is why, at the mere mention of the word time, he is able to explore all of its aspects and go beyond the vast store of knowledge, accumulated by David Bohm about time in his professional way of study for some three decades. Ina flash of lightning, as it were, Krishnamurti is given more knowledge about the various aspects of time and also about the ending of time by man, here in this world itself. Unless time is conquered in mind, mind cannot enter into the dimension of eternity. 'Time is not there in heaven', says the Bible. It also says:'unless ye become like children, ye cannot enter into the kingdom of God'. For the children have not yet developed the sense of ego along with its sense of time. Ego-consciousness cannot be eradicated from one's mind, without destroying the sense of time in one's mind. What the Bible only hints at, Krishnamurti explains in broad, clear-cut, everyday terms because he had developed his insight mind. In fact, he has written a whole book on 'Exploration into Insight'. He called his philosophy, the philosophy of insight.

The vast synthesis of knowledge of Vedanta and western science and its evolutionary theory and beyond offered by Sri Aurobindo in his great world classics like 'Life Divine' and 'Synthesis of Yoga' is another example and evidence of the operation of the 'Insight Mind'.

9. The ninth sense or degree of knowledge as enunciated by Thiruvalluvar is something unique about Tamil Siddha literature. I don't think it is known or mentioned about anywhereelse in world traditions. Perhaps Christ, being a Siddha might have known about it. All the others only talk about it in vague, philosophical terms without mentioning about the physical location in the human head.

It is named by Thiruvalluvar as.

Nun MaanNuzhaipulamillaanezhilnalam

Manmaanpunaipaavaiatru - Kural

The beauty and health of one, who has no faculty of entering inner spiritual sky, is like the painting of a woman drawn by clouds in the outer, physical sky which can be blown away by a small wind. It has no stability.

Here Thiruvalluvar clearly states two things: one, there is an inner, spiritual and divine sky called Chidambaram, a living sky where the Lord is eternally dancing. There is a way and a door, the minutest aperture, the subtlest of the subtle way in the entire creation, inone's head at its centre. The door is now closed. It should be opened. It is called *Thirukkadavamthiratha*by Ramalinga in his ThiruArutpa.

Thirukkadavamthiravaayothiraigalellamthavirthe

Thiruuruvamkaattayo

Won't you open the eternal door?

Won't you remove the veils therein?

Won't you show me your divine figure?

Won't you give me the nectar?

Vallalar pleads with God.

The entrance is the smallest of the small, the finest of the fine in God's creation. One should enter this real temple of real God with one's own consciousness. To do it, one should sharpen and refine one's consciousness to the utmost level, to the level of God himself. That is why, in Tamil God is called as Irai. Irai means the smallest of the small, the microcosm, both in measurements as well as in time [Iraialavu meaning the smallest unit and IraiPozhuthu meaning the smallest measure of time are words used by ancient Tamil poets.]

The grosser levels of consciousness like desire, fear, envy, anxiety, anger, lust, ambition and all the other manifestations of negative emotions and thinking, even thought itself are like large boulders and mountains when compared with the tiny entrance to the inner temple. Jesus compares these grosser manifestations of consciousness to the large size of a camel and the subtle doorway to a needle's eye in his poetic way. He says:

'A rich man cannot enter into the kingdom of God even if a camel enters into the eye of a needle'.

In fact, this is the only key with which all the paradoxes spoken by Jesus in the New Testament especially in his sermon on the mountain can be opened.

Jesus says when a man slaps you on your left cheek show him the right. What does he mean? He warns us to be always watchful of our normal, mechanical, bodily, and mental reactions for they are all gross, habitual reactions like anger, lust, envy, grosser sense of righteous indignation. With these large boulder-like thoughts one can never enter the inner kingdom of God. He is very specific about the location of this kingdom of God. It is not somewhere beyond the outer boundaries of the universe. He declares,'the kingdom of heaven is within you'. Saivite religion says the same thing. This knowledge is given out in stone, in architectural form in the temple at Chidambaram near Pondicherry of South India, in all its elaborations and details. If one wants still more exact knowledge about this inner sanctum sanctorum, one is required to go to Vadalur near Chidambaram, where Swami Ramalinga has built another temple called Uttara [the advanced, the later] Gnana Chidambaram.

Only inside this inner temple of God, one can have God's eternal food amrutha that will keep one free of hunger. Only inside this inner kingdom of God, one can have God's eternal breath, the Holy Spirit which will make one an immortal. Only inside this inner kingdom of heaven, one can see the eternal God himself in the form of vast grace light [ArutPerumJothi].

This is the ultimate siddhi attained by Siddhas such as Christ and Ramalinga Vallalar. That is why Christ says only those who are blessed with a pure heart can see God, meaning, pure consciousness shorn of all gross impurities like lust for power, money, women, vengeance, desire, fear, worry, ambition and so on. Only love and compassion are the subtle denominations of consciousness smaller than the entrance into the inner temple. That is why Christ and Ramalinga emphatically state compassion alone is the key to the door of salvation.

Jeeva kaarunyame moksha veetinthiravukol

Unfortunately,Jesus' compassionstopped with humanism with humans. But Swami Ramalinga emphasizes total compassion towards all beings including plants and animals. Total compassion is a must for attaining divine knowledge or the truth consciousness.

10. The tenth sense or knowledge supreme is God's own absolute knowledge. It is called by Thiruvalluvar as Vaalarivu the knowledge of light. Every aspect of God is of light. Everything about man is dark. That is why the rishi of the ancient Rig Veda prays to God: Oh Lord, Lead me from darkness to light.

This darkness is manifested as matter, in the world and the human body. So the matter in the human body must be transformed into the divine light substance of the body of god. This dark world of matter must be finally transformed into the divine light world of heaven of god.

This is the meaning of the next line of the same prayer;

Oh Lord ! Lead me from *asat* to *sat* from matter to divinity.

This line is unfortunately translated as 'lead me from falsehood to truth'. This philosophical rendering pushes the sense into still more obscurity. Only a scientific rendering can be a meaningful one for the modern mind.

The last line of the prayer describes the last manifestation of darkness in being that is death the termination of being and consciousness. That is why the rishi prays to the Lord;

Lead me from death to deathlessness

Some sixteen scholars have written commentaries on the Sanskrit Vedas, they say. But none unfortunately understood them properly nor exactly. The Vedas were waiting for someone, one inspired by god knowledge to interpret them rightly and scientifically with modern terminology. The concept of the conquest of physical immortality being an ancient Siddha concept, it was rightly understood by Nammalvar the Tamil Vaishnava saint and said so in his immortal classic ThiruVaaiMozhi, the Dravidian Veda. Later it was again rightly understood by the Saivaite saint Thirumoolar and rendered so in his encyclopedic text of yogas called Thirumanthiram. Finally, it was Sri Ramalinga who expounded the teaching in all its scientific and practical details in his philosophy. The total deathless life [maranamilla Peru vaazhvu] - this may be considered to be the most ancient teachingof the world discovered by Tamil Siddhas.

Some seventy-five years after the advent of Ramalinga Vallalar, Sri Aurobindo also surprisingly arrived at the same conclusion that God's absolute knowledge is knowledge of light. The ancient Tamil sage Thiruvalluvar had already said so inhis very second couplet of his immortal, secular, humanist revelation for all mankind, Thirukkural. He called it Vaal arivu. Anyone who attains to this highest level of knowledge verily becomes God. God the most magnificent one will only be too glad to confer the title upon one of his competent sons or daughters. He cannot be a narrow-minded mean and cheap politician to say no tohis own offspring, which act even an ordinary mortal does happily.

Vaal arivu or mind of light is total absolute knowledge born of total compassion. It is always - every timeless or eternal moment knowing and creating all things events and beings everywhere in the universe. It is the 43rd state of consciousness according to Swami Ramalinga Vallalar. Jivathuriya and para thuriya are mentioned in the Upanishads. Siva thuriyawas explained by saintThirumular. Swami Ramalinga goes beyond all those and announces after experiencing them suddha Siva thuriyam and suddha Siva thuriyatheetham. To my knowledge, none in human history had known or divulged all these higher degrees of knowledge. God had blessed only Vallalar with these supreme states of super consciousness.

~~~ ~~~ ~~~

11. RELIGION BASED ON THE BODY

I delivered a lecture on Nataraja Guru at Fernhill Gurukula in Ooty. It was simple, clear and deep. The audience liked it. My strength is to transform difficult subtle and technical knowledge into everyday terms understandable by common men and women on the street. J Krishnamurti first tried this method and succeeded to some extent. He was able to bring the philosophical matter into everyday terms but there ended his success. His methodology of presentation was too logical and intellectual. This limitation was understood by Osho and he rectified it. However, he diluted it too much because his aim was more commercial than esoteric. He wanted to reach the widest possible audience. Ultimately the level of your audience determines your way of presentation. My aim is to dilute the technique but not the matter. I want to come in between JK and Osho. In addition to that, I want to introduce the scientific method of the Tamil Siddhas as well as their knowledge. For I believe that afterthe advent of psychological interpretation of spirituality introduced in the twentieth century by the theosophists and C G Jung the world has entered the scientific paradigm. They explained everything in terms of inner experience or psychology which was not adequate for the common masses. Vedanta and Buddhist philosophies stop here.

Even about consciousness theorists like J.K. and Osho stop here. However, it is not enough in the twenty- first century. Even Sri Narayana guru stops here. For they wanted themselves to be known as neo-vedantins negating the body. They of course did not negate but accepted two of the three major negations of Vedanta and Buddhism namely the negation of the world and negation of life on this world. They wanted to reform and transform this world and this life into a heavenly divine life. However, they were not ready to accept the possibility of divinity of this body like Christ, Sri Ramalinga, Thirumoolar or the Tamil Siddhas. Christ talked about transforming his physical body into a body of spiritual light. Thirumoolar and the Siddhas talked about the physical immortality of this body in its pure form. All the three transformations though they are of various grades among themselves, were only about the physical body. Since the basic premise of Vedanta or neo-Vedanta is that this body is the only obstacle to attaining salvation they could not cross that boundary and so could not enter into the physical scientific paradigm of the twenty first century. They had to stop at atman or consciousness short of the body.

Let me illustrate it with one example. Sri Narayana guru defines atman as i] the enlightening of the darkness of consciousness into one of light and ii] that level of consciousness which is self-aware. Whereas enlightenment is defined by Thirumoolar and the Siddhas in terms of the subtle functions of the body; enlightenment is translated in Tamil as thelivu. Thelivu in Tamil means clarity or purity and in addition to that toddy [kal] shorn of intoxication by the addition of a pinch of calcium. In short thelivu is liquor produced in the pineal gland and secretes into the throat through the uvula or inner tongue. Thelivu [enlightenment] is a thing, a physical object, a drink [it is not only physical, but a spiritual drink suffused with immense consciousness – sithuruvanamarunthu, spiritual medicine, jnana marunthu philosophical medicine [the Siddhas call it] something produced by man's own effort through vasi yoga, a higher form of pranayama or yoga of compassion, in particular. The definition of enlightenment is given in terms that are physical so that it could be verified physically by anyone thus making it more scientific. That was why the mother of Pondicherry said that salvation was physical and she explored the cellular consciousness. Being by birth a western woman exposed to the western scientific atmosphere she couldn't negate the body. Since she was not acquainted with the Tamil Siddha literature she could not travel much in that realm. Her work in the attempt of transforming her body into one of physical immortality was not a total success. She laments in one place that Sri Aurobindo did not tell her about the physical transformation of the body. Through her work of 13 volumes, her agenda was a pioneer work recording her experiments and experiences in the new field, she worked like a lost child in a dark forest. She was groping for a way out for a spark of light. Unfortunately for her not only the way out but also the whole map is available fully chartered, printed and published in the 3000 year old Tamil Siddha literature. The derogatory look on Tamil and its literature and preference of the high-class Sanskrit and English literature has played havoc with some of the greatest minds of the world. With some aid, with some right clues, the mother with her Himalayan will and Herculean perseverance could have succeeded in her attempt of becoming a Siddha and could have conquered physical death. I mention all these to denote the fact that the time is ripe for a paradigm-shift from the psychological to the physiological. I mean the esoteric physiology or the yogic physiology of the Siddhas.

In fact, it is very simple. The milestones or landmarks of the journey of transformation of man's consciousness have been recorded in various texts of esoteric spirituality starting from the Upanishads to Sri Aurobindo, JK, Osho and so on. The Siddhas have recorded their achievements in physical transformation of the body corresponding to the changes in consciousness. World texts of spirituality record only the partial knowledge of transformation of consciousness. On the other hand, the Siddha literature gives us the whole symptoms, process and the results occurring on all the three levels of man –body, mind and spirit. The only obstacle standing in the way, to my humble knowledge, seems to be that the prejudice against the Siddha literature neglected its wisdom all these millennia due to social cause. The lotus may be born in the mire, the pearl of great price in a lowly origin. Those seekers of truth, who want only truth, nothing but the truth will have to come to the place where the real treasure is hidden. Otherwise, the search will be futile. Mankind as a whole cannot move further in its evolution.

Ken Wilber has already done half of the job. He has tabulated all the results of the world's esoteric systems in all their gradations. Now our task is to match those symptoms and landmarks with those of the Siddha literature correspondingly, one to one. The sudden outburst of translations of yogic techniques in the west shows that the time for the paradigm shift has arrived. The advent of yogi Ramaiah and his pioneer work concerning the Siddha literature must be recorded in letters of gold in the history of the world.

Of late a Canadian association has started publishing translations of the major works of the major Siddhas in English. One Prof. Ganapathy who is well versed in the Siddha literature is doing a laudable job. He should be congratulated and encouraged to do more in this direction. Yogadasatsang started by ParamahamsaYogananda introduced the Siddha system, but only in its vasi Yoga [Kriya Yoga was his own terminology] part to the west whereas the medicinal, psychological, social and spiritual aspects of it were waiting to be introduced to the world at large. Saint Ramalinga's works deal with all the aspects of the Siddha literature in clear-cut terms. World conferenceson his SuddhaSanmarga teaching is taking place all over the world. All these are some of the certain indications, I believe, of the radical shift in paradigm, from one of esoteric psychology to one of esoteric physiology, which is the real scientific one accepted by scientists all over the world. A Siddha literally is a scientist, one who has achieved permanent mastery and control over nature, not only in inner nature but also in outer nature like Christ. The day is not far off when the whole of humanity will aspire toward deathless bodies, resurrected bodies, and spiritual bodies of divine light as envisaged correspondingly by the Tamil Siddhas as well as the Taoists of China, by Christ in the west and finally by Sri Ramalinga of Tamilnadu. All these are open possibilities to be explored by scientists in the twenty-first century. Dalai Lama, Ken Wilber, Fritjof Capra and other New age gurus who want to popularize the Eastern esoteric wisdom must be introduced to the immense treasures of these three systems of yogic physiology that deal with physical immortality. When the popularisation of the texts and techniques reach the masses of the world, the total transformation, a literal mutation of Homo sapiens as a species might occur in the near future. This is not impossible.

When one kills a human body or animal body or plant body one kills along withit God also. For the spirit is the dwelling place of God, the real heaven, the kingdom of God. When this truth is realized by all, non - killing will become the number one virtue. Wars will come to an end.

The human body will be worshipped as the true temple of God. For it is accepted by all scriptures of all religions that man was created by God in his own image.

~~~ ~~~ ~~~

12. SPIRITUALISATION OF MATTER

Is it possible to spiritualise matter? Yes, says Indian *tantras*, agamas and the Siddhas.

With Descartes, the world was bifurcated into two fragments: matter and mind. Before that, all the religions of the world and philosophers had accepted three entities. matter, mind and spirit. Inorganic matter and spirit are two poles apart. Their meeting ground is the mind or consciousness. Consciousness is like a spectrum. The first half of it is constituted by matter, the latter half by spirit. Both are joined together in the middle in human consciousness. Man stands exactly in between stone and God. He is both inert earth and spiritual God. If he decided to tilt his attention upon matter and focuses his concentration and mental energy upon matter, like a scientist, he will end up in earth. On the contrary, if he decides to emphasize his spiritual aspect and spends his life on it, he will end up as a spiritual being. Matter will draw him into the region of time, temporality, and death. Spirit will make him cross over the boundary of time and enter into timeless living or eternity. The ending of time in consciousness is one condition of man's entry into the spiritual domain. If it has not taken place in his consciousness permanently, he is still in the domain of mind or subtle matter, however philosophical is his talk or however religious is his behavior.

Is it possible to end time in one's consciousness?

Here is an illustration. In the sixteenth century, when the European settlers went to America, they had to travel on land, by foot, or cart and on sea by ship. Land and water were two mediums, two obstacles they had to endure and overcome. Today anyone can go to America by air. Land and water are no longer the obstacles. A new medium of air travel has been discovered.

Well, we are all like the European settlers of the sixteenth century living in the past as far as our consciousness is concerned. It is still primitive. It has not advanced. It stagnates. A Guru's consciousness is like modern jet travel. Like land and sea our consciousness is bifurcated into two – day and night, light and darkness, intelligence and ignorance, good and bad, all varieties of polarity. Who or what causes it? Time causes it. To be exact, the sun. when it rises in the east in the morning, we call it a day. When it sets in the west in the evening, we call it night. This division is called time and time controls our life.

We are beings of time. We are like fish in the stream of time. We are born in time, live in time and die in time. We are bonded slaves to time. A Guru is not. He has evolved into an amphibian that has learnt to jump over to the bank. He has escaped the clutches of time. He has ended time. Time is no longer a constraint or constriction in his consciousness. 'The ending of time in one's consciousness' is the major difference between a Guru and a layman.

A guru's consciousness does not live in day or night compartments. It lives in an eternal dimension – Atman-consciousness. Day and night must go. That is the real realization of self, the scientific indication and test. A guru also traverses across his day but from a different centre of consciousness, from a centre beyond thought, beyond memory, beyond polarities, from a higher vantage point like from a space craft witnessing the entire landscape of the earth comprising all land and seas at a glance. For, he has attained absolute consciousness. As long as time dominates the human mind, it is only relative consciousness. Only with the ending of time, absolute consciousness comes into operation. Only when the absolute consciousness comes into operation, the apparent world removes its screen and the real absolute reality is revealed to man. Then the very world looks like *Vaikunda, Kailaya*, Heaven like bliss and the eternal face of God, man witnesses for the first time. Until time goes, absolute consciousness remains only hearsay, word of mouth, mere book-learning.

How to end time? A whole book is devoted to this topic by J Krishnamurti and David Bohm, the physicist. At the end of it, Krishnamurti says, thought must end. Only with the ending of thought time can come to an end. For thought is time. Thought creates time. How to end thought? By ceaselessly watching the rising of thoughts without choice. Eventually one day you will realize how cleverly you are fooled by thoughts. And this realization will curb the birth and growth of thoughts. A thoughtless silent state will be born in you and you will be free from time. The ending of time will take place only then.

Thought will breed itself without end as long as desire and psychological greed for more number of things and aspects of living are there. The body-mind complex must be seen by you only as a biological function and nothing more. At this pure state, thought will cease to produce itself. Time will stop. With the stopping of time, eternal living takes over man's life. This is how a real guru lives even in everyday life.

It is not an easy joke, not as easy as it sounds, not meant to be. Suppose I found an ashram tomorrow. With the little bit of esoteric information I have collected for three decades from my reading of all classics of eastern and western spirituality and my association with great saints all through my life, I may even win over a group of gullible people who might call me guru. But is it true? Have I attained a guru consciousness? That is the only parameter. In other words, has time ended in my consciousness?

That is why a guru is equated above and beyond Brahma, Vishnu and Maheswara. All the three are great gods but within the frame of time. One day they are also supposed to die. A single day for them may extend into billions of years, even yugas, but they too are time-bound. A single day in Brahma Loka, they say, is equal to millions of yugas, but still Lord Brahma himself has not conquered time in his consciousness. On the other hand, guru does. That is why he is equated with Param Brahman, the absolute, the Godhead. Guruhood and godhood are the same. An enlightened Guru is God himself.

Is purification of consciousness as shown by Vedanta or in its modern version of J Krishnamurti or the way of Zen – the only way to end time? Or is there any other way?

There is, say the Tamil saints and Siddhas, they go scientifically. They ask you to rewind time backward. How did time first come into existence in a man's life? By his first breath when the child was born into this world and started breathing. Breathing starts the time function in the child's mind. In fact, breath is time. That is why the natal chart, the astrological chart is drawn according to the time of its first breath on earth. The configuration of planets at the time of birth is taken into account. The time frame of the cosmos is made to synchronise with the time frame or life of the child for the next 120 years, that is, two cycles of sixty years and one complete rotation of all the nine planets in a chart. After that you will be free from the influences of nine planets if you are still alive after that long period.

Time itself will leave you after that. This is one way of ending time – living for more than 120 years. That is why the Siddhas want you to take *rasayana* or *kayakalpa* and live for *yugas* or *kalpas* for ages. After 120 years, time releases you from its bondage. Unfortunately, at that time, old age and its ravages would have made you a very sick person like a tattered coat upon a stick – what a beautiful and exact image from the great poet W B Yeats!

Can't we conquer time even while we are very much alive in our younger days? Yes, we can, the Siddhas affirm and offer their vasi yoga or refined version of Pranayama. However, this is a dangerous exercise that is prohibited for the uninitiated. Strictly, one must learn it from a guru who is already practicing it and has a thorough knowledge of its pitfalls and dangers on the way. For, this will finally lead to slowing down of breath and ultimately to its suspension. According to allopathic medical science, if one stops breathing for more than one and a half minutes, the oxygen supply needed by the cells in the brain will be cut off, the brain will have a haemorrhage and death follows instantly. It is too dangerous a game to play. Yet the Siddhas go on that way. That is why it is called 'walking on the razor's edge'. Those who dare to go on that path may write down their will and testament before embarking upon this dangerous quest of a journey.

Your first breath started the inner biological clock ticking and time is running its course in your body like a stream with a source, course and end. When the breath is somehow stopped, time stops. However, you must learn the yoga of stopping the breath and still live and still retain your life on earth. In short, like a Siddha, like a rishi in his *sahaja samadhi*, you should have learned to live without being dependent upon air.

The scientific explanation offered by the Siddhas is simple. The sun and moon that create time for you, every day for you are in fact residing in your body. Breath through the right nostril is known as sun; breath through the left nostril is known as moon. These create day and night in consciousness. These natural ways are to be discarded slowly and gradually for a new way of breathing as taught by the Siddhas. It is called inspiration or inner breathing which circulates inside the body and has no contact with the atmospheric air. This is a secret technique beyond the reach of understanding of modern science. They emphatically say that such a system exists and if you are lucky or destined you don't have to look for such a Siddha for he will come to you. The Siddhas are like vultures that are constantly circling in the sky looking for their prey upon earth.

II

The universe of matter is being spiritualized on the face of the earth. Man is the agent appointed for the task. His body is already doing the task partially without his consent or consciousness. The job of religious and spiritual leaders is to remind him of his task as entrusted upon him by God, in the natural scheme of things and to do it fully consciously. Unfortunately, religions and spirituality have become large institutions catering to the needs and comforts of the power mongers and agents of the devil. Therefore, the intellectual of the world must take over this task in his hand and remind man constantly of his task entrusted upon him by God.

The plant is transforming inorganic, natural energies like sunlight, carbon di oxide, and water into organic food material. Man eats this organic food and converts it into thought or mental matter. This is the stage in evolution wehumans are in now.A yogi goes beyond thought and by awareness and love and compassion creates spiritual matter by his own efforts. A Siddha goes still further and transforms this spiritual matter into divine matter. All the four forms of matter are already in the human body. What distinguishes each of the four levels of matter is their duration or life cycle. Their life cycles in turn are determined by their purity.

In the human body the nails and hair are almost inorganic. All the other three trillion cells in the body are more organic in quality. Their life cycle is about one week. In the next level comes the brain cells. Their lifetime is about one and a half year to two years. Above them in longevity are the optic nerves and other light –identifying cells in the brain. They are almost immortal already. They never die. So, a part of the human body is already immortal. This has happened naturally in millions of years in the course of evolution. Now this process has to be speeded up by man consciously.

The Russian mages Gurdjieff and P D Ouspensky were two such remarkable intellectuals or spiritualists, though they had only distrust for the so-called intellectuals.

Like the ancient alchemists, they had a graded but unified system of matter, mind and spirituality. They posited that all that the universe and man, the micro-cosmos, contained was only matter. However, with man there is a possibility for him to give birth to and develop a spirit or being with his own efforts. The potential of a spiritual being has to be actualized and realized by man by his efforts and understanding. This process was called 'The work' by Gurdjieff – the only work intended for man by God's creation, the work upon himself, upon his consciousness, upon spiritualizing and divinizing his senses and body by intensifying his awareness and consciousness.

The real anatomy and physiology of the human body-mind machine is brilliantly portrayed in the Taitriya Upanishad with its theory of five divisions of the body and the Atman residing beyond them- the food-body, the prana or energy or air-body, the thought body, the pure intelligence body, [the higher intellectual centre in Gurdjeiff's system] the bliss body or love body [the higher emotional centre in Gurdjeiff's system]. One has to travel inside by meditation and cross over the boundaries of all these bodies, according to Vedanta and reach the Atman. Realizing or awakening the power of Atman, the light of it should be brought out and focused upon all the five bodies, transforming them in the process into spiritual entities like Christ did in his body, as Vallalar did in his body.

Some thinkers such as Nataraja Guru and Guru Nitya Chaitanya Yati considered this assumption and projection of the theory of the five bodies that is not mentioned in the Upanishad itself by the rishi is fictitious. Only later commentators added this fiction of five bodies.

Anyway, in such a situation with a different understanding, the aspirant can take the clue from Gurdjieff and Ouspensky and consider everybody as a centre in his body-mind consciousness and learn to separate, identify and operate with its own brand of energy, with its own brand of hydrogen atoms, in the terminology of Gurdjieff's system. Only the roles of the fourth and fifth bodies were reversed in his system. The higher intellectual centre was placed up above the higher emotional centre. Perhaps Gurdjieff's distrust of bhakthi as sentimentality was the reason for it. He said the higher emotional centre worked with hydrogen 12 but the higher intellectual centre needed a still higher and more concentrated energy of hydrogen 6. Gurdjieff was more a philosopher than a bhaktha.

Many people who study the teachings of J K find it difficult to understand them, even after a lifetime of reading. The clue to understanding him is to go by the various dimensions and denominations of energy.

Thought is a material though subtle energy. Intuition is of a different energy and of a different dimension. Insight is a totally different energy of spirituality coming from the total cosmic energy or Tao. Only by dissolving all walls of separation in the human consciousness and then the walls between human consciousness and the universe and God, this is possible. The total energy of the cosmos is available at every moment, in every situation for theenlightened one. This energy of insight is an infallible one. It can never go wrong. For it always acts out of truth of absolute consciousness. Once it is attained, man loses his individuality of consciousness except for his body. The wholeness of life, the wholeness of cosmic life is lived by the guiding voice of insight. That is why J K says, there is no choice in the state of total freedom. For you become one with the cosmos. The voice becomes one. The motive becomes one. Not your welfare but the welfare of the total cosmos becomes your concern like that of God. This is literally God-consciousness, Buddha consciousness, Christ consciousness, Tao consciousness. This is true spiritual energy beyond the material, atomic energy of thought, which is totally different, which always remains a fragment, which always remains a fraction of an individual consciousness.

Both thought and insight are in the consciousness of man. Man is only a cripple with thought, a slave. He should free himself from the chain of thought and go beyond. This is true liberation for man. When the light of insight descends upon his consciousness man's whole body will have a possibility of being transformed into a spiritual one, a true resurrection.

~~~ ~~~ ~~

13. SPIRITUALITY AND DIVINITY OF THE HUMAN BODY

One singular fact about the human body, but a costly mistake, a Himalayan blunder committed by even the greatest of saints and enlightened masters is about the spiritual and divine dimensions of the body.

When you fall physically sick, you go to a doctor and get your health restored. When you fall mentally sick you go to a psychiatrist and get your mental health restored. Eastern spirituality both Hindu and Buddhist claim, and the claim is true, that once a man attains spirituality, he will never fall mentally sick again.

The question is why not apply the same logic to physical sickness also? Is there a science disciplined and formulated step-by-step like Patanjali's Astanga Yoga or eight-step yoga for the permanently healthy and never-sick body? The answer is yes, there is, say the Siddhas. The world should wake up to this light and liberate mankind from disease first. Then, what is the way suggested by them?

The theory is the same. Mind is an impure organ and its activities are the diseases of consciousness: spirituality is a state, which cleanses the mind ofall its impurities or kills it as somewould like to put it once for all. Then there is no possibility of going back or falling mentally sick again. The door is closed forever. Let it be so.

What about the body? Is it not a part of mind-body complex? Or does not body affect the mind, as in psychosomatic diseases? The spiritualists keep silent on this question. At best they reply that it is the nature of the body to fall sick.

The Siddhas offer asolution. As when the impure mind is cleansed of all dross, the mental health is never lost, likewise, when the physical impure body is cleansed of all impurities it attains a state of pure body, an incorruptible body of flesh. This is the first step in real spirituality.

The practical steps suggested are very simple, rational and quite convincing.

i] Just listen to the body. Believe in the wisdom of the body, the wonder-machine created by the omnipotent God. Buddhist Vipasana and modern spiritual teachers like J K advocate self-awareness, constant, choiceless, self-awareness as the way of stilling or killing of the mind and its thoughts. Thought is supposed to be the disease of the mind. When you constantly watch the thoughts of the mind, you understand the mechanism of how your thoughts by themselves will stop arising. Follow the same process with the body. Watch it constantly; its needs, habits, its suggestions and its native intelligence. Slowly the divine intelligence operating the heart, brain and the respiratory system in a divine way, will be restored in the body. Don't listen to the mind. Listen to the body.

When you feel hungry feel how much of fire is there in the belly. Give it only so much of food. No more. Even something less is better than more. This is the

Rule no 1. concerning the quantity of food;

Rule no 2. Deals with the excretory system: once the food is digested and the essence absorbed by the body, don't eat anything more. And here comes the vital point, ignored by modern man and doctors alike. Until the excretory matter, accruing from the food inside, is totally washed away from the bowels, no more food is to be taken. Ignoring this rule is the cause of indigestion, constipation, and subsequently all the diseases. Watch the birds. They eat and excrete the waste matter immediately.

Rule no 3. concerns the selection of food. Though Einstein proved that all matter contains energy, the atomic scientist does not put any or every material into the reactor for transforming it into energy, which is not possible. Great care is taken in selecting the material. Only uranium and its particular isotopes, which have already started emitting energy, are used for fuel. With all that, the efficiency of the reactor to convert it into energy is minimal around one percent.

Man is not matter alone. He is life also. In fact, great care should be taken in the selection of food. The cultured man, in the name of civilization and fads, thrusts anything into his mouth. This is not even common sense. The human stomach, the digestive system is the natural, the noblest atomic reactor ever created. It not only creates energy out of food, but it also sublimates the inorganic matter into organic matter and bio-energy, which is not possible with manmade reactors.

How to select food? By what standard? By the degree of purity of a food. To put it more clearly, all non-vegetarian, animal food must be avoided. Second, only undecaying foods must be taken. If you take into your body a food that starts decaying immediately it corrupts your body and the body also starts decaying. This vital point is again ignored by man. Man should eat not for taste, and not even for nutrition or energy but only for longevity. The purpose of cookingis not to make the food palatable and spicy as the wise Socrates thinks mistakenly. It is to give the food longevity and thereby promoting longevity of man. To arrest the decaying nature of food, to remove the poison and get only the nectar of it. Remove the poison and take only Amrita. All foods are only combinations of poison and nectar. The digestive system does only this. It is the real alchemist. To lessen the burden of the digestive system and do the digestion outside the body was called cooking by Siddhas.

And there are pure foods,undecaying foods like raw sugar and honey and pure water and calcined metals and minerals. A day will come when man will live only on pure water and the 13 biochemical tissue salts discovered by Dr Schussler of Germany. Homeopathy and Biochemistry incidentally derive their philosophy only from the Siddha system of medicine. Selection of foods is a vast science. There are pure foods that are the naturally allotted ones for man and the Uranium of the bio-reactors.

The rule simply says; the food should be by nature the purest of the pure like water from Gangotri, the source of the Ganges in the Himalayas and water from the rain clouds above.

Rule no.4. says the proper balance between the water content, the fire content and the air content must be maintained constantly. Only the imbalance brings disorder called disease. Watch the food you take in. Watch the climate. Watch your mind.

Rule no.5. Watch the economy of energy in the physical organs. The output must never surpass the input. By practicing continence or Brahmacharya and Pranayama this can be properly maintained. Cut out all of your unnecessary movements.

~~~ ~~~ ~~~

14. FOOD PROBLEM OF HUMANKIND

Akkuzhithoorumazhukkuatrapothey- Thirumanthiram

The pit of the stomach will be filled up permanently only when there is not even an iota of excretory, waste matter. Then the pure body starts producing its own food, nectar. It starts production and the brain or the pineal gland secrets the nectar, the real – *KanchiVellam* – into the throat. One drop of this nectar, the Siddhas say, is enough food for man for twelve years. It contains so much of concentrated energy. Then the stomach, the digestive system realizes its full potential of a bio-atomic reactor. It is the scientific way of spirituality. Then sleep and its offspring death will be conquered forever. 30 grams of food will be converted into energy by the bodily reactor equivalent to that energy released by exploding six hundred tonnes of TNT as the atomic science and Einstein's famous formula $E=mc2$ proclaims.

Then the higher Alchemist in the mind the psychic equivalent of the digestive system, will give man the true and direct perception in an instant and every instant without the intervention of memory or knowledge accumulated in the past into her words, mental excreta. Every experience in every moment of life will be unique, joyous like that of a child or a Wordsworth or an enlightened master in *Sahaja Samadhi* such as Vallalar. Every moment will exist by itself producing only joy, without leaving any waste matter or thought behind. Immediately, only the essence of the experience through the perceptions of the five senses will be absorbed by the totally awakened intelligence, and insight will be always in operation all through the day giving always the right answer and solution to every problem that arises in life. Like the gods and angels, man will be eating and absorbing only the essence of food through the five senses, only the nectar. Not even an iota of poison will be admitted into the body or mind. The separation of poison from the nectar in every food and experience will be done outside the body. The digestive system and the mind-psychic digestive system will be spared the excretory matter. The human body will become a real temple where you don't find toilet-rooms. Gods are supposed to eat only the essence of food, the spirit of it only. Man will also ascend to that level. The human body will slowly lose its excretory systems.

The three-step formula to attain this stage of pure-body is this:

1. To eat only vegetarian food. Otherwise, you cannot escape death. To some extent, the possibilities of escape from death are increased by this habit.

2. To eat less food. Limit your movement like a plant. Sit in one place. Do not waste your physical energy by excessive mobility.

3. The final stage is to do away with food – total negation of food, water and air. There will be another type of food, another type of breathing and another type of water. Jesus hinted only at these three in his teachings when he said the following: 'I have some other food you don't know', 'the water of life' and 'unless you are baptized by spirit you cannot enter into the kingdom of God'

This dependence and reliance upon the corrupt food of the outside world must go. Only then doors to the spiritual possibility will be opened. Man will be taught by nature, masters or by God about these different types of food, water and air. Only then and not before. Purification of body, breath and mind is the job of man. Only when man has done his part, the help from the spiritual realm will come. This understanding of the danger of food must be instilled in man's mind first. Then consumerism will be known as man's number one enemy in his upward journey in evolution. The other steps and aids will automatically follow after this realization. 'Man does not live by bread alone'. The meaning is: he dies by bread. It is only a slow death, animperceptible one like the march of time. Overeating killed Gurdjieff, said the doctors who did autopsy on his body.

Does it not sound paradoxical or even absurd to state that food kills man when statistics declare that a large portion of the child population of the world, in Africa and other underdeveloped countries is dying of starvation, malnutrition and inadequate diet? The answer to this question is yes and no. It is true that it sounds paradoxical as quantum physics sounded paradoxical when it was discovered and announced to the world. Now it is an accepted fact that Newton's and Einstein's laws of macrophysics do not work in and not applicable in the microphysical world of the quantum or sub-atomic world. There the laws are different. Macrophysics and Microphysics are only complementary to each other. Similarly, up to certain point, it is so determined by the quotient of efficiency of the nuclear reactor in man's stomach, lungs, and brain. The utterly inefficient way, say 0.0000001 percent of its real potential in which they are functioning now demands a quantity in kilograms for every meal. When the genes are reprogrammed and the efficiency of the digestive system increased a thousand-fold or even a million-fold and Einstein's formula $E= mc2$ is actually realized inside the human atomic rector also, perhaps 1 gram of food might be the need of man for a day. The change in the programming of genes, the change in the efficiency of extracting energy out of matter or food – when this will occur or how long it will take for man to accomplish this revolution or the next biological mutation in man, could be answered only when the importance of this problem is fully understood and the concentrated attempt is made by all the scientists in the world, say by scientists from a combination of various disciplines in science like atomic science, human biochemistry, nutrition, transpersonal psychology and mysticism. How much time will this require? Who can say? This could happen even next year. It depends on the speed and concentrationof our collective effort. Mystics such as J.Krishnamurti emphatically declared that mutation in man could happen in an instant. Perhaps he was talking from personal experience. As for myself, I believe that some kind of mutation has taken place in his mind or consciousness, though not in his body. The unique discoveries by him in the field of consciousness, the way he could apply his whole mind and total energy of his body-mind-being complex on problems and solve them in an original and creative way provide ample evidence of the truth. The way of nineteenth century Tamil Siddha Saint Ramalinga and the way he transformed his physical body intoa spiritual body of wisdom light could throw light for scientists entering this field. The way he took less and less of food and finally the way he did away totally with food is a revelationin the science of evolution of man. To put the matter in physical, scientific terms, when the two-stroke engine in the human digestive system is replaced by four stroke engine, this two wheeler of the human body will also give more mileage and will release more energy out of the same amount of food. By an increase of even 1 percent in the efficiency of the digestive system, we could solve the food problem of the world to a considerable degree.

When the efficiency is increased a hundredfold, there will not be any food problem in the world. This is not utopia or dream. This is real science, science of the real future. When billions of dollars are spent on research and development for increasing the fuel efficiency of cars and two-wheelers, in Japan and America why not in this two-wheeler of man? The discovery of theanswer could not only solve the food problem of humankind forever but also it could make profits in billions of dollars. Once the food problem is done away with, then humankind could concentrate its energies totally on cultural andspiritual activities. As Swami Vivekananda rightly pointed out, a hungry stomach does not need Bhagwat Geeta or a Bible but food first. Serve food and then give him the scripture. This is the right, and meaningful procedure. All these millennia, man has been putting the horse before the cart and the cart has been pushed backward. To change the order of priority and to aim at the permanent solution is the only way left for man.

How can one get such a pure body? What is the process? How can one cleanse the impurities in the genes, in the *vasanas* of the mind? An astonishing and at first an unbelievable fact by way of answer is given by the master Siddha, Thiruvalluvar. He says there are two ways of purifying a man. One is by water, which purifies the outer. The other is by truth or confession as practiced in the Christian religion before a priest, or God as in Hinduism.

Cleanliness of the outer is by water;

Of the inner by confession of truth.

Puram thuimaineeralamayum

Ahamthuimaivaimayalkanappadum.

The above meaning is the normal one given by the commentators. However, there is one more subtle, esoteric meaning aimed at the initiationof Siddha yoga. The outer body for an initiate is not only the physical body but it also includes the five senses as well as the mind. Which means even the impurities of the mind can be cleansed off by water if it is pure enough. The degree of purity of water determines the power of its penetration into the mind-body complex of man. That is why man is asked to take only the purest of the pure water, the rainwater, inits pure form, or the pure water of the Ganges at its source or the spring water uncontaminated. Saint Ramalinga urges his disciples to take only hot water after condensing it by two-fifths. Take five litres of water, boil it down to two litres andthen drink. If one can purify it still more, thebetter it is. If water is purified morethan seven hundred times, it loses all its impurities and becomes the purest water. Its very quality changes and then it is potentized enough to cleanse the body or mind of all its dross and convert it into a pure body.

Ecology is a spiritual science in the literature of the Tamils. Man's body is classified into two: *Akam* and *puram*. This is the classification of the Tamil literature. The scholars know only about these two. On the other hand, there is one more classification in the Siddha and *Bhakthi* literature of the Tamils. The two are subdivided further into four. They are *Akam, Akappuram, Puram* and *Purappuram. Akam* means the spirit. *Akappuram* means the individual *jivan* or life. *Puram* means mind. *Purappuram* means the body and five senses and the world. Therefore, the body, senses and the outer nature are all one. Whatever change occurs in the senses of man, the brain of man, and the mind of man [*akappuram*] will be polluted also. There is no escape. *Puram* the outer operates at three levels, the world or the senses, the mind and the individual soul of man. Only God or Atman the pure spark of God will remain pure always. The remaining three have a taint of corruption or the outer matter or *puram*. Thus for our purpose here, the *puram* or the outer that is the body, the senses, the brain, and the mind also could be cleansed by water alone provided it is purified to the degree and its nature changed to the level of nectar. Saint Ramalinga calls the pure rainwater as; *purapuraamudham*, external nectar.

That is why yogis go to the Himalayas where they can have the purest water from the source of the Ganges. There they can also have the purest, unpolluted air. The purer the oxygen, the more potent and the more energizing its quality. The heat he can create by himself by his pranayama and concentration. By closing his eyes and focusing inwards and upwards upon the Agna Chakra or the place between the eyebrows where the pineal gland is situated he can create enough heat for cooking the spiritual food needed for the growth and development of his spiritual child at Sahasrara Chakra at the crown of the head. Lord Muruga, the spiritual child will be born in the thousand-petaled lotus of the brain. As this spiritual child grows by the spiritual food produced in the body, the transformation of the physical body into a resurrected, spiritual body begins. The allotted period of growth and complete transformation is 12 years according to the scriptures. Then the spiritual child Muruga, Lord Subramania attains puberty and readily destroys the Asura the physical in the body and converts him into the spiritual, his vehicle the peacock and flag, of the cock, omkara in video and audio forms.

For the yogi in his last stage of yoga pure water is both food and water. This is the real meaning of the couplet;

For the Siddhas, the pure rainwater is both food and water.

Thupparkuthuppayathuppakkithupparku

Thuppayathummazhai. - Kural

Thuppar means the Siddha, the intelligence-awakened one. *Thuppu* means two things in Tamil, intelligence or cosmic intelligence and the spit. Saliva is more than a secretion of the body. It is external nectar also. The habit of kissing between male and female is based on the exchange of saliva implying the exchange of intelligence or spiritual power.

The normal or usual rendering of the meaning of this couplet is that rain is at once a food for man and water quenching his thirst. It is also the reason for the growth of plants which become food for man. The real inner meaning is derived from the significance given by repetition of the world *thuppu* six times out of seven words. Thiruvalluvar was not an ordinary poet who would waste words unnecessarily.

Thuppu is the purified salt of Jesus, when he says, 'You are the salt of the world. When the world loses its salt, with which it could be salted again?'. Here the salt implies the intelligence, the virtue and the spiritual power of man. The pure rainwater is enough for the sustenance of a master yogi such as Jesus Christ and saint Ramalinga.

With pure water, pure air and eyesight focused inside, man's seed or woman's seed sprouts into a tree of life and develops into a spiritual tree.

This tree produces the fruit of life, 'thuppu- or real Kanchivellam' the spiritual gruel and the brain secretes it into the throat via uvula, the small tongue. Whoever takes this fruit and water of life becomes immortal. This is the meaning and only purpose of man's body – not wasting it upon sensual enjoyments and thereby dying, ending up as dust or ashes. One who ends up in death is a fool and one who becomes an immortal resurrected body is the wise man. This is the secret, inner meaning of the following couplet, not profit or loss in a business transaction as given by commentators.

Pethaienappaduvathuyathenilethamkondu Uthiampogavidal - *kural*

Consciousness will become a Siddha. Here the medical system is not only a system of medicine but also a system of yoga, a gnana. Again it is lamentable that the present colleges where the system is taught ignore this vital factor of the holistic approach of the Siddha.

Anyhow, after proper purification, the food is cooked. The purpose of the science of cooking is not to add flavor or to make the food tasty and palatable as the wise old Socrates of Greece says in the Platonic Dialogues. It is to add longevity, to add life to the food. Fried food will start decaying soon. Baked foods will always be slow in their decaying. There are 32 ways of cooking or prolonging the life of a food or medicine or extending the expiry date of a food or medicine as given in the textbooks of Siddha medicine. There are hundreds and thousands of such textbooks unused, unexplored, unclassified and unverified. Palm leaf manuscripts alone number more than five thousand. Another five thousand such manuscripts lie unused, untranslated in the Chinese language by the Taoist Siddhas. It is a sorry affair. Siddha or Taoist the knowledge contained in those manuscripts belongs to all the sons and daughters of humankind. Perhaps the globalisation movement will initiate the interaction and exchange of medical knowledge of all traditions of the world. UNESCO could form a committee to go into the details of this programme and unearth the treasures of human knowledge buried under the earth for ages. This is a real task before us, not to buy foreign things that could only enlarge the coffers of the already super-rich men of TNCs and MNCs.

~~~ ~~~ ~~~

15. THE YOGA OF RESURRECTION OF THE BODY

The process of converting this physical body into a spiritual body is called Resurrection. It has three steps:

i] Man does not live by bread alone. He also lives by the word of God. Bread gives fire and warmth to the physical body. Word is also fire but subtle fire needed by the spiritual body.

The more you take in of God's pure words into your body through the ears, the less of bread you will need. At the final stage, like a Christ, you will not be in need of the bread, absolutely. The physical matter would have been transformed into a total spiritual body. Words replace food. The purer the word is the better, Gospels and Revelations of the world are the best spiritual food. Next comes the inspired poetry of great poets. Only inspired portions of them. They are really the daily bread for man. Lastly the words of the inspired philosophy like Plato's. For example, the Garden of Eden of Genesis was translated into philosophy by Plato, the mystic as the world of ideas.

His archetypal idea of the world was, the Garden of Eden; the idea of man and woman were Adam and Eve before the fall. Every tree, every animal, everything was described pictorially by the Bible whereas the same things were treated philosophically by Plato. In addition to the idea of Heaven or Ideal Garden, Plato also described the condition and world of man after the fall, as the cave. In the allegory of the cave, the cave is the present physical world. The shadows are the physical bodies of men and women. The oozing light into the cave is the sunlight of this world. Those who escape this dark cave and enter the world of true light or spiritual light like Christ escape through the small hole with their fine and refined spiritual bodies or resurrected bodies.

ii] Man does not live by water alone. He also lives by the water of life.

Purity is the only yardstick and difference. The pure in heart shall see God. Why? God is nothing but a state of purity. Purity is God, spirit is consciousness purified. Matter is consciousness darkened. Remove the darkness in your consciousness. You are already spirit, already God. What is darkness? Your ego.

In the same way, for creating and sustaining spiritual body take only the purest of the pure water. Drink only pure rainwater or water from Gangotri the origin of the Ganges in the Himalayas. Or purify the water 700 times; you will have the purest water. Drink only this water.

Every once in five minutes, swallow your own saliva. It is also another form of living water created in a living body. Kissing was introduced to drink each other's saliva only. Saliva is nectar.

Another form of water of life is semen in man and sronitham in woman. This must not be wasted, even a single drop of it. Conserve it. This is the only way to become a genius and to have a resurrected body. Become eunuchs to enter into the kingdom of heaven, said Christ. He meant only this habit of conserving and preserving your chastity and continence. This is called 'brahmacharya' in India – practice of protecting Brahman the ultimate. Here only the human seed is openly declared to be Brahman or the absolute God. God created man in his own image. So man is a potential God. Man is only a developed, grown-up seed. So seed is God. 'Don't throw your wild oats in the wind'.

a] By avoiding thoughts on sex b] by always concentrating on your forehead between the eyebrows brahmacharya can be successfully kept up. This is the place where resurrection takes place. This Aagna chakra is the gate to the kingdom of God, the Chidambaram where the Lord Nataraja is dancing eternally, his dance of creation converting matter into spirit. That is the meaning of creation. This place is the ideal city of Jerusalem with 12 gateways. Head is kabalam with its openings.

iii] Man does not live by oxygen alone. He also lives by inspiration from the Holy Spirit or God the subtle prana, different from the atmospheric air.

Adam was infused with God's breath or inspiration and became alive. He did not need oxygen because there was no physical body and no physical air in the Garden of Eden. Everything was spiritual. So if you want to enter into the spiritual heaven of God you must know how to get and breathe this spiritual air. This is the ultimate secret of Siva Yoga. Jesus meant only this when he said: 'unless you are born of spirit, you cannot enter into the kingdom of God'. Spirit means spiritual air, nothing else (prana).

An advanced yogi in Samadhi state lives for years with this inner breathing or inspiration. He does not need oxygen for his survival. This suspension of outer breath is called yoga. Along with the breathings, thoughts or the mind will also be suspended. For both the breathing and mind are twins, two sides of the same coin. The physical is nothing but the image or thought that is noise. The spiritual means silence. Love.

A poet in an inspired state suspends his outer breath and receives the inner spiritual breath of God. Along with this inspiration, he sees some glimpses of the spiritual reality.

These sights he puts down on paper. A poet is the least of the spiritual man. Therefore, art simply means a way to acquire this faculty of inner inspiration and suspending the outer breath. Shakespeare was the supreme example. Michel Angelo was another. Who is an artist? One who has the inner breath. What is art? The product of man under the spiritual breathing. This was what happened at Pentecost.

A plant creates food or chlorophyll in its leaves with three things: fire or heat from the sunlight, air from the atmosphere and water from the roots down below. Inorganic matter is converted into organic matter or made edible for animals and man.

By concentrating his consciousness and eyesight [fire] on the region of the third eye, man combines the water from the roots or *mulathara* called semen and inspiration through the subtle door at the spiritual centre of the head, the pineal gland he cooks spiritual food. This spiritual food or gruel will trickle down his physical throat and transform his physical body into a spiritual body. Once this nectar is produced and tasted by man, he will have no need for any physical food, water, air or warmth. He enters another dimension, the spiritual dimension. This is the final step. This focusing of the sight of closed eyes on the inner third eye is called Kesari Yoga, the yoga of the Lion.

The third eye or the pineal gland can be opened only by God or another spiritual being like Christ or Vallalar. With his subtle and minute spiritual body he can enter this place the size of it being compared to the eye of the needle and open the gates for the spiritual air or prana to enter directly. This is the function of the Guru.

To teach this ultimate science called Siva yoga and open this secret door in the third eye of the initiates are the only functions of a guru, a spiritual being with a resurrected body. This resurrected body is immortal and will never die.

~~~ ~~~ ~~~

16. YOGA OF SUDDHA SANMARGHA

Why start with the purification of the body? For two reasons: first it is possible, yes, it is possible to cleanse the body of all impurities and have a pure body. All these millennia it had been thought by philosophers and saints of both east and west that it is not possible to cleanse the body of all its mala or impurities. Now it is proved that it can be done, well evidenced in the lives of Jesus Christ and saint Ramalinga, saint Thirumoolar and other Siddhas.

Second, all these millennia, philosophers and saints started with the mind and its purification. This is a colossal task like cleansing of the stables by Hercules. Individuality [Anava Mala], residue from the past [karma] and ignorance [maya] have been accumulating in man for innumerable births. Even if one doesn't take into account the truth of reincarnation as in the case of Christians, all the three impurities have been accumulating from day one of man's life on earth. In addition to that the impurities generated by the physical body added to the burden. Man had to fight the combined evils of both the mind and the body. It is too much to be done by an ordinary human being. Extraordinary beings like the Buddha and J

Krishnamurticould do it to leap over the vast chasm at one go. Ordinary mortals have no such energy. They have to go at it one step at a time.

So, the Siddhas devised a plan to divide and conquer the enemy. Purify the body first. When it is over and you get a stable, uncorrupt and incorruptible body, that itself will be an aid to you in conquering the battle against the mind. Convert the body into an aid from being an enemy.

Further the body acts on the mind and the mind acts on the body. The process of generating impurities both by the mind and the body is unfortunately supplemented and complemented by each other. Cut the problem into two halves and solve each half separately. Stabilize yourself first in one.

This is the theory behind the formulation of the concept of a pure body by the Siddhas. There is another advantage in this system. One can simplify the work of yoga by this method. Correct yogic posture, correct breathing, right mental atmosphere, the balance between the inner and the outer focus of consciousness will be done easily and effortlessly by the pure body, with its uninterrupted universal intelligence. The wisdom of the body is unimpeded and uninhibited by the mind or tradition here.

The traditional way of saints of all religions was through mind and its control and subsequent eradication. This is a slight alteration at the initial stages in the way discovered and practiced by the Siddhas. They want to purify the instrument of body first. And this seems to be scientific also.

The weight of body and the physical habits of the brain are pulling down man in his efforts to rise to the spiritual domain. J Krishnamurti could counter and win over the inertia of the body by devoting more than four hours a day on the exercising of his body and silencing the ever-working brain cells. This helped him go beyond into eternal timeless living of the absolute consciousness. However, an ordinary human being can do it only one at a time. Transforming his impure body into a pure one and concentrating all of one's forces and attention on it are easier when compared with the all-out attack of the traditional method.

SuddhaSanmargha is the way of enlightenment and immortality and divinity discovered by Swami Ramalinga Vallalar of South India. According to him, 'Yoga of Compassion' directed towards all sentient beings, human, animal and vegetation is the foremost yoga. In addition to that he prescribes purification of body, senses, mind, psyche and atman in his 'daily regimen'. This impure physical body is to be transformed step by step into a pure body, sound body and light body of compassion. He has given us a complete science of these triple transformations. He accomplished it in his own body. We will deal with it in the later chapters.

17. THE WAY OF FUTURE EVOLUTION OF HUMANKIND

I – Meaning of evolution

The concept of evolution was not originated in the west. It was first proclaimed by the Tamil grammarian, Tholkappiar. Unlike Charles Darwin who believed in mechanical evolution shaped by natural selection, Tholkappiar believed in creative evolution. According to him the life principle wanted to realize its full potential and proceeded to liberate itself from the dark inconscient matter and evolved sense by sense. The inner urge of the life principle wants to conquer and transcend all limitations imposed upon it by nature, particularly the limitations of time and space.

Every step or stage in evolution brought forth a new faculty. And the burning desire and earnestness for a new faculty at last materialised itself into a new sense organ. *Orarivathue uttrarivu.** The amoeba had only one sense, the tactile. This sense of touch reached its culmination in the plant. It learnt to grow by eating. Later it learnt to create its own food by photosynthesis. The plant was a successful demonstration on the part of the evolutionary force, which liberated itself from everlasting inertia and death of matter.

To a very small extent, the limitations of space, distance, time or death were conquered.

The urge to go, to move from one place to another manifested itself in the sense of taste and in the organ of tongue. Some more refinement in consciousness resulted in motion.

The third sense developed was smell and its corresponding organ nose. The fourth was the sight and its organ eye. The fifth was hearing and it produced the ears.

II – The Third Eye

Eventually in man, the all-conquering faculty of mind was born. What was the organ for the mind? Of course, the brain. That is what modern science says. It is only partially true. The whole truth is that mind, to bring forth its full potential of the conquest of space and time has developed inside the brain, an exact organ called the pineal gland. This is the organ known in the Tamil Siddha and Saiva literatures as the third eye of Lord Siva.

Modern science is yet to know the purpose and function of this organ. Until recently, a surgeon accidentally touched a patient's brain with his knife during a brain operation, western science was in the dark. Unexpectedly the patient developed para psychological senses like telepathy. The doctor was surprised and recorded the patient's paranormal experiences in a medical journal.

But this was common knowledge here in Tamil Nadu among the Siddhas. Saint Ramalinga says 'by any means, get your third eye opened'. He also gives out the ways to open it. 'Keep your attention always focused upon it. Meditate upon that point, imagining that a light is burning there'. He also comes out with recipes to clear out the passage to it blocked by the mucous.

III – Thiruvidam

The point is, long before saint Ramalinga, long before Tholkappiar, the originators themselves of the language of Tamil had known this fact of the use of the pineal gland. This is known as the very letter "ak" in the Tamil alphabet. It denotes the third eye, the place in between and behind the eyes. The Chinese Taoists called it 'the sacred square inch of immortality'. The Tamils called it, the temple of God, 'ThiruChitrambalam' where the Lord is eternally dancing'. It was also called 'thirunilai' the place of immortality. Refer to swami Ramalinga's verses;

> 1. *Thirunilaithanivelisivavelienumore*
> *Arulvelippathivalararutperunjothi*
> *-Agaval poem (ThiruArutpa)*
> 2. *Thiruneriuttren*

The great Tholkappiar has stopped with the sixth stage of evolution, with the rising of the phenomenon of man. Though he knew the secret of further evolution through the pineal gland to the seventh stage of intelligence, spirituality, it was reserved by God for another saint to be born specifically for that purpose in the nineteenth century, swami Ramalinga. Out of compassion for mankind was revealed by him all the secrets of God's creation. That was why he was fondly called "Vallalar' the philanthropist.

For some 3000 years after the advent of the Upanishads, there was no new thinking or original thinker in the Indian subcontinent. Every philosopher was repeating or only modifying or complimenting the teaching of Vedanta. Nevertheless, all thought, the whole tradition of Indian thought Hindu, Buddhist, Jain, Carvaka, and so on, had acknowledged the undeniable and unsurpassable fact of death. After a very long stretch of darkness, a new dawn broke out in the land of the Tamils, the land of the immortals, '*Thiruvidam*' that became later *Dravidam*. The new bright effulgent sun was known by the world as '*Thiruarutprakasavallalar*', swami Ramalinga.

The new thought proclaimed to the world in clear cut terms by him was the conquest of physical death. The message was not shrouded in any ambiguity. Not only the hypothesis but also the exact scientific process to make it into a reality, in all the exact details, was given in clear prose and immortal verse. Most importantly, the experiment was carried out in his own body successfully. The result was the glorious body of light, a body of indestructibility, immortality and total consciousness with the five Godly powers of creation, sustenance, destruction, clouding and enlightenment.

When European thinkers such as Herbert Spencer, Darwin and Nietzsche were speculating about man's evolution, there was a man who had evolved into a superman with an indestructible and deathless body of light. The whole science behind the process was promulgated to the world in detail.

Man's body is not only a tree of knowledge but also a tree of light. The fruits could be different, either of mere consciousness or self-consciousness or absolute consciousness. This fruit can be created in the body either naturally and mechanically or fully consciously.

IV – Thirumoolar
The four stages of creation of light in the human body are vividly described by saint Thirumoolar.

Maanudaraakaivadivusivalingam

Maanudaraakaivadivu Chidambaram

Maanudaraakaivadivusadasivam

Maanudaraakaivadivuthirukkoothe

- Thirumandiram

Man's body is Sivalingam

Man's body is Chidambaram

Man's body is Sadasivam

Man's body is dance of creation [the spirit or immortality]
[*Aakkai*], in the form of verb [*aakuthal*] means to make or
to create.

Sivalingam is the fusion of eight [A] and two [U], the body
and soul into an everlasting indestructible pure body
[*suddhadhegam*].

Ettodeyirandaiyumserthuennavumariyeer

You don't know how to add 2 and 8 and count – Vallalar

Ettumerandumsernthathe lingam

Lingam is the conjunctin of eight [A] and two [U] – Saiva
Siddhanda text.

In the Siva temple, we are worshipping only the number
ten, the number one above the zero, the vertical one above
the horizontal zero.   Long before Einstein and other
scientists, the Tamil saints and Siddhas gave knowledge to
the world in the form of mathematical formulae.

To fuse together the body and the soul or to make the body
into a fully alive body – all the matter in the body is
transformed into live or living matter.   This is the first
permanent transformation, according to Thirumoolar's Siva
yoga.

This pure body [*sivalinga*] is changed into space-body or
Chidambaram.   Saint Manickavasakar attained this level of

space body and entered into the empty space in the sanctum sanctorum of the temple at Chidambaram. Chidambaram means space of consciousness. This is the second transformation into *PranavaDeha*.

The space body is converted into a body of *sadasiva*. *Sadasiva* means both form and formlessness. This is the third transformation.

In the fourth and final stage the very human body attains the level of divinity of light of compassion or godhead and starts the act of creation. It becomes a part of Siva.

V – Light

Light is the link or bridge between matter and spirit. Matter is darkness. Out of matter is born light – the physical. The physical light, say, from the sun, is transformed into life, which is the light of consciousness. This transformation takes place in the body of plants. The light of consciousness is transformed into the light of mind or intelligence partially in the body of animals and fully in the body of the human beings. [Makkal]. In the bodies of some special human beings like the philosophers and thinkers, this light of mind is transformed into self-consciousness. However, man's body has the potential for one more transformation, the transformation of the light of self-consciousness or reflection into the light of spirit, pragnana or cosmic consciousness. All the practices of yoga or gnana are aimed at the last transformation. For with the first three transformations the products are liable to fall back to the dark stage of matter. The plant, animal and common man are prone to decay, disease and death and become dust once again. Only in the fourth stage of transformation into spiritual light or spiritual consciousness, stability is attained. Only in the fourth stage of transformation, nature and its laws are conquered and man attains the control over his body and destiny consciously. In the first three stages man is only a puppet in the hands of nature. Only after the last transformation, he starts the eternal dance of creation. He gets the five powers of the Lord himself. This is the final attainment.

Swami Ramalinga got his cue from Thirumoolar and Manickavasakar. Manickavasakar calls this process *poi kettumeiaathal* [losing illusion and becoming truth] in *Sivapuranam*. Thirumoolar calls it *Thooyaneri*[the pure way].

VI – Love
Swami Ramalinga changes the terminology, simplifies the process and supplies the scientific details. He equates light of consciousness with love and its denominations. In matter there is no reproduction or sublimation. In plants, animals, birds and men, love is expressed through the reproductive organs and sex. It is only sexual love, the instinct for mating and maternal instinct.

In man, this instinct for love grows into friendship and platonic love or mental love without needing the physical contact. This develops into devotion or bhakthi toward the Lord, or even into mysticism.

Furthermore, the Swami says, this love for one or for a few beings must grow and develop intoa cosmic love and encompass not only human beings but also all sentient beings.

According to the new equations given by the swami:

- The light of life or mere consciousness = sexual love
- The light of mind or self-consciousness = friendship and devotion
- The light of super consciousness = total compassion for all beings
- Jeevakarunyam, karuna, dhaya = compassion is all yoga and gnana.

Anbesivamaavathu– Thirumoolar.

Love only becomes Siva through various transformations. Love is the only power or force that creates the universe and sustains it. This is the ultimate message as well as the ultimate science, according to Swami Ramalinga and the Tamil rishis.

VII – Entropy, Life, Love and Spirit

According to the second law of thermodynamics, entropy causes disorder and death in man. Life is the fighting agent against entropy. Life brings in order. Science accepts these two facts. But here, the Siddha system of scientific spirituality takes over. Life fights against entropy and succeeds only up to a certain level and then loses. It is always a losing battle. Life always ends in death. In the battle of matter versus life, matter always wins. To prolong the fight, life discovered a device, offspring through sex. The parent dies, the offspring continues the battle.

The law of entropy operates only in the dimension of matter. Life has no law of entropy. Unfortunately, man's body needs both matter and life.

Science has known what matter is. It doesn't know what life is. Life is defined as the ordering principle, the growing principle, the bio-heat, or consciousness. Here is where the scientists go wrong. The Siddha scientists say life is love-energy, not merely consciousness.

Anbinvazhiyathuuyirnilaiakthilaarku

Enbutholporthaudambu. - kural

Only through love, exists life. The love-less have only a bone-structure blanketed with skin.

So, love is life. This is the first law of life. The second law states that death occurs when there is no love in the body.

Enbilathanaiveyilpolakayume

Anbilathanaiaram. - kural

Sunlight kills the boneless creatures. Likewise, the law of justice kills the loveless.

So in the course of evolution, the bone structure is given by nature only to those species that have love in them, atleast toward their offspring. Bone is the physical carrier of love. This is a scientific fact, adiscovery by Thiruvalluvar, ignored by the modern scientists, which is yet to be clinically verified. The amount of love-energy in an organism determines the amount of life-energy in it and also its longevity.

The third law of spirituality says: 100 percent love becomes compassion and compassion is spirit. Not even a single iota of dislike or any other negative emotion should be there in the mind. Only love remains there, compassion toward all beings, even toward enemies. This Christ-consciousness is spirit.

Matter is darkness, ignorance and death. Life is light. Love is more light. Compassion is total light, the light of consciousness. And compassion is spirit. Once this state of spirit is reached, there is no going back, and no more falls for man. Compassion is spirit, light, wisdom and immortality. Only in love and compassion matter is conquered and turned into life and then into spiritual matter. Love created the universe and sustains it. Love is the way of mutation.

Love is the only antidote to entropy. With compassion bone will be melted and turned into light and physical body resurrected.

VIII – Vaasi Yoga

In addition to love and compassion, Siva yoga or SuddhaSanmarga yoga, being a scientific process, emphasizes 'Vaasi yoga'. Man must learn to transcend the process of outer breathing and attain the level of inner breathing or inspiration or cosmic prana. In the raja yoga Swami Vivekananda calls it chit prana. Brihadaranyaka Upanishad calls it sutra atman. The Tamil saints and Siddhas call it gathi. Learn to master gathi, you can master your destiny vidhi; then only you can attain the level of guru consciousness, says Arunagirinathar:

Gathiyaividhiyaiguruvaivaruvaiarulvaigugane

Swami Ramalinga also says;

Oh lord! Grant me the power of transforming this air-body into a 'Gathi-body'.

Arulvai, katraaleaagiyaivvudalgathiyudalaamaare

Man to evolve into superman, the way shown by swami Ramalinga both in his books and in his body was perhaps the only complete and successful way. Other thinkers either remained merely theorists or fell short of attaining supermanhood in their bodies.

IX – Conclusion

Nietzsche's theory of 'will to power' was basically wrong. By getting more and more power, one has no chance of breaking free of the ego-consciousness. 'Will to compassion' is the right antidote for it. Power makes you more of an individual andlove more of divinity. Power narrows down consciousness. Compassion enlarges it.

What is the light that your eyes emit? That determines your state in evolution. If you emit only the physical light, you remain an animal; if love, a human being; if compassion, a spiritually enlightened master or superman.

Charles Darwin was only a speculative thinker and theoretical scientist. He did not think about the future prospects of man. Teilhard de Chardin was more interested in propagating and justifying the truth of Christ than in showing mankind how everyone can attain to the level of a Christ.

The efforts of Sri Aurobindo and the Mother are laudable. Perhaps their mistrust of body-transformation of the Tamil Siddhas and their early faith in Vedanta held them down from attaining the physical transformation.

Swami Ramalinga has given to humanity the blueprint for attaining a new mutation and evolving into super humanity.

~~~ ~~~ ~~~

18. SCIENCE OF IMMORTALITY

The philosophy and yoga of Thiruvalluvar

Vedanta and Buddhism emphasize only the liberation and self-realization of the spirit, negating the body. The Tamil Siddhas emphasize both; the body as well as the spirit. The body must be transformed into an immortal one and the spirit into eternal consciousness. Why did they think so? For they were the first scientists. Science wants control over nature both outer and inner. The keyword here is control. Are you controlled by nature or you control nature? Does nature impose upon you death and then birth ina different body? It may be even the body of a heavenly being, a god. The process is unconscious, carried out by nature.

One fine morning you find yourself inside the body of a god or a man. Even this realization could happen only on condition that your consciousness becomes fully self-conscious and reflect upon its own condition. Even a *deva* a god does not know anything about his previous birth and the interval between his death and the rebirth. This weakness and limitation of ignorance must be conquered.

For God does not have this limitation. Creation is in his own hands. Man's role model must always be God. He should take over the control from nature into his own hands. That is why the emphasis is put on attaining both the powers of a Siddha, the physical immortal as well as the *muktha*, the eternally awakened consciousness. Man should become at once both a Siddha and a *muktha* like God. This is total transformation. This is total evolution for man. This is total control over and conquest of nature or *prakrithi*by man.

In the sixteenth century, saint Thayumanavar talked about such a synthesis of Siddha and muktha.

Vedanta siddhantasamarasavithagasiddharganame.

Oh! Immortal Siddhas who have attained the synthesis of Vedanta and siddhanta!

Thiruvalluvar one of the forefathers of the Tamil tradition had already realized this synthesis some two thousand years ago, with an acumen and foresight all his own. All the later literatures of Siddhas, saints and poets were only commentaries on his ageless work Thirukkural.

Malar misaiekinaanmaanadisernthaar

Nilamisaineeduvaazhvar. *- kural*

Only those who attained a space body as light as to sit upon a flower will have longevity upon the earth.

What is the object that exists forever upon earth without changing? Sky, Akash, space, heavens. It is the first and the subtlest of the five elements [*panjaboothas*]. From space came air, from air came fire, from fire came water, from water came earth, says "*Taitriya Upanishad*".

Thus, in this world, space is the subtle, unchanging, first mover. God dwells in this world only in the form of pure space. He is more subtle, more rarified than a flower. He can sit upon a flower. He is all love. Love is the subtlest thing in creation, the only transformer of gross matter into subtle, spiritual thing. The author says elsewhere 'Love is more refined than a flower [*malarinummelliyathukaamam*]'. Therefore, God who is all love, who is purer and subtler than space is living forever upon this earth. By imitating God, by becoming all love, one can transform his gross body into a subtle, space-body and live forever, or with greater longevity on this earth. Saint Manickavasakar attained this rare feat, says saint Ramalinga. He addresses him as,

Vaankalanthamanickavacaga!

He merged with space. He became space in front of a large gathering of devotees in the temple at Chidambaram. He entered the vacant shrine and disappeared. It was witnessed by everyone present.

At death, common man merges with earth or matter is turned into ashes after being burnt. One cannot step upon a flower, with gross feet but only with feet as light as space. *Maanadi* – means space-feet; *maan*means space in Tamil. In another couplet the author says,

The physical beauty of one who does not have the intelligence or skill to enter the inner sky is like a painting done accidentally by the clouds on the sky which can be blown out by a small wind.

Nunmaannuzhaipulamillanezhilnalam

Manmaanpunaipavaiatru   407

Here *manmaan* – means the sky of the earth visible to our eyes. *Nunmaan*means inner space visible only to the inner eye of enlightened masters, Gnanis during deep meditation. The suggestion or the implication is this: only the gross physical body is the cause of man's early death. It is susceptible to constant and accelerated form of change and decay. Make your body as light as possible to sit upon a flower-like an angel. You will have super longevity or immortality. Make it into a pure body [*suthadeham*] shorn of all impurities. This is the way – the purity of the body is the way of attaining longevity and living upon earth for a very long period. All Siddhas followed this method of transforming their gross physical body into a pure space body. The great avatar, Babaji, the founder of YogadaSathsangam, who is supposed to be alive even today with a body as old as six hundred years is a fit example. In the nineteenth century in Tamilnadu saint Ramalinga elucidated this process in an elaborate manner with all the details in his poems and prose works and also proved his theory by attaining the pure space body [Pranavadeha] and even going beyond it into a body of light spiritual.

How to do it? What is the yogic process? In China, this secret process of immortality is known as Taoist yoga which is beautifully given in detail in the immortal classic, 'The Secret of Golden Flower'. It is available in English translation with a commentary by the world-renowned psychologist C G Jung. He calls it the way of spiritual alchemy.

II

There is a second interpretation for this couplet. Some say, this refers to and sums up the Chinese Taoist Yoga explained in the Chinese yoga classic 'The Secret of the Golden Flower'.

Inside the decaying death-prone physical body of man there is another undecaying death – defying, indestructible immortal body of light. This was referred to as *'Mei'* or *Makara Mei* – by the Tamil Siddhas. Unfortunately, this is only in the form of a seed now, only as a potential. It must flower. It must blossom fully. Then only man a potential God becomes an immortal.

This is the *mei* [consonant] of the Tamil grammar [spiritual] referred to by Tholkappiar. When Saint Manickavasakar in his *'Sivapuranam'* calls the process of his yoga of transformation of body as [*poi kettumeiaathal*] he means only this indwelling immortal diamond body. The flesh and blood physical body must go and be replaced by *mei* the divine body of light that can live forever.

The ritual called '*makara jyothidharsan*' at Lord Ayyapan's temple in Kerala on the day of makara sankaranthi implies only this fact that every man and woman must see and give birth to his/ her own immortal body of light.

The word [malar] in Tamil could be split etymologically into two syllables [m+alar]. Alar means to blossom forth, [virithal] to expand M or Mei, which is now in the potential form of a seed, must blossom forth into a flower of gold whose carat-value is immeasurable.   Only upon such an immortal golden flower, God the eternal being can descend and live forever. This fact is mentioned by saint Ramalinga in his famous hymn on Lord Nataraja.

> *Matruariyathacezhumpasumponnemanickame*
>
> *Cudarvannakkozhunde*
>
> *Kootruariyathaperumthavarullakkoilirunda*
>
> *Gunapperumkunre*

Oh Lord of Golden body of infinite carat value!

Oh Immortal red sapphire!

Oh! Fire hued eternal youth!

Oh! One who dwells in the heart temples of immortals that conquered death with great penance!

Oh! Great Mountain of character!

Man, the Spiritual Tree

Man also is a tree but a spiritual one that is intended for producing spiritual food either for himself or for other higher beings.

Unfortunately, photosynthesis does not take place fully. In a tree mineral water is sucked from the ground by the roots and sent above to the leaves; air from the atmosphere is sucked by the leaves. Heat, needed for cooking the food is received from the sun. Fruit is the food produced. A part of the produced energy is taken by the tree itself for its maintenance and growth of limbs. Extra energy is given out in the form of fruits for the purpose of propagation of species, its offspring.

With man, a change in aim and motive comes in. He not only wants to propagate his species through his offspring, but also wants to live forever as an immortal, to evolve into a higher species. Thus, he has to produce a higher kind of food by taking which only he could develop into a higher being.

Where is the leaf in which this photosynthesis of a higher food takes place in the human body? In the Sacred Square Inch between and behind the eyes, in the place of the third eye. Rishis in puranas did penance or tapas for 12 years to produce such a higher food, the spiritual fruit. This fruit is supposed to be the nectar, amrita that will convert man into an immortal. This spiritual juice will get collected in the pineal gland and start secreting after 12 long years.

The mineral water to be sent above through the trunk or spinal cord is the semen. The power of sending it above, which a tree possesses by instinct, man has lost. It has to be learnt and practiced consciously. This practice is variously called kundalini yoga by trantra, vasi yoga by Siddhas, kriya yoga by Yogananda and immortal breathing by the Taoists.

Sexual thoughts will pull this energy downwards and waste it. Thoughts on God who dwells in the crown will send it upward. This is called 'brahmacharya' in Indian spirituality. All eating and drinking through the mouth are done only to produce the semen. This is the mineral water from the ground to be sucked by the roots of the spiritual tree.

Air is inhaled through the nostrils and sent down to the lungs. As semen is the essence of food and water produced in the factory of the alimentary canal after digestion, absorption, elimination of waste, and up-gradation into bones, blood and finally into semen, the air of the atmosphere also is digested, the waste thrown out, and the essence or milk produced. This essence or milk of breath must be sent upwards to the place of the third eye. This is the process of purification done by the respiratory system.

Further, pure heat must be produced. This is done by the eyes, ears and mind. The light of both the eyes is focused on the place of the third eye. Musical mantras and other sounds are heard through the third eye, by focusing the attention there. The mind is always focused on the inside of the sacred square inch believing God exists there.

The aim of producing the spiritual food is never forgotten – even for a moment.

Not a drop of semen is wasted by sexual thoughts or sexual activity.

Not an iota of breath is wasted by over-exertion as in running, deep sleep, and in anger. The body or mind is not allowed to agitate and waste the breath. The body is mostly seated in a relaxed posture or allowed to move in a gentle way.

No thought is wasted. If one has to think he can think of God inside or focus his thought-energy only on the third eye. For thought is the subtle energy, which can produce pure heat and also one of the three raw materials of food.

This is a life-long process. To produce results, a minimum of striving for 12 years is required. If the practice continues for 24 years, the aspirant can attain the seat of a Rudra and with the practice of 48 years he could become a sun, say the Indian scriptures.

Like a tree that learns to be rooted in a single place, learn to sit in *saazen.*

Like a tree learn to send upwards your mineral water. Learn the technique from a master who knows it.

Like a tree, learn to be thoughtless.

This can be done in 4 ways;

1. By *vipasana* or watching your thoughts or Raja-yoga
2. By practicing *pranayama* or breath-control
3. By focusing your attention on the third eye
4. By eating some yogic herbs like *'thoothuvalai'*

Unlike a tree, be always conscious. For individual evolution can be done only consciously.

COSMIC BREATH

Adi in ancient Tamil means *kaal* and in modern terminology it also means air, *katru* or breathing. *Maanadi*means cosmic feet or cosmic breath or cosmic prana, or inspiration of God that was blown into theclay-body of Adam to awaken him into life eternal. In Chinese Taoist yoga, this cosmic prana or *maanadi* is called as cosmic chi; in Tamil Siddha literature it is called – *Vaa chi.*

Ordinary breath or respiration of air is only a vehicle that carries inside it the prana energy. Only on pranic energy man lives. Swami Vivekananda, in his famous classic on Raja Yoga calls this energy *chit prana*.

Man in his present stage of evolution cannot take in prana directly. He can take it only through the vehicle of air or oxygen through his nostrils, as he can take in the energy of sunlight stored up in vegetables and greens but not directly. The fish is still worse. It can take prana only through the vehicle of air contained by water, that is twice removed.

The evolution can be measured by the form in which prana can be taken in by the animal or being: From fish through man to the immortal who can directly take in the cosmic prana. This state is called sahaja Samadhi which is living on the earth without breathing air. Such beings, the immortal yogis breathe the pure cosmic prana through the invisible subtle channel of *SuzhiMunai* which runs from the centre of *mooladhara* at the base of the spine to the crown centre of *Sahasrara*. The habit has to be newly learnt by man in his future evolution. One who has completed learning and mastered the process becomes a superman and lives like an immortal on earth.

To know and use the cosmic prana is the yogic wisdom referred to by the sage in this couplet.

In the Ramayana, Hanuman is blessed and credited with immortality. He is figuratively known as the embodiment of *mukya prana* or cosmic prana. He is also known as *siranjeevi*, meaning one who lives by the crown or crown breathing. We ordinary mortals live by nose breathing of air.

In the *Vaishnavaa* literature, Hanuman is given the status of guru. The qualification of a real guru is to know and practice cosmic breathing and live like an immortal.

This cosmic prana is also called *gathi* in Tamil. Celestials live by this *gathi*. Only those adepts in yoga who have learnt to master the cosmic prana or *gathi* can understand destiny [*vidhi*] and become a guru. Guru is one who has mastered *gathi*[cosmic prana] and destiny [*vidhi*]. One can understand destiny only by mastering cosmic prana. This science of cosmic consciousness is pointed out by Saint Arunagirinathar in two of his hymns.

Vidhi kaanumudambaividavinaiyen

Gathi kana malarkkazalenruarulvai?

Oh! Lord! When will you reveal to me your blossom-feet of grace, so that I can see gathi, the cosmic prana and end this karma infested body given to me by destiny?

Uruvaiaruvaiulathaaiilathaai

Maruvaaimalaraaimaniaaioliaai

Karuvaaiuyiraaigathiaaividhiaai

Guruvaaivaruvaaiarulvaaigugane

The last two lines clearly state the progressive line of evolution to attain the level of guruhood.

uyiraaigathiaaividhiaai

Guruvaaivaruvaaiarulvaaigugane

Now we are only beings endowed with life. We have to acquire the habit of breathing cosmic prana or gathi. Then we can become onewith destiny and change it consciously. One who has mastered his own destiny alone can change the destiny of others. He alone is a guru, like Hanuman or Lord Muruga – both immortal yogis par excellence.

Saint Ramalinga in his '*Arutpa*' requests the Lord to grant him with a similar boon of gathi or cosmic prana body.

Enruarulvaai

Kaatralaagiyaivvudalgathiyudalaamaare

Oh Lord! When will you grant me the boon of transforming this body of air into a body of cosmic prana or *gathi*?

Eternal living begins with the ending of time. The ending of time can be brought about in two ways. 1] by the ending of thought by the way of Vedanta, Zen, and J Krishnamurtiand 2] by the ending of breathings by the way of the Siddhas and Taoists. Both are extremely dangerous paths. They may lead one into madness or even into death. Therefore these experiments must be carried out only under the expert guidance of realized masters and adepts in yoga, not under charlatans with mere book learning.

As far as I know, there are places in the world, where this knowledge of cosmic prana available in a practical scientific way 1] The vasi yoga literature of the Tamil Siddhas. 2] The ashrams established by SivanandParamhamsa of Vadakarai of Kerala, 3] ParamahamsaYogananda of YogadaSatsanga at Ranchi in India and California and 4] Sanmarghis of Vallalar.

The title Paramahamsa means one who has mastered the art of breathing cosmic prana.

The fabled bird Hamsa could separate milk out ofwater contained in a vessel. The real meaning is this: the vessel is breath. The water is air or oxygen. The milk is cosmic prana.

Only those who have transformed themselves into Hamsa birds by imbibing cosmic prana can fly in the eternal sky and live everlastingly and in an eternal, timeless way.

Meditation: 1. Meditate on 'Malar'.

2. meditate on "Maanadi'.

Cadaari = cada + ari = [a pair of feet] cutting the inorganic air of forgetfulness.

When you go to a Vishnu temple you are given after *aarthi* – light of the lamp in front of the deity - some

*Tulsiteertham*that is water with a basilleaf in it. Furthermore, avessel-likecrown is placed upon your head. If you watch, you can see a pair of feet engraved upon it. Whose pair of feet are they? Why a pair, instead of a single foot? These questions are important, also the answers for them.

The feet belong to Sadakopan, Nammalvar, the guru in Vaishnava tradition, who never breathed in his life right from his birth till his last breath or no breath upon earth.

Guru is one who has mastered the technique of Samadhi or suspending his breath forever and learnt to live with cosmic prana which is made up of light and consciousness instead of air and oxygen.

Every one of us must transcend this human stage and go beyond to the state of Sahaja Samadhi. That is the meaning and purpose behind the act of placing *cadari* on our heads.

Cada+ ari = *cadaari* means one who sawscadam or atmosphere air, one who has done away with air. Space has become his medium transcending that of air.

Why the pair of feet? The first step of suspending breath starts with changing our normal way of breathing. To indicate this step, Nammalvar's two feet are put on our head. This new form of breathing is called 'double breathing' that is breathing through both the nostrils instead of through the right or left at a time. With practice this new form of breath will subside by itself and outer breath will be suspended of totally. Inspiration or inner breath will take over.

Inaiadi

Parallel Feet or pair of feet

Whenever the holy feet of a guru or the divine feet of God are mentioned, they are mentioned only as a pair, not singly. Why? This is an esoteric, yogic secret. The word in Tamil for 'foot' is 'adi' or 'kaal'. Both the words mean in yogic terminology breath; the left foot meaning breath through the left nostril and the right foot breathing through the right nostril. When the pair of feet are mentioned, it means both nostrils. 'Irukaalumpoorikum' says Thirumoolar. What is the benefit of such breathing? This is the short cut discovered by Indian yogis for unifying and integrating body-mind-soul complex of man. In modern times various attempts have been made by masters in physiology to unify the personality of man. Everyone has tried in his own way claiming his own method is the best. Yet no one has touched the core of the problem except the Indian yogis such as Thirumoolar. Let us see and analyse some of these methods.

CLONING

Cloning is the discovery of twentieth century technology. A single cell of a living organism of a sheep is taken from it and the whole body is duplicated out of it and grown into a fully developed new body. This is the artificial way of reproduction of living organisms.

In the natural way of reproduction, 23 chromosomes of the male sperm and 23 chromosomes of the female egg join together to make I cell of the future offspring. On the other hand, in the artificial cloning method, asingle cell from any one of the seven systems of the body except the reproductive system [for its cells will contain only 23 chromosomes of either male or female gender] is taken and it contains all the 46 chromosomes; it is developed into a full organism in the laboratory. However, the problem with such cloning is that, a cloned Hitler will be exactly a Hitler. The unification or purification of consciousness has not taken place. Therefore, this method will not help in the spiritual development of man.

TWO BRAINS THEORY:

Recently it was discovered by surgeons and later proved by psychologists that man's brain operates in two separate ways. The brain is bifurcated in the middle. The left-brain takes care of certain functions like logical thinking, quantification, argumentation and everyday acts of prudence. The right brain is spontaneous, artistic and intuitive. Only rarely they act in a combined way. When they act in co-ordination they produce genius. But mostly each side of the brain functions separately. How to make them work always in unison is the million-dollar question yet to be answered.

Vasi yoga of the Siddhas is the simple and right answer for the combined functioning of both the brains.

Whole brain thinking, holistic thinking and right-brain thinking are some of the practical concepts used by modern psychologists and various techniques have been devised by them for this purpose. But none has given the desired result. Genius has not been created so far in such artificial methods.

In fact, this double functioning of the human mind is very ancient in origin. In the west Socrates was the first man to record it. It is found in Plato's dialogue, the 'Symposium'.

The book is about sex and man's fascination for it. Why is there physical attraction between man and woman? Socrates quotes an ancient myth by way of the solution.

In the beginning man was whole, complete containing both male and female. His power kept on increasing. God wanted to punish him and so he divided him into male and female and put them in far-off places. Therefore, every male or female is only one half, constantly searching for his own, exact half. When the right half is discovered, satisfaction follows, otherwise not. There will be only conflict in the relationship.

Here, the chances of unification of male and female parts are possible perhaps one in a million. Out of billions of human beings, the right man must find out his own other half.

When an atom is split into two, one part is attracted towards the other even if it happens to be placed in the other corner of the world. Their bond and memory are so strong. On the other hand, in man and woman, memory is too weak to remember the most ancient bond between them. Therefore, the Socratic method of unification of both the parts remains only literary and utopian.

Anima, Animus and Individuation of C G Jung.

C G Jung the psychologist, taking the cue perhaps from Socrates gave a similar theory in modern psychological terms.

According to him, every man has a woman in his mind, every woman a man and they are called ANIMA and ANIMUS. These two dark aspects of the minds must be discovered from dreams and behavior patterns and consciously developed fully. Then only man's mind will become whole and complete. Such a whole mind will be safe and healthy. Other minds, though normal are not healthy. They can become neurotic at any time. The process of wholeness was called 'The Individuation Process'.

This remains only as psychological theory of mind, which is opposed by exponents of other schools of psychology.

Integrity of Mind by Emerson:

Perhaps C G Jung got his idea of 'Individuation' or wholeness of mind from the nineteenth century American thinker, Ralph Waldo Emerson. Emerson was a man full of insights. He valued any man by the number of insights he discovered all by himself. Man's life is a mental life, an adventure into ideas.

To delve deep into the ocean of mind and come out with the pearls of insights — that was how he envisioned a scholar's life. He called his philosophy '[Whole'] Man thinking', instead of a portion of man's mind the understanding alone thinking.

'Nothing is sacred at last but the integrity [that is, integration] of your own mind'.

Man's mind or energy works in parts. Full mind or total energy does not come into operation at any time. This happens only rarely. In such rare moments, man is blessed with insights into reality and touches reality truly and directly only then. Otherwise, he is kept in abeyance, in his own shell of ego-consciousness. At one time, man either senses, feels, thinks or is in emotion. All these functions do not come into operation at once. In the same way, every sense organ like nose, eye or ear operates singly in any given moment of time. All the five sense organs and mind do not combine their energies at any moment and work in unison like an orchestra. This must be understood consciously and made possible.

The faculty of understanding, the sense of gain and utility, egoism and egotism of man, separation of man's mind by walls of prejudices – these are some of the reasons why man is not able to bring into play his full power or potentials.

Though Emerson had intuited rightly, he was not able to suggest practical ways of realizing one's full energies. His generalizations, though profound and deep, were very vague and even great thinkers such as Herman Melville and Nathaniel Hawthorne were not able to follow his sublime ideas, let alone the common man on the street. The mental and spiritual revolution, he hoped for in the minds of his countrymen did not take place.

Wholeness of Life –Philosophy of J Krishnamurti

After going through the complete works of Emerson and J Krishnamurti and after thoroughly and deeply perusing them, I have come to the conclusion that J Krishnamurti was an extension of Emerson. Standing upon the shoulders of Emerson, Krishnamurti saw farther.

Most of the generalized and obscure expressions of ideas by Emerson get clarified when Krishnamurti takes them into his own hands and ruminates over them part by part in simple everyday words, but of course in a scientific manner. I can quote hundreds of parallels between the two; I want to call them the 'Twins of American Thought'. Though by birth Krishnamurti was an Indian, he was thoroughly American as a free thinker and had deeply absorbed and assimilated Emerson's basic, seed ideas.

Emerson's concept of '[Whole] Man Thinking' was given a new and full treatment by Krishnamurti. What Emerson called understanding he called thought or intellect and what Emerson called Reason or Intellect, he called insight. Man thinking was translated into, 'wholeness of life' or unfragmented mind.

Like Emerson, he said, 'thought is number one enemy of man' because it fragmented or bifurcated his consciousness and the energies of it. Thought only creates ego-consciousness and all sorrows of man follow suit. Go beyond thought and in that silence all problems are solved for then the whole universal energy of life is available for you and it is at your disposal. Unfortunately, man identifies himself with a tiny speck of his mind called thought and makes use of a three voltage battery when the whole energy of the cosmos is waiting for his use at his fingertips.

Krishnamurti was right in most of his discoveries and insights. Unfortunately, he confined himself to the problem of thought only. Man has also got another treasure with him- his body, which is a miniature cosmos, a micro cosmos in every sense of the word.

Though in his personal life, he took great and meticulous care of his body, he did not talk about regulating and sublimating the energies of the body. Every day he spent nearly four hours for maintaining his body in top form, with total alertness and awakening.

The first thing in the morning, he did yogic exercises for 45 minutes and pranayama for 30 minutes. In the afternoon, massage on his body was performed for 30 minutes. In the evening he walked for more than an hour. On his return from walk, he again performed pranayama for another 45 minutes. All these details are given in his photo-biography, 'One Thousand Moons' by its author, Asif Chandmal.

To keep his body and mind totally awake, alert and attentive and to ward off sleep, he did all these things in personal life. However, these yogic exercises and pranayama are not given importance in his teachings. Pranayama goes a long way in warding off sleep and bringing in a steady state of alertness. In fact, saint Thirumoolar says the right way of doing pranayama is the only way to conquer sleep, lethargy, inattentiveness, laziness and procrastination in man.

Instead of eating with the left hand or right hand,

eat with the proboscis;

You will conquer laziness; thus by conquering sleep

you need not die,

you can be forever. – Saint Thirumoolar.

[Edakkaivalakkaierandiyummatri

Duthikkaiyaalunnavallarkkuchoravumvendam

Urakkathaineekiunaravallarkku

Erakkavumvendamerukkalumaame].

With right pranayama even sleep can be conquered permanently. When sleep is conquered, death is conquered, according to Thirumoolar.

The work of Gurdjieff and Ouspensky:

Another mighty thinker of spirituality of modern times was GI Gurdjieff (and his disciple- collaborator P D Ouspensky). His way is called the work – he borrowed this word from western esoteric tradition. Even in Tamil, it is called the work *[velai]*. *Thani velainigalthidalum* says Saint Arunagirinathar.

He rightly understood that sleep is the root cause of man's ills and it has to be conquered at any cost, so he waged a 'war against sleep', in the words of Colin Wilson. He emphasized 'extra-effort' in the form of exercises, dances and mental exercises like constant self-remembering, stop-exercise, doing everything with total attention and so on. Nevertheless, he forgot to include in his curriculum, the simplest but most effective way of fighting sleep – pranayama.

He was again right when he said that pranayama is a very dangerous thing. True, it should not be practiced without the guidance of an expert. One runs the risk of madness, even death. Therefore, he did not prescribe pranayama in his system.

But prana, breath is the first most important thing in the transformation of man. Breath links the physical with the subtle and spiritual. When Jesus Christ says, 'you cannot enter into the kingdom of God, unless you are born again of spirit', he meant only 'breath', the subtle breath or cosmic prana, the Sutra Atman of Brihadarayaka Upanishad. Spirit or pneuma is only cosmic breath.

The legend of ArthanaariEswara of Lord Siva and Parvathi holds true even today. Every man's and woman's body even today is in the form of ArthanaariEswara, half man, half woman. Not only the mind and the brain are bifurcated into two, but also the body is split into two. This can be verified in the case of paralytic patients. To unite and unify the two sides of the body there is only one way - vasi yoga. Only through proper breathing it can be done.

By nature, man does not know how to breathe. He must learn afresh. It is a complete and most difficult art, like any other art. In the same way, man does not know how to make use of any of his sense organs. He does not know how to see. This was proved by Aldous Huxley in his classic 'The Art of Seeing'. If you want to see properly learn to draw and paint.

In the natural state man does not know how to hear. He has to learn music in the right method. Shakespeare rightly said: if you have not learnt music, you are as good as deaf. There is such a vast difference.

In the same way, every sensory way of experience has to be learnt afresh by man. Only for that purpose, every art was born, dancing for the tactile sense, cooking for taste, reading for mind and so on.

VAASI YOGA

Coming back to our point, 'Double-breath', as prescribed by Thirumoolar is the shortest way to unite the two parts of the human being. For breathing is living. When breathing is understood and mastered, you enter spirituality, the realm of angels and God.

That is why Thirumoolar and Thiruvalluvar emphasize worshipping 'the pair of the divine feet', meaning double-breath or vasi yoga.

'While inhaling and exhaling,

no one knows the exact ratio,

nor the double –breathing'.

198

Yetrierakkiirukkaalumpurikkum

Katraipidikkumkanakarivarillai

Why the name vasi yoga?

Va means Vama. Vaamapagam – para shakthi, the female part.

Ci means sivan – siva the male part.

Irukkaalumpurikkum, inaiyadimantiram, two feet in cadari all mean only one thing. Double breathing, breathing through both the nostrils all the time. What normally happens is that, we unconsciously breathe through the left nostril for some time and through the right for some time. This habit must be changed.

Why adimudiarithal, to know the feet-crown – the legend of Annamalai? Kaal means both feet and breath. According to the yogic lore, vasi the cosmic prana travels from the foot to the crown. This passage of subtle prana inside the body must beunderstood consciously by us. Control comes only after understanding. That was why Buddha asked us in his vipasana meditation to watch the breath, to keep on watching. One day you will see its origin in the body through the heel [adi] and its termination at the crown [mudi]. When prana is consciously seen for what it is, we can have control over it. Though we are alive, we don't know normally where our prana in the body is.

Yoga means only two things: 1] understanding of bodily processes, 2] and conscious control of them. When each and every process in the physical, subtle and causal bodies of man comes under man's control he is truly liberated from the iron claws of nature. His limitations in consciousness like time and space are conquered and cosmic consciousness attained.

The simple, secret way is to unite the male and female, yin and yang in man through 'double breathing' – breathing through both the nostrils at once keeping your mind focused at the sacred square inch of immortality on the inside of forehead, behind and between the eyebrows. This is called the immortal breathing in Taoist yoga and vasi yoga by the Tamil Siddhas – by some it is done from the base of spine, by some from the throat. Learn from the adept or master. Don't practice by yourself. This is too dangerous and strictly prohibited.

When this new breathing takes over from the older one, after some time, the outer breathing will be slowly suspended. From the physical body the function of prana would be shifted to the subtle body.

What happens after death, you will be able to do now here upon earth; physical breath will be suspended but you will be very much alive. Air body, *katralagiya udal*, will be replaced by cosmic prana – body *gathi udal* like that of a Rama or Krishna, the avatars.

Now air is the link between the physical and the subtle. Air is the lorry the goods-carrier, prana shakthi being the goods. We are incapable of taking prana directly from space. We can take it only through air, as fish can take oxygen only from the medium of water. Man is one up than fish. He has done away with the medium of water. Now his medium is air. This also must go. Limitation of air must be transcended. Then man will always be in a state of *Samadhi*. In *Samadhi* state, there is no breath. Hence, no thought. Then his energy is not bifurcated. Whole energy of the cosmos is available for him. Man tackles any problem immediately with this cosmic energy. No problem is difficult for such a liberated man.

6. Porivayileyenthavithanpoitheerozhukka

Nerinintrarneeduvazhvaar- Kural

Those who transcend their five senses and attain to the level of unbreakable consciousness will live long and attain immortality.

Here is another couplet that talks about immortality or longevity or both. To attain longevity here on this world is the aim of materialists. To attain eternal life in the other world is the ideal of all religions. Thiruvalluvar aims at both by the phrase, *NeeduVazhvaar*. For God lives like that. He is here in the physical plane as well as in the spiritual and divine world. For Thiruvalluvar, the goal of man's aspiration should be to follow God's way. To worship

God's feet means to follow his footstep and go on the path shown by him. God is always whole, never fragmented. Thus, humans should also aim for such wholeness, being his sons and daughters, made in his own image.

What is the way shown here, in this couplet, by Thiruvalluvar? The way is indicated here in two steps. The first step is to transcend the sense-pleasures of all the five senses. For every sense operates singly and claims to be the only knower of reality at the time of perceiving. They may alter among themselves or succeed one another but they never organize themselves into one unity and operate as a whole. When one sees, he only sees. When he wants to see, hear, touch and taste simultaneously he has only a blurred or a foggy image or impression. That is why when one wants to listen totally and concentrate on a piece of music, he closes his eyes and channelizes all his attention only through the organ of hearing.Similarly, when one wants to think continuously, and concentrate on an object, he closes down all the five senses and enters into his own mind. This is called meditation.

The secret to be understood is this: consciousness is life. Cessation of consciousness is death. To have control over consciousness is to gain control over death. Therefore, the removal of obstacles on the way to gaining total control over total consciousness is the way to longevity and immortality.

Death occurs in three ways. One way is to die permanently; the body is separated from consciousness. This is called clinical death, certified by the doctors.

The other two ways occur while we are alive, while having a living body. Here death is partial. It is a training or exercise to go into the land of death permanently. Living through the senses, perceiving through the senses is one way. Sleep is another way of practical death. Thiruvalluvar calls these two live-deaths by the word [poi] or cessation of consciousness or the operation of only a fragment of consciousness and the remaining parts of it inoperational or non-functioning. Which means, man even while alive is only partially conscious, that is partially alive and partially dead. He is not totally alive, not totally conscious. His consciousness is not totally enlightened. Sense living is partial sleep or partial death or partial cessation of consciousness. During sleep most of the consciousness is dead. There is a break in the flow of consciousness. For some hours, the waterfall of consciousness goes dry. Man loses control over his own consciousness. As long as this control over one's own consciousness is not totally won over one cannot conquer the death of consciousness or the death of body.

God is total consciousness operating simultaneously everywhere. Man should aim at this model. But what is happening to him now, in his body? His each sense fragments and narrows his consciousness. Though one is supposed to be alive during sleep he has in reality lost contact with reality and for all practical purposes dead. The phrase *'poitheerozhukkaneri'* means the way of unbroken consciousness like the fall of oil,*thailathaarai.* The main thing is to be with no break in the functionality of consciousness. In short to conquer sleep forever is to be enlightened. Not to lose consciousness even for a second is the way to immortality. The body is only an instrument. It can go to sleep. The body can take rest like a machine. Even a machine needs rest, but consciousness – never. Consciousness must never go to sleep, not even for an iota of a moment. That means gaining total control over your consciousness. This is known by Thirumoolar as *'Thidampadameignanamserthal'* – *jnana* means enlightened, awakened consciousness, continuous uninterrupted flow of consciousness through waking hours, dreaming hours, and sleeping hours. This eternal vigilance of consciousness must be kept up. That is *'meignanam* – true *gnana'* or turiya the fourth state of consciousness. Then one conquers the laws of physical nature and goes beyond and enters into spiritual reality.

Ozhukkam – means flow, to fall continuously. (*MookilSaliolugukirathu,aruviyilneerolugugirathu.*) Examples can be multiplied. Like that consciousness must flow constantly.*poi* means interruption, break in continuity.

We say in Tamil – *Mazhaipoithathu.* It means rains did not come. Manifesting itself at one time and not manifesting at another time is called –poi in ancient Tamil. To be always there is denoted by *mei. poi theer* means eradication or destruction or cessation of interruption in short to be uninterruptedly, to conquer the break, to be forever, to be one and not to be fragment.

So *poi theerozhukaNeri* – means the way of having a continuous flow of consciousness and not to lose control over it.

Avithal has two meanings in Tamil; both extinction and cooking – cooking something to a more sublime state. To remove the dross and ennoble the essence and make it endure for a long time. *Idleeavithaan* means to cook the rice cake. By cooking the rice into a cake in an oven, its longevity is extended. It is more palatable and made easily digestible. In short the process of transcendence is taking place. In the same way, all the five senses are cooked, their limitations are removed. This means they are made to act wholly, in unison, as different instruments in an orchestra. They become fragments in a whole, water drops in the flow of a river. This holistic state of consciousness is achieved through true love as seen in the couplet;

My organs of sight, hearing, eating, breathing and touching

Are all with that lass of lightning – creeper

[Kandukettuunduuyirthuutrariyumaimbulanum

Onthodikannae ula]

In short, the fragmentation of consciousness is death which must be foregone to achieve total, whole, continuous consciousness of God. When such a state of consciousness is achieved, man can have a long life as well as eternity.

For this to be achieved, the narrowing down of the five senses and forgetfulness and sleep in man's present consciousness must be fought against and transcended.

The implication of the couplet is this: only the five senses and a fragmented and often-interrupted flow of consciousness pave the way for an early death of man. In short, senses kill man. Antithetically, control of and command over senses and sleep will give longevity and destruction of them immortality.

Pori – means an instrument or machine or technique. All instruments limit, and narrow the consciousness. Any instrument or technique of consciousness is an enemy to the total, cosmic consciousness. J Krishnamurti says: all techniques are false. Understanding alone liberates. He is only a present-day echo of the eternal wisdom of the great Thiruvalluvar.

Porivayileyenthuavithanpoitheerozhukka

Nerinintrarneeduvazhvaar.

The most significant word, the word to be meditated upon, in this verse is 'eyenthu', number five. The five denotes five sensory organs that are channels for five senses to sense five boothas or five elements, which are earth, water, fire, air and space. These five elements must be transcended, or sublimated or conquered or cooked in the poet's words. Why? Because they only kill man, since they are constantly changing, since change is their very nature. Where change is the order, one cannot help undergoing ups and downs, pains and pleasures and all sorts of polarity. To attain the unchanging, eternal para-nature these five must be feared, fought and conquered. One who knows thoroughly, scientifically the very nature of these five elements alone can aspire for immortality.

One can ask if there is any evidence for my argument. Yes, the Tamil Siddhas like Thirumoolar claim to live for billions of years:

Ennilikodiyugamirunthenikkaayathae

I lived in this body countless millions of years, like the legendary figure of Hanuman of Ramayana, the Guru of all gurus, the eternally famed '*Anjaneya*', the son of *Anjana Devi*. *Anjaneya* is called *Siranjeevi*the immortal, one among the seven immortals of the Hindu puranas.

*Siranjeevi*means two things – an Immortal and one who lives always in *Siram* or head, is one whose consciousness always remains in his head and never descends below. Anjaneya is always in the consciousness of Brahman, always chanting God's name Ram, never forgetting even for a second the thought of Brahmam.

It is strange but true that anjaneya becomes the embodiment of the definition of this couplet. To become an immortal two things are necessary, according to Valluvar:

i] poitheerozhukanerinitral – conquering cessation of Brahman-consciousness.

i] eyenthuavithal – conquering the five elements both in the outside nature and inside the body at the five outlets or sense organs.

A hymn to a God usually reveals his nature. It is a meditation. The hymn to Anjaneya by the immortal Tamil poet Kamban, the vaishnavite, goes like this;

Anjileonrupetraan, anjileonraithaavi

Anjileonruaaraaga, aaruyirkakkaegi'

Anjileonrupetra, anangaikkandayalaaruril

Anjileonruvaithan, avanemmaialithukkaapaan

- Kamba Ramayana

Aujulayaanaiadaviyulvazhvana

Aujukkumanjezhuthuangusamaavana

Anjaiyumkoodathaadukkavallaarkarke

Anjaathiyaathiakampuka lame

208

-Thirumanthiram

Even Thirumoolar, the saivite saint says the same thing.

Normally emphasis on a point is shown by an ancient poet by the technique of repetition. In the above-mentioned hymn the word 'anju' is repeated several times, which goes to show that it has got special esoteric meanings.

Irrespective of their religions, both the poet and the yogi say the same esoteric and spiritual truth. Note this point.

Here anju means only one thing; five elements. The only thing man must be afraid of, must fear is the power of five boothas, five elements, the real ghosts that kill man. This is the natural, scientific fact. This body is made up of five elements and their nature is to change. That is why this body is called by saint Manickavasakar in SivaPuranam as,

Maatram, change, in

Maatrammanamkaliyanindramarayone'

[God is the hidden one, living beyond the Vedas, standing beyond body and mind that change constantly]

Saint Arunagirinathar also calls this physical body by the name of maatram change as in

Maatramenumciraikootaividukelai

You are reluctant to throw off this prison house of the body, which always undergoes change.

Then what to do, after discarding this changing, decaying body? You can get an unchanging, immortal divine body, like a Christ or like an Anjaneya or Vallalar. Saint Manickavasakar says

Poi kettumeyaanaar

One who destroyed this fictitious body and had a true, resurrected, eternal body. Because one cannot live in this other, ugly, decaying poisonous, egg:

Vetruvikaaravidakkudambaikutkidapa

Aatrenyemiyaaaraneyoenrendru

Potrippugazhndirunthu poi kettumeyaanaar

Poi kettumeiaathal –means resurrection, transforming this lie of a body and getting a body of truth, of spirit.

Anjaneya is supposed to have such a body that is not made up of five elements. That is why, Valluvar says elsewhere, that

Anjuvathuanjaamaipethamaianjuvathu

Anjalarivaarthozhil

Not to fear those that must be feared is foolishness, meaning death; to fear those to be feared is the task of the wise.

Though the surface meaning is about prudence, the real, spiritual meaning is clearly pointed out by the four-time repeated word Anju, meaning five, the five elements. This is a technical word [kuzhuvukkuri] used by the Tamil Siddhas. Valluvar also uses this five in a concrete way meaning the five elements in another couplet,

Suvaiolivooruoosainaatramendru

Eyenthinvagaitherivaankatteulagu

The world belongs to him who knows the functioning of the five elements.

So here the poet exactly means only the conquest of the nature of the five elements and their functioning in the human body.

To achieve a state of Mei or truth by cooking, purifying and sublimating the ever-changing five elements. This unchanging state is somewhat similar to Plato's ideal forms of purity. Siddhas believe there is such a pure state in nature, like gold. In short, nature can be modified and purified to a clean state, they believed. This is the state of immortal body of an avatar such as Rama, Christ, and Krishna – AprakrithaDeha in Sanskrit of SrimadBhagvata. According to Vallalar, this pure state is total compassion.

Kural10. Piraviperunkadalneenthuvarneenthaar

Iraivanadicerathaar.

Those who attain the feet of God will swim and cross over the ocean of birth, others will not.

There are in fact three different interpretations or meanings for this ambiguous couplet. Variations are caused by changing and manipulating the order and sequence of words, which is allowed in poetry. Moreover, they are based on assumptions as to where the author Valluvar put his emphasis. Whether he emphasized more of human effort or God's grace or whether he believed in one birth or many. Every change in emphasis and perspective rings out a different meaning. The words of the couplet have been selected and placed in such an ambiguous way. Poetry means ambiguity of course. Though Valluvar was a great poet like Dante, he was also a philosopher and scientist with an exact meaning. Though this poem could be a beautiful illustration of William Empson's theory of poetry as ambiguity as he explained in his masterpiece of literary criticism 'seven types of ambiguity', it also illustrates amply valluvar's emphasis on the prime importance of human will and effort.

The usual interpretation offered by the ten ancient commentators is this: Samsara or life is an ocean of maya or illusion. It is also an ocean of births and deaths. Man by himself can never cross over this ocean. He needs a boat with whose help he can cross over to the other shore of heaven or salvation. And this boat is the foot of God. The commentary runs somewhat like this: only those who catch hold of God's feet can swim and cross over this ocean of births and deaths, others cannot. This meaning is derived from the emphasis given to the supreme fact of God's grace or human inadequacy. The philosophy of Saiva Siddhantha and that of Ramanuja's Visishtadvaida are based on this foundation of God's grace. Without God's grace man is an absolute nonentity. Human will and its power is almost negligible when compared with the awesome difficulties facing man in life and in death. Man is a zero and god is infinity. This one view is the view of devotion.

An exactly opposite view is offered by the Buddha who did not accept the existence of an omnipotent God or his grace. He accepted the other shore and the concept of salvation and the crossing over of many births and deaths. However, he questioned the role of God's grace in this endeavor. He asks: suppose a man wants to cross an ocean and reach the other shore. How does he do it? Either he swims across like an Olympic swimmer, like a Mihir Sen with the strength of his own hands or he fashions a boat and an oar with his hands and with its help, he crosses over. No sane man would expect the other shore [meaning God] would draw by itself towards him. No amount of crying or devotion would do it. It is simply impossible and shows only ignorance on the part of the reason of the man.

On the other hand, the bhaktha counters this argument in two ways: by taking pity on the disciple on seeing his love and earnestness, God sends his help in the form of a boat which is the symbol for his holy feet. Secondly, god is not an inert shore made of earth. He is an alive being, the supreme power that erected this billion star- studded cosmos and still is maintaining it with his power. For such a powerful being, to offer help to a friend or bhaktha to crossover to the other shore of enlightenment is not a difficult thing.

But Buddha's meaning is clear: what nobility or dignity is there forman's effort when the problem is solved for himby God? The ultimate degree of effort using his whole body, mind and being is needed by man for conquering this Herculean task. When he succeeds, he deserves to be a god. Otherwise not. Moreover, when it is accepted that man is zero, most of man's self-confidence will be lost. A man devoid of self-reliance is already dead. It is a kind of character assassination. To prove his point, the great Buddha attained salvation by his own effort. Hence, the second interpretation offered by Buddhists and agnostics goes like this.

Only those who swim and cross over the ocean of *samsara* of births and deaths all by themselves can attain the feet of god or the state of enlightenment called Nirvana. Others cannot.

The third interpretation is offered by those who believe in only this life on earth. Not only the materialists but also the Christians adhere to this point of view about life. If there are innumerable opportunities to achieve something, the urgency, the intensity, the earnestness, the fire will not be there. Without the enthusiastic fire, nothing can be achieved. We know neither about our past births or the future ones. What we know is only this life on earth and fortunately it is a human birth with an adequate body and a spark of divinity for man. He must fight it out with might and main. The problem of the birth and death of consciousness must be solved once for all. This magnetic centre of a refined and purified consciousness is called cosmic consciousness. The word –piravi stands here as a singular noun.

We can see one idea running through all the three interpretations. People might differ among themselves about the existence of god, about the number of births, but everyone is after salvation, after attaining the cosmic consciousness in one way or the other, with total human effort, with devotion, with god's grace, with an all-out intensity. This present narrow consciousness of the fictional ego must go. Whether one calls this superior state of consciousness as god's feet as Thiruvalluvar calls it or nirvana as Buddha called it, or as advaita as the vedantins called it does not matter. A rose by any name is a rose. It smells the same.

The school of Saiva siddhanta has a beautiful expression to denote this union of man and god called *thaadalai*. It is a unified single word made up of by two separate words: Thaal + thalai meaning God's feet and man's head. This wise technique solves many problems, for example, god and man are not separate. Where does god live? Where is god's holy feet? Inside the head of man, inside his consciousness, inside his pineal gland. Thus man-god is to be sublimated into god-man. Only the seed is to be grown into a tree. However, one must be aware of the fact that the seed is a special one containing within it, the very tree of god. Man's consciousness is a seed of self-consciousness. This self-consciousness by its reflection upon its own limitations or thoughts must outgrow itself and tear open into the tree of cosmic, total consciousness. The seed of individual self-consciousness or semi consciousness must burst into the tree of god-consciousness. This is the reason why Thiruvalluvar uses the word god throughout – to indicate the goal of man's inner journey to make him not to forget even for a second that he is a potential god in his consciousness. Only it has to be taken to the bank and encashed or realized. Behind every word or syllable he uses, the great sage is very particular about its usefulness for man. Thiruvalluvar was the first pragmatist, in the true sense of the word, a practical teacher, par excellence.

~~ ~~ ~~

19. THE EVOLUTIONARY THEORY OF SIDDHAS

With the advent of man the species called homo sapiens, the evolutionary force reached its penultimate stage. There is only one more step to reach the ultimate stage of man, that of supermanhood or godliness. So far the evolution has been a movement of unconsciousness conducted by nature through instincts. All sentient beings, of plant kingdom, animal kingdom and the like have been only sleepwalkers, automatons activated by nature. They were born in sleep, lived in sleep and died in sleep. With the advent of man, evolution has come to a halt. It has given the reins into man's hands. It has given him freewill. Now it is man's destiny to continue the evolutionary movement consciously or to retrograde and regress into unconscious animal living.

The Guna system of Indian philosophy classifies the created universe and all sentient beings into three categories; *tamas* or sleep, whose various gradations being procrastination, forgetfulness, sloth and sleep leading into death;*Rajas* or all forms of aggression like ambition, dominance, violence , anger manifesting in all gradations of overactivity and excessive energy motivated by egoism or self-interest; and finally *Satwa*or goodness seen in co-operation, sympathy, empathy, love and compassion emanating from peace of the soul and motivated by altruism.

The mineral kingdom and the vegetable kingdom represent *Tamas* or sleep or darkness. The animal reveals the Rajas. Man acting with the character of self-consciousness and love for other beings alone represents *Satwaguna*. However, most of the time most of the human beings are still at the animal level only. For man still carries on his shoulders the burden of the past, the aggressive, animalistic tendencies of the animal kingdom as well as the sleep and sloth of the mineral and vegetable kingdoms in his consciousness. Every human being should always, every moment be aware of his inheritance of this dark past in his consciousness and act accordingly. That was why spiritual teachers like J.Krishnamurtiand Vallalar repeatedly stressed that man should empty his consciousness. Yoga systems want man to consciously stop the mechanical reaction of man in both *tamas* and *rajas gunas*. It wants man to be always in *satwaguna* or peace in soul and in love and then act not react.

So far, these religious philosophical teachings and the technology of consciousness called yoga have not given the desired result. Most of the humans remain as before, as animals only. They are not able to conquer all their own aggressive, animalistic egoistic tendencies of self – interest. Religion, philosophy and yoga have failed though we cannot refuse to give them the credit for properly laying the foundation stone for building the structure of the species of home sapiens, that is, with self-consciousness, love, compassion and moral living. But these ways of illumination were not enough for man to combat the downward pull of instincts inherited from the mineral vegetable and animal kingdoms because these instincts are based in and arise not from mind or consciousness only but mostly from another source, the human body and its makeup and source of food. This was the unique discovery of the Siddhas and alchemists of the world. For, they were the first evolutionists of the world.

First let us define who is an evolutionist and who is a religious thinker. An evolutionist believes in the truth and hidden potential of matter, in the true, scientific manner. He believes that only from matter, life evolves and from life mind evolves and from mind spirit evolves and from spirit or soul, the oversoul or god-consciousness evolves. It is only one, unbroken ray of creation from the inert inorganic stone to the absolute, omniscient God. They are only different gradations and levels of one reality. Man stands in the centre exactly at about the middle point between the unconscious stone and all knowing, omniscient, absolute consciousness of godhead. In the ladder of evolution man is the only conscious climber as well as the unconscious rung. All the other species remained only as rungs of the ladder. Nature or evolutionary force was the only mover, the only climber. Now nature or evolutionary force has climbed on to the back of man and has taken rest from her long and arduous ascent from stone to homo sapiens and has started enjoying her ride on her vehicle – the man. It is now man's duty to climb to the summit of consciousness called god.

Here the aim and ideal is the same for the religious thinker as well as for the Siddha and the alchemist. A Siddha in his aim goes far above and beyond the alchemist who only wants to find out the secrets of transformation of base metal into faultless gold. It is only the first step in his agenda. The second step is to test this proven exercise on his body. The physical corruptible body is first turned into a copper like metallic-organic body and then with the secrets of transformations of alchemy like the philosopher's stone, water of life and so on, into golden organic body. Third it is transformed into a diamond organic body of light. This light body is then finally converted into a body of resurrection like that of Christ, Taoists and saint Ramalinga Vallalar of Tamilnadu, India. This is a body of divine light. It is incorruptible, everlasting and also possesses the properties of sustaining itself everlastingly by secreting nectar its own body. It is not dependent upon any outside source for its sustenance. For it is similar to the body of god having absolute, eternal, supramental consciousness. But the religious thinker does not accept the truth of matter and its divine potential or evolution, its unfoldment. He negates matter totally and absolutely. Matter is only an illusion, an error of the mind of man to be removed permanently by true knowledge, the mistake is only in identifying wrongly the rope for the snake. The snake was never there. Only the rope exists. Man's illusory mind is the only culprit. Once this truth is known and understood man will come to the light of liberation; it is the only liberation from the illusory nature of matter once for all. There exists only the spirit. No matter ever existed. There may be variations and gradations and degrees in various theories and philosophies of religions and idealistic philosophies, but the basic assertion, assumption and premise remain the same.

Along with matter, most of these religions and idealistic philosophers negate the truth and potentialities of the human body. Vedanta, Buddhism, Jainism, Christianity and all ascetic training systems blame the human body as the culprit not allowing man to attain salvation or release from suffering. It is only through the body the tempter Maya operates. It is only a lavatory constantly producing the waste. It is the embodiment of ugliness, decay and death - in one word of negativity. Shun the life of the body and take to the life of the spirit – is their declared way of life.

Is the human body a lavatory or a temple of god? Along with most of the Indian philosophies such as Buddhism, Jainism, Vedanta and Vaishnavism the interpreters and commentators of the Old Testament as well as the new negate the body as defecation causing death - death not only to the physical body but with it the death of consciousness also. But the true teaching of the Bible, the old as well as the new testaments only reiterate the Siddha's point of view about the human body, that is, the human body is the temple of god. Not in its present condition of course. Now it is functioning like a waste producing factory only. But its true nature when it was created by god was not like that. It was meant to produce nothing but nectar and it was a bliss body. The present ugly lavatory is to be demolished slowly and gradually, the place purified totally of its present contamination and in its place reconstructed a beautiful sacred temple of god where god himself would be willing to live forever. In fact, they claim god can live only in such a conscious human temple, not in structures of brick and mortar nor of stone granite or marble however vast and artistic the architectural design.

According to Siddhas this body is no lavatory. In fact, this is the only vehicle man is blessed with to take him to salvation. A Ford T model car has to be upgraded and transformed into a jet-propelled sports car. And if the car is not capable of taking you to moon, don't blame the car and throw it away. Transform it into a rocket. The human body is the greatest machine ever invented and yet to be invented in times to come. It contains in itself all the mechanisms of all the machines. It can adapt itself to any level and any type of mechanism. Only our ignorance is the cause of its mismanagement. Suppose you use diesel or kerosene for a rocket, what would be its function? In the same way man even now doesn't know what is the real fuel for this wonderful machine of the human body. If properly taken care of, it can do the functions of a rocket as well as those of a microscope or a telescope.

In fact the human body is only an indicator of the human mind. They are like two sides of a single coin. One reflects the other. The body-mind complex is a single unit, says modern medical science. The same point of view is upheld by the Siddhas. Psychosomatic is nothing new. It was the most ancient thought of them.

Moses says the spirit dwelling in man is a spark of God. Christ exhorts: destroy this temple, I will rebuild it in three days.

How could he fulfill his claim? He could and he did, say the New Testament, but added a conditional clause. Only he could do it, being the only son of God. None other could. Here the Taoists of China and their counterparts the Siddhas of India, along with some true, realized Christians such as Joel S Goldsmith differ. They say Christ is not a person but a stage in spiritual evolution of man, something like the Supermind of Sri Aurobindo or *guru-thuria* consciousness of *Saiva Siddhanta*, a stage to be crossed over before attaining the absolute consciousness of Godhead. They claim it is the birthright of every being, human or otherwise, to reach the absolute consciousness which is only the top rung in the ladder of consciousness. Now in this present stage of evolution or in a distant future, every being is destined to pass through that stage and attain divinity.

Then why is this mortal body given with all its decay, disease, old age and death? What is the reason? The Semitic religions put the blame on one mythical pair of Adam and Eve and their transgression of God's command, resulting in Original sin carried over by all humans descending from them. No scientist today would accept this myth, whatever hidden truth one may ascribe to it. Science accepts only facts, not myths or allegories.

All the other answers provided by other religious teachers and philosophers can be broadly categorized, classified, and abstracted into three ways of salvations namely;

1. The way of pure speech or pure *Vak* or Revelation or the word of God
2. The way of pure consciousness, or pure mind
3. The way of pure body

The first way, the way of the word of god, is the way offered by the most ancient religions. It is offered by the Bible, both in Judaic Old Testament and in Christian New Testament.

They build their theory on the fact that man alone of all beings of creation is blessed with speech. And they consider speech only as an instrument of communication as it is thought today in the secular society of scientific temperament. Which, in their eyes looked only as the result of a fall, called by them as original sin but in reality, as a fall from God's word, or God's breath blown into Adam's body of clay to give it life eternal. Various religions call it by various names but all of them have understood its ultimate significance as the penultimate rung in the ladder of creation, next only to God, the absolute consciousness. The Koran calls it Rhua. The Upanishads call it, the Mukya prana or essential universal prana whose embodiment is worshipped in Hinduism as Hanuman, the monkey God. Hanuman can enter even those places where air cannot enter, is a proverb of Hindus, implying Hanuman represents the Cosmic prana embedded and hidden in oxygen or air.

Man does not live by air or oxygen but by Cosmic Prana Energy which is all pervading unlike air, whose pervasion is limited to the atmosphere or ionosphere measuring upto about five miles above the earth. Oxygen is only a lorry, a goods carrier, the real goods being the cosmic prana. It is the cosmic prana or cosmic breath pervading the whole universe. It is the real sustainer, the real food of all beings the Manna of Old Testament, the *vak* of the Hindu Vedas, and the Chi of Siddhas, the Psi of the Taoists, the Rama's arrow of the Ramayana and so on.

This is what is meant by the bible teaching when it says, man does not live by bread alone but by the word of god. I mean this word of god that really sustains man. If man could live on bread alone, he/she should not die. On the contrary he/she dies. So if he learns to take in the word of god or manna, or cosmic prana he won't die. This is the real meaning of god's word and some other teachings of the

Bible such as: In the beginning was the word, the word was with god and god was the word, and word made flesh was Christ. The word of god, Christ, the Holy Spirit – all these words mean the same thing.

Breath or spirit of god, god's power of creation and sustenance, was the first, illimitable, infinite power that created spirit, life, mind and matter. This is the real source of all power, animate and material in the whole of creation. Once a being knows this source and identifies with it and learns to apply it, he/she becomes Christ or a Siddha or an immortal. This science of vak or pure speech or revelation is almost lost except in the writings of the Siddhas where one finds almost the whole of it, intact, in all its details, theory as well as practical application. The real theory of evolution of the Siddhas is based on this science of Chi of cosmic prana or the word of god.

According to the scientific evolutionary theory, from the fish, the amphibians evolved and from the amphibians, the mammal, from the mammals, the Homo sapiens. It is an evolution by the variation of organs. The Siddha's theory of evolution centers not only in the variations of organs or organism but also mainly on breath or the respiratory system of them. But the basic premise is this: All sentient beings are sustained, only by cosmic prana. [In the last century one evolutionist believed that even stones grow; they breathe in their own subtle way and develop. Later this theory was discarded not by disproving but by the latest prejudice or in the name of scientific temperament.]

All sentient beings breathe and through their breath, they take in the cosmic prana in any one of its manifestations, gross or subtle or pure. The plants take in the cosmic prana from the carbon-di-oxide of the atmosphere. This is almost a coarse way thrice removed from the original source. From carbon-di-oxide, oxygen is separated from oxygen, cosmic prana is separated and taken in. In the case of fish, the water is gulped, the oxygen in the water is separated and then from oxygen the cosmic prana is separated and taken in. This process is twice removed from the source of original pure cosmic prana. The apparatus suitable for this is the gills of the fish. Then arrives in the evolutionary sequence, the amphibian like frog or a crocodile which can live both in water and on land. They developed a different system of respiratory apparatus with which they can take in oxygen from water as well as from the atmosphere. The next development occurred in man who can take in oxygen only from the atmosphere. So evolution, according to Siddhas is a process of arriving at the source of pure cosmic prana and taking it directly instead of through oxygen or through air or carbon-di-oxide.

Here once again man faces a transition, the stage of an amphibian like that of a frog. Now the future amphibians are expected to live both on oxygen and without oxygen, directly imbibing the cosmic prana without any sort of adulteration. So man has to develop another organ for respiration to take directly the cosmic prana apart from his nostrils and lungs with which he is enabled to breathe.

Some yogis such as swami Rama of the Himalayan institute of India have already reached this stage of the next amphibian.

In 1970, in the Menninger Foundations in America Swami Rama demonstrated in the presence of a large audience of doctors and scientists that he can sustain himself and live on cosmic prana alone. He proved to the audience, he could live without oxygen far beyond the time-limit of say one and a half minutes after which a normal human being would die for lack of oxygen supply to the brain.

Swami Rama was seated in a glass cage with all the desirable medical apparatuses like ECG and EEG attached to his body. There were two colored bulbs red and green placed with the switches inside the cage. With the red signal from the yogi, oxygen from the cell will be sucked out and a vacuum created. The yogi should live without oxygen and only on the subtle cosmic prana which cannot be known by any recording of the presently known apparatus. And the yogi entered his trance-like living without oxygen. Later after more than five minutes he came back to his normal consciousness and switched on the green light. After the green signal, normal air was pumped in. Swami Rama, once for all proved that man with proper yogic training could live only on cosmic prana as well as on oxygen like a future amphibian. Only after this experiment, the westerners flocked to India to know the secret of yoga. They were not satisfied to the point of conversion even by the great teachings of Sami Vivekananda, ParamahamsaYogananda and other Indian saints and yogis.

The next and final stage beyond the amphibian is to do away with oxygen completely and live only on cosmic prana alone. Then there won't be any use for the respiratory apparatus of man like nostrils or lungs. He will directly breathe the cosmic prana by some other organ in the brain. The Siddhas say it is the pineal gland that is inactive in man. This fact is also mentioned in the bible: Trust not the man who breathes through his nostrils. For according to Siddha teaching, the breath through nostrils creates the mind and its ups and downs, dualities and polarities. Its very nature is to corrupt the mind and the body. The *Ida kala*, breath through the left nostril and *Pingala*, breath through the right nostril are breaths of death or causing death [*saagumkalai* in Tamil]. There is yet another breath breathed directly from above through the aperture in the crown. It is called *Sagaakkalai* or deathless breath. One who has learnt to breathe it like Jacob of the Old Testament will not die. The place where god is seen is denoted by the name pineal. It is not the name of a geographical place on earth but a place inside the human brain where Jacob saw and wrestled with god.

Kabala is the name of the esoteric school of Judaism, which explains the inner, esoteric meaning of the Old Testament. Kabala in Tamil and Sanskrit the ancient languages of India, means the human head. There are many similarities in the teachings of the Siddhas and kabala. Kavna is the Jewish word for meditation and contemplation. Kavanam in Tamil also means the same thing. In the first century before Christ, there was shipping transportation between South India and Israel. In the annals of Israel, we find mention of the feathers of peacock and pearls of great price to have been imported from South India. One left hand branch of saivism was known as kapalikas who wore mistakenly garlands of human skulls. They also ate and drank in skulls like Lord Byron, the English romantic poet. For kabalists, kapalikas and the right-handedsaivaites and Siddhas, the key to human salvation lies inside the human skull. For them, god can be seen only inside one's brain and never outside. The famous saivite temple at Chidambaram, near Pondicherry in South India is the architectural portraiture of the same idea.The temple built by Vallalar atVadalurdevelops the idea further.

~~~ ~~~ ~~~

20. AS ABOVE SO BELOW

This is one of the famous sayings from the green emerald tablets of thrice great Hermes. Hermes was the god of learning in Egypt as well as in Greece. He was also the god of alchemical lore. Alchemy was the ancient equivalent of the theory of evolution based on the truth of matter and its potential for being transformed into life, mind and spirit.

In the first stage, the alchemist learns to transform the base metals into the pure metal gold. Once this process of purification and transformation that takes place at the molecular and subatomic levels is mastered by the alchemist, he tries to apply this process on to his own body. For this to take place, he discards gradually and step by step his vegetable and animal foods and opts for only calcined metals, like copper and iron and minerals and the purest of the pure water. Like copper that is constantly producing stain of a green taint, this human body is also prone to producing shit in all its varieties through all the nine apertures of the body.

By slowly taking in the calcined metals and minerals instead of regular diet of vegetable and animal food, the alchemist is first converting his body into a living mineral or living metallic body. Later by applying the same method of purification and transformation on to his body, his base metal-like body is transformed into a body of living or organic gold. C G Jung calls this philosophic gold. It is not like the inorganic metal gold. It is far purer and superior in carat value and living quality. It is durable for thousands of years and almost everlasting. Instead of producing waste, it will start producing ambrosia or nectar or *amrutha*. *Amrutha* means the life – giving medicine that fights and conquers death, *mrithyu* in Tamil. It is also called *amuthu* meaning a potion that fights and conquers old age. Immortality without eternal youth will be an everlasting hell, an unendurable torture.

Once this golden body is achieved, the alchemist next tries to transform it into a diamond body of light. Like a glass, it will be transparent and light will pass through it. There will be no shadow for this body. Swami Ramalinga calls this body a pure-body [suddadeham] and describes its qualities in all detail, from his own experience.

The next stage is to convert this pure-body into a letter-body or sound-body called pranava-body or mantra-body. This is like the bodies of angels and gods. Like a letter, say 'A' it will have form [video] and sound [audio] but no substance concrete and material.

The final stage is to attain the meaning body or wisdom body of pure consciousness of light. It will not be visible to the naked human eye. This is similar to the body of god himself. It has no limitations; it can travel at the speed of light and more. It is not physical light that travels at the velocity of 3,00,000 kilo meters per second. It is divine light, the causal light whose science has not yet been discovered by modern scientists. According to saint Ramalinga Vallalar there are many varieties of heat and light, but basically three: 1] physical or impure heat and light 2] pure or subtle heat and light [e.g., love, friendship sympathy etc] and 3] divine or causal heat and light [e.g total compassion towards all beings without discrimination]

It can be everywhere at once. All the eight qualities or attributes of god, this *gnanadeham* will be blessed with. With this attainment, the process is complete, evolution is complete.

Well this is the picture, of course the ideal picture of future evolution of man in ages to come. The aim is declared, the destination is announced, and the path is neatly laid. Only humanity is to walk on it.

Now one can ask, is it another kind of utopia? Is it possible at all, this assumption of man becoming godlike?

The answer is an emphatic yes: For the simple reason that one man Saint Ramalinga has already attained it. He has also revealed to the world this secret, esoteric, divine science in all its details as he experimented it in his own body. This science is available to us now in the form of ThiruArutpa containing about six thousand immortal verses and scientific prose of about six hundred pages.

Before the advent of Tensing and Sir Edmund Hillary, it was believed by all humankind that Mount Everest can never be scaled or reached by man. In that high altitude of some 29000 feet above sea level, oxygen is very scarce. The temperature is below zero degree centigrade. The hardships on the way were innumerable and insurmountable. But all these superstitious beliefs were destroyed once for all by the conquest of Everest by Tensing and Hillary. After their successful climbing, many have followed their way and triumphed.

In the same way all these millennia, mankind has falsely assumed that conquering death was not possible, even by so called scientists like J B S Haldane [read his essay, the possibilities of human evolution]. It is more superstitious than any religious superstition and the way he makes fun of George Bernard Shaw is nauseating. Once Bertrand Russell asked in an essay, 'Is science superstitious'? It could be. Limitation is the only sin, said Emerson. Both G B Shaw and Emerson may not be academic scientists like Haldane but their minds were more free, uncluttered by any prejudice of science or the limitations it might impose on the human mind and its possibilities. He had assumed that all men are mortals. Who said that? How could you know for certain? Like David Hume, the Siddhas question this very basic assumption of mankind. Just because most of the students fail in their examinations and only a few score about 90 or 95 in mathematics, one cannot rule out the possibility of one getting hundred out of hundred. Saint Ramalinga asserts and declares, by mistake all men die, by wrong choice of food, by wrong habits of body and mind and mostly by the wrong belief deeply ingrained in their DNAs of the assumption that all beings that are born must die. All this false brainwashing, all this wrong conditioning of mankind must go, the human body is created to last forever, say the Siddhas. Its potential is really godly. When the Old Testament says god created man in his own image, it meant that man is verily god himself not only in form but also in power provided he is as pure as god both in body and in mind, in his intentions. God's intention is always and eternally to have compassion towards all his/ her children. In the same way if a man /woman could ascend in consciousness towards that summit of total compassion for all beings, lodging not a single idea of separate, egoistic disturbance in mind he would also be blessed with god's eternal body, eternal mind and eternal powers. Saint Ramalinga names this all-compassion attitude towards all being as *anmaneyaorumaippadu* or the integrated soul-love which is common ground not only for human beings but also for all sentient beings.

To become godlike through love and compassion - this is the ideal of life or end of life or *purushartha* of the Siddhas. This is different from the traditional four *purusharthas* or ends of life as offered by Hindu spirituality which was meant for all common folk namely dharma [righteousnesss] –*kama* [pleasure], *artha* [money], and *moksha* [liberty from bondage of the cycle of birth and death].

Here not self-realizations [*atma vidya*] only, not even god-realization [*brahma vidya*] but becoming like god himself in form, in body, in mind as well as in his powers, - this is the ultimate wish and ideal of mankind. Because god alone is totally free from bondage, from nature and beyond it. Unless man attains the level of godhead, he could never be absolutely free. Logically this holds good for all beings. Even for gods. Here a question arises: is it not the same poison of ultimate ambition Lucifer drank and fell into sin and subsequently into hell? No. One wants to attain the level of god not for his powers, not out of pride but out of compassion and love, in order to serve all sentient beings eternally like Christ. The intention is different, not to rule but to serve and sacrifice.

In India also the same question was raised against this ideal of SuddaSanmarga: is it not the same poisonous ambition of Ravana and other asura-kings of puranas? Again the answer is no. Their intention was to conquer all worlds and rule them eternally. Here the intention is totally a different one. To serve all beings in all worlds, to teach and help them in their evolution.

If this is a real though ultimate, science, what are its laws? How to know them? How to practice them? These questions have been answered by the Siddhas, by saint Ramalinga in particular.

What are the differences between God and other beings, gods as well as humans and animals and plants? Basically, there are three differences. All the other beings except God are dependent upon god or outside sources for three things in order to survive: i] food ii] breath[prana] iii] knowledge [impressions]. God alone is self-sufficient in all the three. He is not in need of any of these three. In fact, he is the source of all these three. So if man wants to be free from the human condition and attain the level of godhead, he should be capable of producing in his own body food, breath and knowledge necessary for his survival.

In fact, this knowledge about three kinds of food necessary for the survival of man was known to most of the religions and their esoteric branches. Gurdjieff's system called 'work' is particularly known for its teachings upon this fact. Gurdjieff's teaching upon Hydrogen the basic energy and its denominations is well known. But what Gurdjieff did not know was that there are higher forms of food, breath and knowledge available in the human body itself. This secret teaching is available only in the Tamil Siddha system of which unfortunately Gurdjieff was perhaps not familiar.

The real inner and more secret meaning of the dictum 'as above so below' eluded Gurdjieff's grasp as it eluded most of the world's masters. This happened in two ways, for two reasons. First, they were not aware of the real and total significance of the uniqueness of the human body and its god-like potential powers; secondly they did not belong to a tradition where this teaching was given.

This is the unique and most important discovery of the Tamil Siddhas, particularly saint Ramalinga Vallalar. He was fondly called Vallalar, the Munificent, mainly for declaring this secret to the world.

Not only Gurdjieff and PD Ouspensky but also most of the world gurus like Sri Aurobindo and the Mother were not aware of the secret because they were not familiar with the Siddha tradition. Here the tradition plays a vital role. A single human however great he or she is even an Aurobindo cannot discover all the facts of a science all by himself. A tradition is the accumulated wisdom, like modern science of all the discoveries of all of its adherents. Since the Tamil Siddha tradition remains to the world a hidden tradition its discoveries and knowledge are not available to it. Who is the loser? Ofcourse the world, the common humanity.

Gurdjieff thought he had found a scientific way of transforming physical energies into spiritual energies by giving them names of denominations of hydrogen and discovered a whole system and developed it. Some people say Gurdjieff took the cue from Madam Blavastsky's 'The Secret Doctrine' and developed it. When I triedto verify this fact, I found some similarity between the two teachings. But what is unfortunate for mankind was that both Madam Blavatsky and Gurdjieff were not aware of the total science of bio-energetics available entirely in the Tamil Siddha system. The sad thing is that Madam Blavatsky established her headquarters of theosophical society in Adayar, Chennai but she was not told about the teaching of the Siddhas. Even Gurdjieff had visited Tamilnadu during his travels across the globe in his search for the truth. Again, bothSri Aurobindo and the mother arrived in Pondicherry near Tamilnadu and founded their ashram there. They thought that they were the pioneers of the idea of transformation of the body and the material world into spiritual and divine one. But these were very ancient ideals of the Tamil Siddha system and they were openly announced and practiced and perfected long before them by saint Ramalinga, into a fully developed and exact science called SuddhaSanmarga.

Well, the time is ripe now for the followers of Gurdjieff and Sri Aurobindo to take note of the Tamil Siddha and Sanmarga traditions in Tamil if they sincerely want to go further in the way of human evolution and secular scientific spirituality.

Or if they want to talk only politics, it is only they that will be the losers. Mankind is one. We are living in the days of globalisation. All teachings of all the traditions of the world belong to mankind. Even a small hitherto unknown tradition might also have and offer a unique solution in the form of rare knowledge to solve the eternal human problems of death, immortality and further evolution. We should have an objective, impartial, scientific attitude towards any idea, we should not see where it comes from, that is politics perhaps spiritual politics, nonetheless politics, let us ignore it – but see whether it is worth and add to our present fund of knowledge.

Well, let me come out with the secret meaning of the Hermetic saying 'As above so below'. In Tamil this is known as '*AndathilUllathupindathil*'. *Andam* means the universe the macrocosm. *Pindam* means the human body. Whatever the universe contains, the human body also contains. Whatever mechanism the scientific community has discovered so far, the rocket, satellite communication, TV, nuclear reactor and whatever mechanism is yet to be discovered in times to come, this human frame already contains it in a miniature form. That is the apparent meaning of the above dictum. Even Emerson accepts this meaning.

But there is a second secret interpretation for it in Tamil. Only Sri Ramalinga opened that secret. *Andam* in Tamil means not only the universe but also the head, the human skull. *Pindam* means the body below the skull. So applying this new interpretation we get the meaning for the saying as above so below, the inner wisdom teaching like the following: As in the head so in body. Just invert it. As in the body so in the head.

All the functions performed in the lower body below the head must be transferred to the head above. For Saint Ramalinga says that the head is heaven and below it, the body is hell.

What are the functions done in the lower body? i] Physical movement with legs and hands, ii] sexual reproduction, iii] digestion of food in the body iv] respiration of air or prana in the lungs.

When consciousness is perfected and the light body of wisdom attained, physical movements will not be necessary. Thirumoolar says 'a Siddha is one who has seen Siva's world here itself, [siddharsivalogamingeyadharisithor – thirumanthiram] reaching the outer worlds through the inner, says Joseph Campbell.

Concerning the transference and displacement of sex from abdomen to the head, a lot has to be said. Even Sigmund Freud talks about the sublimation process of sex energy into creative intellectual energy. Long before Freud, the Hindu yoga tradition talked about the effects of sexual continence or Brahmacharya. Brahmacharya means to preserve Brahman or the semen. Semen only becomes Brahman when properly transformed and transmuted. With human sexual copulation and reproduction only one out of more than a million sperm cells is turned into a human baby. Whereas through Brahmacharya practice, all of the sperm cells are preserved and transformed, as it were, into a multi-human form or a thousand –headed, a thousand bodied God of purusashuktha or like the god Muruga or Subramania conceived by Lord Siva in his third eye.

The third eye is the place known to the Chinese Taoist masters as the sacred square inch where divine, spiritual sex takes place and one gives birth to oneself as a spiritual child. Siva gives birth to himself as a spiritual child Muruga. Every jeeva, every being is potentially Siva capable of giving birth to a spiritual child like Muruga.

The third eye is known in Saivite literature as Chidambaram. *Ambaram* means firmament or sky. *Chit* means life, spirit, divinity the power of creation of god. So Chidambaram means the spiritual sky. It is already there in the centre of the human skull.

According to Siddha system of philosophy, every event, physical or mental or spiritual must have an exact location in the human body. This is almost a law. This law is not recognized or accepted by Vedanta, Buddhism and other systems that negate the wisdom and truth of the body.

Anyhow, let us follow our argument. The sexual apparatus we have in the abdomen is duplicated above in the brain. According to some Siddhas, the pineal gland is the upper penis. [Watch the etymological roots of both the words, pineal and penis. In the Old Testament, Jacob wrestles with god throughout the night and this place is named as pineal and the pituitary gland is the vulva, the female reproductive organ. Watch the word. Pit is the depression, the dent. Utery comes from uterus, the female womb]. Modern science knows about the functions of the pituitary gland but almost nothing is known to it about the pineal gland. Some scientists like Lyall Watson try to prove that only the third eye has turned into the pineal gland in man.

In some animals, the third eye is still a protuberance in the forehead.

So the upper or higher copulation must take place between the pineal gland and the pituitary. The upper semen [melsukkilam says saint Ramalinga] must be produced in the pineal gland and secreted into the pituitary gland. Then the spiritual child is formed. This was known to the Chinese Taoists, they describe this process in their classic 'The secret of the golden flower'.

Pituitary is the female. Thus, all humans are female in the spiritual aspect. The only male, the Lord is still dormant and not functioning in us. He will operate when the pineal is activated.

Now through the pituitary, only the soul force goes down to all the cells of the body to keep them alive. This is like having only the moon light for the world and the solar eclipse is for always. When the pineal is activated through love, compassion or vasi yoga, the lord's power, the chit prana [para nadi] will radiate throughout the body. In the idol, lingam of a Siva temple, we see only this copulation of the upper lingam, or penis inside the upper female reproductive organ, lingam inside aavudiyar. The male is known as A or 8. The female the individual self, jiva is known as U or 2. When joined together we have the number 10. In the Siva temple we find it as 1 above 0. If one knows the meaning of the number 10 one becomes a Siddha. Long before the scientists like Einstein the Siddhas codified their knowledge in numbers and formulas. They were the first scientists of the world.

Even Gurdjieff was perhaps wrong in thinking that sexual daydreaming or sexual fantasy was a wrong functioning of the centers. This was natural evolutionary happening. Only the negative manifests at large first. Its real true positive counterpart has to be consciously separated and distilled from the raw ore by man. With all my humility and high regard for Gurdjieff as an enlightened master I request his followers to consider this and try to find out the truth. If I am proved wrong, I will be all the more happier as a disciple of Gurdjieff.

Next is the food problem. Amrita will secrete in 5 places in the head, says saint Ramalinga, as soon as one stops taking food from the outside. Those who want to have more details are requested to listen to the author's lecture on 'the yoga of food'.

The function of breathing must also be transferred from the nostrils and lungs to the centre of the brain. There inside the space in the pineal gland is the tiniest and minutest aperture in creation. One should consciously enter it; inside one will find Chidambaram, the divine sky, where the divine breath of the Lord is available in golden color. It is inexhaustible. It is always circulating inside. One should learn to breathe this chief prana or *mukya prana* in *Upanishadic* terms directly. This is known as undying breath. Or God's breath. In Tamil it is called

Sagaakkali,amudakalai,vegakkal. If one learns to tap this divine breath or chit prana one becomes a Siddha and becomes an immortal. All lessons in *pranayama* or vasi yoga are only preliminary lessons to enter and reach this inner sanctum sanctorum.

As for self-sufficient unlimited knowledge of God, it is available inside this inner temple as vast grace light or ArutPerum Jothi. Whoever witnesses this light can have light knowledge or *vaalarivau* in Thiruvalluvar's terms. Ramalinga Vallalar calls this inner education as non-learning wisdom, [othathuunarthal]; it is integrated, total and absolute knowledge. The sage Thiruvalluvar calls it *vaalarivu* or mind of light as it was later called by Sri Aurobindo.

In a nutshell all the functions of the lower body must be transferred to the head. The possibilities are already there in the human body. We are born with it.

Once all these lower-body functions become refined and eternal functions of the head, man becomes man-god like a Christ like a Saint Ramalinga Vallalar. He becomes not only one with God and self-sufficient but also blessed by God with godly powers of creation, sustenance, destruction, veiling and grace.

Perhaps Sri Aurobindo and the Mother were mistaken in thinking about bringing down the supramental consciousness of God from beyond and above the physical sky. We, humans according to the Siddha lore, already possess them in our heads, we are born with it. Only we have to consciously refine our consciousness into so fine and thin a nature so as to enter into this inner aperture and see the Lord dancing there in the form of light and bring it out consciously into the cells of the body and thought and our eyes must look at the physical world and transform it by this inner light power into a spiritual divine world.

The secret traditions of the Alchemists we find in all countries, throughout history. But the complete science of evolution, namely transforming matter into life, spirit and divine matter, a natural process of millions of years speeded up in a short span of a human lifetime, I find only in the Tamil Siddha system. Evolution is summed up by swami Ramalinga in 6 forms of matter namely 1] inorganic matter 2] organic matter [life] 3] mental matter 4] psychic matter 5] spiritual matter and 6] divine matter. Sri Aurobindo in his spiritual classic, The Life Divine, offers a similar form of evolution. That is why I think, the Tamil wisdom tradition must be the root, the most ancient of all esoteric and spiritual systems. The glory of it is that it is based on science. That is why I think that when this Tamil secular scientific spiritual wisdom reaches the western scientific community, the next development in science will automatically occur. The third renaissance of the world will happen, I believe. And the Homo-sapiens will ascend not only to the next rung in the ladder of evolution that is superman but to the final destination also: To become a God like species.

21. COMPASSION IS THE WAY TO IMMORTALITY

Why should one be granted an immortal life while other beings pathetically die every moment at the tender age of a few months or years due tonatural causes like volcanoes, earthquakes, tornadoes, tsunami etc or diseases? There should be a convincing reason for God to bless one with such an extraordinary boon. Is it because one has done a lot of penance, prayer, yoga or meditation? What is the motive behind all such acts of conscious suffering and enhancing one's consciousness? If the motive is one of really getting interested in the welfare of and care for others, God could also be interested in it. When God is convinced absolutely that there is no iota of hatred or dislike towards other beings or self-interest in your mind, He could have no misgivings or reluctance in granting you immortality. I think it is fair enough.

Of course, all of us are children of God. Certainly, we are not children of Satan. But almost all of us almost all of the time forget this truth and act only with an intention of gaining something for us, and for our kith and kin. What is in it for me? That is the only question always driving us on. We narrow down our consciousness and focus our attention only on our own survival and security and prospects.

247

Even when we become members of a society, the circle is expanded only a little more. From being egocentric our consciousness becomes ethnocentric caring only for the welfare of the groups we belong to. We never become world-centric, caring for all the beings. We constantly forget the fact that all of us are children of one father in Heaven. Our affiliations to smaller groups like caste, creed, gender, color etc are the walls created by our ancestors among humankind and sustained by us. The consequences of practicing this law of the jungle are feuds, conflicts, wars, concentration camps and unimaginable suffering by millions of people. Unfortunately, the brain of humanity, the scientific community armed with their unique knowledge of higher sciences like quantum mechanics atomic physics and information technology stand first in aiding this destructive tendency and animalistic behavior of our leaders. What could be the end result of this madness? It is quite obvious to everyone: total destruction of all forms of life on earth. Now thatall the sides of conflicting forces are armed with nuclear bombs the next major conflict could only end in total extermination.

Do we have the moral right to do that? Think twice. Think a hundred times. Do we have the right to destroy the future of our own children? In fact, it is our duty as parents to leave behind us a better world than what we enjoyed. Where are our consciences? Why do we allow them to go to sleep? Why do we allow others into brainwashing us to go into slumber? Our very survival depends upon these vital questions.

There is yet another question to be answered by every humanbeing. According to science, the big bang took place some 13.5 billion years ago. Some two millions of species evolved and lived here before Homo sapiens arrived about two million years ago. Man is the latecomer. Infact we are guests in the house of plants and animals. They have been not only our hosts, but they have been our food. More truly, according to the evolutionary theory they are, in fact, our ancestors. Now think and ask yourselves: do we have the right to destroy their ancient house? Is this the way to show our gratitude to them?

Man is supposed to be a moral being endowed with a conscience. Thousands of books on morality have been written by hundreds of philosophers from the beginning of recorded history. All religious teachers unanimously preach only morality, though their own brands may vary. And this is the most important and most urgent moral dilemma facing humanity.

Can man create a blade of grass? When you cannot create life, do you think you have the right to destroy it? No animal would consent to destroy all life on earth. Is man far below the level of animals? Then, why talk and preach about God and religion?

The only solution to this vital problem is to plant in the mind of every human being jivakarunya a compassionate way of looking at other beings and rendering service to them.

And as far as I know, the science of compassion has not been taught in all its dimensions and details by any other worldteacher than Swami Ramalinga Vallalar [1823 -]. His gospel of total compassion called, 'The Discipline of Compassion' was written and published by him in 1867 at Vadalur, some thirty kilometers away from Pondicherry in South India.

There are many good qualities and traits in the human soul such as self-control, parental and fraternal love, devotion to God, thirst for knowledge etc. So far compassion has been considered one among the other good virtues. And the dire consequences of following such a policy we have been witnessing through history. Now we are at the edge of survival, like cliff-hangers. Our only chance of survival is to change the priority of virtues and place compassion at the highest pedestal where it truly belongs. In ever so many ways, religious, philosophical, psychological, scientific, moral, economical, social and evolutionary Swami Ramalinga Vallalar argues his case for compassion. And he does it with utmost impartiality, taking into consideration the welfare of all beings in the world. Not even a single soul must be harmed- that is his only motto and prayer to God.

CELLS AND CANCER CELLS

Are we cells or cancer cells in thebody of God? If you are a regular cell in the body of God, you will be provided with food [manna] and oxygen [holy breath] by God, and you will live an immortal life with God. For God's body is a body of light cells of total compassion. If you are a light cell, you can remain in thebody of God forever. On the contrary, if you are ahuman cell with self-interest, with 'I and Mine consciousness' you become a cancer cell in the body of God. You steal the food and air sent to other cells for their survival. And they die. The regular functioning of the body of God is disturbed. Friction, strife and violence are introduced in the very atmosphere of love and compassion. You are the cause of this entire malady. So God wants to cut the root of the cause of disease and you will naturally be cut off from the body of God like cancer cells during an operation by a surgeon.

So why man dies? What is the cause? Because he turns into a cancer cell in the society. He doesn't identify himself as a cell in the body of God. Rather he identifies himself as a human or an animal with a human form. A cell in the body of God is made up of love and compassion. A cell in the body of a human or animal is all self-interest. So in order to transform oneself from the human condition to the immortal condition of Godhead, man's consciousness should be absolutely compassionate. This is the only way to illumination and immortality. All the other factors causing death are only secondary. And all the other ways of immortality are only half-measures. Some two thousand years ago the great sage Thiruvalluvar summed up this eternal law in a couplet: As the hot rays of sun kill the boneless easily, the law of justice of the cosmos kills the loveless.

THE POSITIVE ASPECTS OF COMPASSION

In the first part of this article, we saw the evils and dire consequences arising from lack of compassion.

Now we are going to see the benefits accruing from a compassionate way of life. The benefits of compassion are of two types: 1] in an individual's life and 2] for the species Homosapiens.

First, in an individual's life, compassion shows one a frictionless, stress-free way of behaviour, a mode of non-confrontational, affectionate conduct towards other beings. Where there is empathy, there is no sorrow or fear. Where there is no stress, there is no cause for diseases physical or mental. One's health is improved. When one is always in a state of compassion Swami Vallalar says, nectar is produced in the body and the immune system is boosted. All the other thoughts, emotions and moods except love and compassion produce only poison in the body. When this poison gets accumulated in the body, it manifests itself in the form of disease, old age and death. So compassion, according to Swami Ramalinga is the universal remedy for all kinds of diseases.

One reaps what one sows. If one sows the seeds of goodwill by the way of compassion, the accumulated goodwill, will be returned by God with interest in the form of wealth. So compassion becomes a way of wealth-creation too.

All of our ills and sufferings can be attributed to two causes: 1] our past karma in previous births and 2] carelessness. Compassion, the Swami says, is the only antidote to past karma. It can offset all the evils of past fatal and chronic karma manifesting in our lives in the forms of diseases, poverty and other forms of sufferings. Compassion, Swami assures us, has the capacity to save us even from natural catastrophes like tsunami, earthquakes, etc. At the time of these occurrences, one who is leading a way of compassion will be taken away from those places of danger under one pretext or another.

According to Yogi Patanjali, yoga means stilling one's thoughts, the waves in the ocean of the mind. Confronting, overcoming and subduing thoughts are Herculean tasks to be continued in many births. Vallalar shows a shortcut to evade and bypass this obstacle. By compassion, his consciousness has already crossed the boundary of mind and its thoughts, and reached the soul. The ego-consciousness is transcended. In a true state of intense compassion, one's soul starts melting. The I-consciousness and mine-consciousness do not function then. One is already a yogi. So compassion, like Zen, becomes an instant way of becoming a yogi. One reaches a state of love beyond thoughts of self-gain. And love is neither a thought nor an emotion of the mind but the energy of God with which He creates and sustains the universe.

For all intelligent beings, compassion is the only true way of worship. Because one sees God everywhere, that is in every being. Everybody, every being is the real temple built by God-himself. All the other temples are built by man with brick and mortar. And God's house is built by God himself. [Citrambalam or Chit Ambalam means temple of Gnosis]. So when one serves a being in suffering, one truly serves God with true love. So compassion is the true way of worship.

Can a householder attain Gnosis or Gnana? Yes, it is possible, says Vallalar, provided one's lifestyle becomes compassionate. What is gnosis? To feel atone with all souls; advaita, not two but one. The identity changes from selfishness to altruism, from egocentrism to world centrism. When one feels the sorrow of another being, realizing one's own brother or sister is suffering, one has already understood the fact that beings are children of one Father, God. His soul melts at the sight of another being suffering. One has realised the eternal bond of Universal Soul Love of all beings. In the eternal, universal body of God, I am one cell, you are another cell, and all the beings are cells. When your foot is hurt by a stone, the eyes weep. In the same way, when some cells in the body of God suffer, you suffer with them and you try to alleviate that suffering. So compassion becomes a way of self-realisation or gnosis.

Can compassion give one salvation, enlightenment and God-realisation? Yes. When you are giving what you have got to other helpless beings, you are performing the act of God. God is instantly pleased with your behaviour. You come under the personal surveillance of God himself, particularly when you save a being from getting killed or hurt or when you pacify the hunger of the poor. These two acts of charity are called by the Swami as Para Jeevakarunya or Acts of Divine Mercy. You become the real representative of God's work upon earth while you shed your smaller egoistic self. You act from your higher self or spirit. For the first time in your life, you act according to His will. The spiritual transmutation has already taken place. You are acting like a jeevan-muktha upon earth. Total compassion is nothing but the supreme state of super consciousness or Sahaja Samadhi, the highest level of Samadhi.

Also, according to Swami Ramalinga Vallalar, total compassion is the way of immortality. There are grades and levels in immortality such as 1] pure body attaining which one can live hundreds of thousands of years upon earth with a golden body like a Siddha, 2] Pranava body or Mantra body of gods and goddesses with which one can live for aeons and yugas and finally 3] Divine body of Godhead made of light of total compassion or grace.

When God is satisfied with a being's state and behaviour of total compassion, the ultimate boon of the final body of light of compassion is conferred upon him or her. The process is scientifically described by the Swami: When one attains total compassion [arulnilai] and gets stabilized in that state forever, Causal Heat is produced in his head. The human head is transformed into God's head. Along with the causal heat, causal air or holyspirit and nectar of grace are produced in the head. When one consumes this ultimate form of Divine Nectar [Arul Amudham] and breathes the Divine Breath [Vegak kaal] one enters the Hall of Divinity [Chid Sabha]; the very body, mind, soul and spirit, all the four parts of a human are transformed permanently into ArutPerum Jothi, the Divine Light of Total Compassion.

This was what happened to Swami Ramalinga Vallalar in 1874 at Siddhivalagam in the village of Mettukuppam. This transformation has to take place in every human body. In fact, the homosapiens, as a species are undergoing such a mutation. In the 1960s, Sir Julian Huxley, the then president of UNESCO revealed this scientific fact to the world. He called this new species yet to arrive as 'Neo Humanism'. A hundred years before Julian Huxley, Vallalar declared, God has revealed to me: 'Except those that kill other beings, all the others are qualified to become mutants of the new species.   And you are the first born of my species.'

Let us lead the way of a compassionate life and reap these godly boons and benefits.

~~~ ~~~ ~~~

22. THE DAWN OF THE AGE OF SCIENCE AND TECHNOLOGY

The Greeks from the days of Democritus had known about the existence of atom. But they did not attempt to develop it into a science, nor into a technology with which they could produce atomic energy. For they did not want to. Their aim was different, so their methodology and consequently their way of life were different. Their aim was only to know the basic laws of life. In other words, philosophy was their aim and the only end of life. They did not want to improve the lot of humans because they had a large community of slaves to take care of their mundane works and menial jobs. And they were able to concentrate on their contemplative life which according to Aristotle was the best way of life. For, man was defined by 'the philosopher' as a 'rational animal' and the contemplative life was the only way that offered the possibility of developing reason. And they were satisfied with that end of reasoning and philosophy. Almost all the energies of their greatest thinkers were concentrated on knowing the laws of nature and human nature. The only utopia conceived by the Greeks was done by Plato in his theory of Ideas which was some sort of other worldliness like that of the Heaven of the Christians. Both did not attempt to alleviate the sufferings of the humanity but built utopias in other worlds after death. So the knowledge of atom did not develop into an atomic science.

The same thing happened in India also. The philosophers of the school of Vaiseshika had known the fact that the world and all the matter in it were composed of atoms. They too stopped with forwarding arguments for the existence of atoms as the ultimate particles of matter. They too did not attempt nor want to develop it into a science or its technology, because they lived in a world which they believed to be illusory, something to be left behind as soon as possible and enter Moksha, a state of liberation from the natural cycle of birth and death. And their philosophy offered a way of salvation and they were gratified with it. They never considered that their ideas when developed into a technology could help humanity to free itself from its ills and agonies. For their menial jobs were taken over and performed by the three lower castes. Their only privileged way of living was to develop philosophy, have darshans or visions of the world, atman and Brahman. They never bothered or worried about improving of the lot of humanity. They rather preferred the status quo to continue. Hence, their neglect of science and technology of atomic energy.

But in the West, after the advent of reformation and Protestantism, there began a radical change in the aim and utopian plans of the Europeans. The German people had always hated the ideals and practices of Hebraism. It is history. Their archetypes hated anything Jewish. Hence their hatred for Jewish ideals and other worldly utopias. Finally, this long suppressed racial antagonism erupted. Their representative or new prophet Martin Luther declared Protestantism and waged war on the Jewish tradition including its continuation in the form of Christianity and its revered leader the Pope.

The major result and consequence of the reformation movement was a rebellion against the ideals of Judaism and Christianity such as faith in other worldliness. The emphasis shifted towards the welfare of mankind in this world, here and now. And the atmosphere was a favourable one nourished by the Renaissance Movement. The European countries were flooded with the old classics of the Greeks and the Latin that emphasized philosophy and arts and reason. So, the European thinkers mainly the Germans were newly armed with weapons of reason and philosophy to fight their battle with faith and religions. This new trend of rationalism developed and fully flourished into a mass movement in Germany. And the world witnessed the rebirth and resurgence of philosophy as the foremost value in a society like that of Athens. Great philosophical thinkers like Immanuel Kant, Hegel, Fichte, Schelling etc., were seen as national heroes and respected by the people. Intellectuals from all over the world like Cobridge, Wordsworth and Carlyle from England, Emerson from America, Soren Kierkegaard from Denmark and many French philosophers like Sartre rushed to

Germany to learn the German language and the German philosophy.

Our point is that along with all such tidal changes, the ideal of utopia shifted from faith and other worldliness to reason and utopia upon the earth itself. This ideal culminated finally into Marxian utopia through political economy by way of industrial revolution. Marx entitled his theory as 'Scientific communism'. In the meantime, such a shift in utopian ideal had already taken place in the previous three centuries. Sir Thomas Moore of London had written his own utopia. Sir Francis Bacon also wrote his version of utopia and called it 'New Atlantis', where a league of scientists were the rulers and developers of society. His prophesy has come true now, to some extent. Science and technology have literally become the masters of our world and rule our lives.

A society free from disease, old age and even death and all forms of suffering was the ideal and utopia of the Siddhas like Thiruvalluvar and Thirumular some two thousand years ago. 'To live in this world like gods forever and fully develop oneself into a superhuman and finally into a divine person was the aim and ideal openly declared by them in their books. And the Siddha movement culminated in the system of science called 'SuddhaSanmarga' of Vallalar which showed the scientific method for humans to evolve into Mukthas or enlightened beings, then into Siddhas or supermen and finally into godlike, divine beings with indestructible, eternal bodies of light of compassion. The way, the stages, the difficulties one would encounter on the way of transformation, and the remedies to counter and conquer them are all given fully and totally, in all scientific details by Vallalar. No one in the recorded history of humankind has, as far as I know, divulged all these secrets of nature [*pasagnana*] of human nature [*pasugnana*] and divine nature [*pathignana*]. If the humanity does not avail of this freely available treasure of knowledge, its very survival will be jeopardized. If it accepts the saint's way and travels on it, it will reach the higher levels in its evolutionary course like Superhumanhood and Godhead. Otherwise, it might be doomed and come to extinction, the sixth one like the five before that exterminated all beings upon earth before the advent of man. The choice is in our hands. And with our free will, we are free to choose either the upward path shown by Vallalar or the downward path shown by other thinkers who believe in violence, such as Nietzsche, Dostoevsky and Darwin.

We are living in a period of transition. We may also note that some changes have taken place in the evolutionary force. For one, it has stopped its natural course. It has transformed itself into a cultural evolution. It has given its reins in the hands of humans, its highest product because of his self-consciousness. Nature is acting through the agent of man. The second noteworthy point is that it has changed its direction. From operating through external circumstances, it has turned inside human consciousness. As Teilhard de Chardin rightly pointed out in his classic on

'The Phenomenon of Man', evolution hereafter will take place in the consciousness of man, in its higher levels. It will be measured in future by the gradations of his superconsciousness as Sri Aurobindo and Vallalar before him have foretold. And the organic evolution of Darwin will also take place along with conscious evolution. The higher levels of consciousness will produce the needed new organs for their full functioning to take place such as the third eye, replacing the anatomy and physiology of the present waste producing machine into one of nectar – producing factory. Instead of blood and oxygen circulating the body and providing food and air to the cells, nectar will be circulating the body. Instead of the brain producing thoughts, it will produce *amritha* or ambrosia which will feed the cells of the body and nourish them. The Pineal gland will be fully activated and man will act like superman with paranormal powers. All such physical, mental, psychic and spiritual transformations that are going to take place in future man were all written by Vallalar in his *Agaval* poem in the section on 'Transformation of the body'.(2).(See Chapter 33)

The ancient Siddhas had not only known about the existence of atoms but had discovered the atomic science also. They were able to exploit the positive and health-giving radio-active, vital energies of some 120 minerals and metals [*uparasas*] including mercury. Only in the fifteenth century, the western Siddha Paracelsus was able to make medicine out of mercury whereas the Siddhas were able to convert all metals including mercury and all its varieties into medicine some two thousand years ago. With their vast and deep knowledge of the herbs, they were able to bring out the health-giving atomic energy of metals. First, they purified the metals and removed the toxins in them that could harm the vital organs of the human body. They were transformed into calcined metals. Next their potencies were increased million-fold by alternately grinding them in a mortar with a pestle adding juices of relevant herbs millions of time and infusing into them their own consciousness by chanting life-affirming mantras of God like *OM NAMASIVAYA* thereby converting them into medicines with consciousness. They remain by such treatment no longer inanimate, inorganic and toxic metals but nectar-giving, vitality-increasing, edible and highly energized, spiritually charged medicines. These medicines were classified into 32 varieties according to their durability and lifetimes. The highest two such medicines called '*kattu*' and '*kalangu*' could last, according to the texts of the Siddhas for eons and could revive dead bodies into live beings. Some of the other medicines could make a man enter Samadhi state of consciousness. When one enters Samadhi, his body will have all the symptoms of a dead body such as no breath, no pulse, no warmth etc. But it will not decay. After the effect of the medicine is gone, the man will come back to life. Once again his body will start breathing, his blood will start circulating, his brain will produce thoughts, he will be able to get up and move around. He will be after such a deep sleep and total rest will be rejuvenated. His body would have grown stronger, his mind developed para-normal powers and so on. He would become a superman.

This strange and superior potion that could make man enter a state of death, stay in it for some time and revive later, must have been known to Shakespeare who lived in the sixteenth century. For he writes about such a potion in two of his plays, Romeo and Juliet and Winter's Tale. There is a speculation that Shakespeare who had his education only upto high school was able to become a great world poet only by taking such a potion that was called by the alchemists of his day as the 'universal medicine'.

Another guess among the historians of ancient Mystery Cults such as Eleusinian mysteries and Orphic mysteries is that the initiates into mysteries were given such a potion. They were able to enter death, experience its dimension and were able to come back. So they, like Socrates, were able to conquer the fear of death and become suddenly wiser than their fellow beings.

The aim of science and technology, according to Bacon is to alleviate the sufferings of mankind and to make his life upon earth as blissful as possible. The causes of man's sufferings are the limitations of his body, the perversions and limitations of his mind and the disadvantages given to him by harsh and hostile circumstances. How to eradicate all these problems and create a perfect man and transform him into a divine being in a divine body with all the divine powers over nature through the technology of love and absolute compassion was shown by Vallalar. He has given us a blueprint with which we can build a house with all the desired advantages for humanity. He has given us a road map, a GPS, with the help of which our species can travel safely on the road to superhumanhood and divinity. We shall all, in due course, become perfect like our Father, the supreme God-head who is forever living here upon earth immanently inside every atom and transcendently beyond the universe by being and living with absolute compassion. For according to Vallalar, it was the omnipotent power and omniscient wisdom of absolute compassion out of which all creation was born and is being sustained by it. Even if a particle of dust is imbued with all-compassion, it will have all the five powers of God.[4]So the aim and ideal of science and technology can be fully realized and the dream that has waited for too long can come true by following the path of science shown by Vallalar.

He claims to have conquered all forms of sufferings and was blessed by God by way of reward for his all-compassion towards all beings without any difference or discrimination with a body of bliss.[5]This divine body of bliss had the attributes of all knowing divine wisdom, all-pervading power, producing the ultimate nectar of compassion [arulamutham], ever-growing, with no limitations whatsoever including time and distance etc. It possessed all the divine powers.

23. SCIENCE OF MATTER AND SCIENCE OF CONSCIOUSNESS

These two forms of science are always supposed to be antagonistic to each other. Some historians like Edward Gibbon, Buckle and philosophical historians like Bertrand Russell affirm such a conviction and demonstrate ample evidence for it throughout their books and some scientists like Richard Dawkins literally live it in their lives.

But is it the truth or only an opinion taken from the ancient tradition without thoroughly analyzing the issue and its roots in all their perspectives? History shows that such a dichotomy, such a dialectic runs through it all the time. The spiritual philosophers call them exoteric and esoteric garbs of truth. The so-called materialists and their offsprings like the rationalists and the scientists who base their beliefs and reasoning only upon the empirical, sensory data accept only the exoteric facts and condemn all esoteric teachings as baseless and fictions created by human imagination and childish hopes. It is a way of escapism, they accuse, and a distraction that deviates from the real task of facing real problems in this life. Esoterism might offer other worldly solutions for the present problems and agonies like hunger, disease, war, old age and all sorts of human miseries and sufferings. They might offer as solutions the discovery of atman, God, Heaven etc., which can never pacify hunger nor cure diseases.

When religious people claim that a great esoteric master like Jesus fed more than five thousand people with two fishes and a few crumbs of bread and cured all incurable diseases like leprosy, they only laugh at them and pooh pooh them for believing such nonsense. They don't believe these miracles and call them as comics like superman comics and spiderman comics of old times believed as true only by children. If it was science, why don't they happen now? Everyday hundreds of children and adults are dying for want of food and proper medicine. When these facts stare us in the face, how can these religious people go on reiterating these tall claims as scientific truths? These followers of such miracles-making prophets and Sons of God, they question, why don't they create food for the hungry and make the lame people walk? If it was possible for a man two thousand years ago, why not now? If it was a science, what happened to it? Where is it? What are its rules and technology? Why is it hidden? Why is it not revealed fully to the world? Either there was no such science or there was no compassion to reveal it to all. But science means and demands that knowledge should belong to all and it should be available to the public. Modern science reveals all its discoveries and inventions the moment they are discovered. The ample truth of it has been well demonstrated in the world for the past three centuries. Cholera, leprosy, smallpox and most of the so called epidemics and incurable diseases have been cured and the handicapped made to walk with artificial limbs. A tree is known by its fruits. The tree of knowledge, science is always learning and giving out fruits whereas the so-called tree of life of religions and esotericism are fictitious drawings on the black boards, they are not true even if the drawing is repeatedly drawn millions of times all over the world, all through the year. A drawing of Holy Bread can never pacify the hunger of a child.

The above arguments of the materialists and scientists are too factual to be refuted. As long as humans live upon this earth, this life, though it might be called as apparent, illusory or superficial by the religionists and the spiritualists, they are facts at the apparent level. For a man or woman who is always in a higher dimension of spirituality or divinity might have known the secrets of conquering hunger, disease and death. But it is not the practical truth or a way of living for the common humanity. They cannot live in such fairy castles built in the air. Their only salvation is science and technology. For the first time in world history, at least, a major portion of the humankind live in comfortable, care-free conditions. What were once supposed to be luxuries that only kings and lords could afford have become comforts enjoyed by all, such as cars, air-conditioning machines, television, smart phones etc.,

The only way out for the spiritualists is to reveal their so-called spiritual truths in provable, demonstrable and quantifiable ways. Here yoga has stood such a test of the scientists to some extent. That is why it is gaining popularity all over the world. It keeps people healthy physically and mentally.

So the science of matter has triumphed over the ancient science of consciousness at the present and got the upper hand. But obviously it has not solved all the problems of the humankind. Furthermore, science and technology have created more problems for humans which were not there before. These man-made problems such as atomic catastrophe, global warming etc, could totally exterminate all life on earth. Scientists are everyday coming out with warnings of 'the day after', 'the sixth extinction' and so on.

~~~ ~~~ ~~~

24. SCIENCE OF MATTER AND SCIENCE OF TECHNOLOGY

The materialist scientist Sir Charles Darwin discovered and proved as true the law of Natural Selection. He also said and his followers to the day like Richard Dawkins affirm this law is operating in nature at random. But logically it is not viable. Because the very word 'law' implies intelligence, atleast memory however negligible it might be or at least a pattern of recognition. Again the word 'selection' implies choice which means some agent is selecting certain thing or species and avoiding others. Again this implies there is a cause behind the selection. And this cause or aim is obviously 'evolution' or evolving of species from a simple state to a higher and more complex form or intelligence. Mutation might happen as these materialist scientists argue very slowly, in millions of years and in a non-linear way. But the law of time operates in nature, according to Stephen Hawking in a straight line, like an arrow, from the past through the present towards the future. If this law of time is true, evolution being the biological dimension or variation of time must also be true. This straight line operation of time must operate within the field of evolution also. The most apparent evidence of this fact is the factor of aging in all beings. Every being is born, grows into adulthood, declines into aging and finally fall into death. This pattern proves that the law of change, as the Buddha and the Greek Heraclitus and Empedocles discovered long ago, is a constant process of nature. And evolution only adds that this change is always for the higher mode of living and for a more complex way of living by species and their beings, in short, towards higher intelligence. From inorganic gases to amoeba through the plant kingdom and the animal kingdom to homo-sapiens and beyond man into a superman and beyond – this is the picture of evolution evidenced in the record of fossils. The next stage of superhumanhood has been achieved in recorded history by a few exceptional humans like the Buddha, Christ, Thiruvalluvar, Thirumular and Vallalar. Which fact is only an indication of the direction, the way forward in which homo sapiens are expected to travel in future if they aspire towards higher levels of intelligence, wisdom and compassion. Here Vallalar differs from other supermen like the Buddha, Christ and others in two ways.

This superior existence as supermen or superwomen is possible, according to them only in another world or in another dimension and that too is possible only after death. This is not science but religion and philosophy. If it is science and evolution the mutation into superhumanhood must take place here upon earth. And the second difference is the changes in the human body after mutation. According to Darwin's evolutionary theory, evolutionary force operates and is evidenced only by the change demonstrable in the forms and organs of the bodies of various species. The Buddha and Christ and other spiritual leaders accept and declare that the superman state is desirable and the only possible way of conquering the ills and problems of the human condition, but they don't explain scientifically what sort of bodily changes can occur to accomplish this superhuman feat. In the case of Christ, a resurrected body is mentioned, but how he got it, what was the process and what new organs it had? Such scientific details are not given in the gospels, whereas Vallalar openly publishes all the details of transformation of his physical body into a pure physical body and next into a spiritual body and finally into a light body of wisdom or absolute compassion.[6] And more importantly he did not guess or speculate about these details of bodily transmogrification.

He conducted all these experiments of physical transformation on his own body, observed the process, noted them down exactly and published them like a scientist in all their details. If the species of homo-sapiens are to be transformed into superhumans and finally into godlike beings what will be the processes and new habits of body, mind, soul and spirit that are to be adopted by them? All these processes and changes of habits are elaborated in the scientific scripture called 'ThiruArutpa' by Vallalar. For the whole species to undergo collective mutation, how many millions or billions of years it will take? For it took for nature to accomplish this feat of transformation from inorganic matter to man nearly 3.5 billion years. And for the next transformation to take place in man from the human condition and form to the divine condition and form may take another 3.5 billion years. How to expedite this process? Vallalar shows the way. He cut short 3.5 billion years to a single lifetime of 50 years 3 months and 24 days. Because natural process of evolution is a very very slow one accomplished in millions and billions of years. Nature has got all the time in the world. Unfortunately, man's lifetime is very short. He has to accomplish all that he wants to achieve within a short span of a lifetime of a few decades. Since man is a small microcosm that contains all there is in the macrocosm and secondly now that nature has given its reins in the hands of man and thirdly, the time for species-level mutation for homo-sapiens has already arrived, Vallalar opted for it and successfully completed the operation of transformation in his own body, according to God's will and order. That is why he urges all to join him to accomplish this unique feat of the species-level transformation from being humans into Divine Beings.

So Vallalar being at once a scientist of matter and scientist of consciousness, was able to give to humankind both the needed processes and details of transformation of body and consciousness. Though the latter part of the great work was known and declared by almost all the saints and spiritual masters of the world, the first part of biological immortality was either neglected or rejected as nonsense or impossible. Only a small segment of thinkers such as the Tamil Siddhas, Chinese Taoists and alchemists of the world accepted it as a possibility and worked their way to attain it. It was a sad thing to note that even very advanced spiritualists considered the human body, its conditions and needs as obstacles on the way to the enlightenment of consciousness. Finally, it was only thanks to the divine knowledge of Vallalar the world got clarified on this age-old riddle of man, the mystery of all mysteries.

Natural selection implies there is constant interrelationship between nature and species, between the inorganic world and the organic beings. Both are parts of a whole. One cannot exist without the other. Whatever change takes place in one will automatically take place in another.

'Adaptation to environment' is the way to survival for beings. Why? Only the environment provides being with provisions they need for their survival such as food, *prana* or air and knowledge. Unless all these three are adequately available in a circumstance, the living beings cannot survive there. So far, this was the story of evolution. But, now, at this juncture of evolution humans are required or compelled by a higher law to change and reverse this law of adaptation. Instead of adapting himself to nature and its conditions and demands, man has started ruling over circumstances or nature. They should adapt themselves according to the whims and fancies of man. This is what modern science and technology are doing in the world today. Man with the help and aid of instruments provided by technology has learnt to survive in hostile circumstances such as in space travel where atmospheric air is not available, and travels in deep underwater, in oceans in submarines. Genetically Modified foods, cloning, homosexual marriages, genetic engineering, robotics, pills once a week instead of normal foods for astronauts are some of the indications of this new trend or reversal in the course of evolution. This trend, as some traditionalists fear and warn us as symptoms of impending danger to the very survival of homo sapiens may take us to new heights and powers, physical and mental, psychical and spiritual undreamt of and never seen before. Our steps should be measured and cautious and thought out a thousand times before action. Not mere knowledge, proud knowledge but wisdom only can save us. The value of the body, the significance and reverence for life and foreknowledge and insight are what we need now, in this time of crisis and transition.

The wisdom of the Siddhas like Thiruvalluvar, Thirumular and Vallalar is what the world needs now. For, they are adepts in the science not only of the enlightenment of consciousness but in the immortality of the physical body also. They claim to have lived for eons and will never die. They also claim to have the fine divine powers of creation of universes and beings, sustaining them, destruction of them when their evil exceeds the limits, veiling their knowledge to suit their lives and conditions and finally offering them grace for salvation and empowerment as spiritual and divine beings.

According to them all*jivas* or beings are potential Sivas or God. In the mythological figure of Lord Siva, they embedded the physical changes yet to take place in the human body in future evolution such as the Third Eye, the androgenous whole Man [*Arthanareeswara*] of the Symposium of Plato instead of the half man and half woman as we are at present, the ten places in the human body where it would produce its own food called nectar or ambrosia to replace the foods from the external nature of the plant and animal kingdoms which produce poison in the form of waste matter that corrupts the body and cause it to undergo disease, old age and death. Finally, these dark matters coming from food, air and material data are deterring the human body from becoming a light body and cause all the limitations of it, physical and mental, psychical and spiritual. And the Siddhas and Vallalar in particular offer us alternatives to our food, air and knowledge which they used in their bodies and found them good in transforming the dark matter of the physical body into a pure light body. And, I think, it is high time, humankind gave these Siddhas a chance. By doing so we are not giving a chance to these higher beings but only to our own selves. They don't need any of our favours. They don't depend upon us. Rather we are in need of them. For they are our only chance, the last refuge. Because they are the only Masters who have mastered both the science of consciousness and the science of matter. For evidence of what we mean, one can look at the marvels of their achievements in their Siddha system of medicine in which all metals, minerals even gem stones have been transformed into edible medicines, including the nine poisons from which system the German multi-linguist Hahnemann learnt and formed his own system of homeopathy. It is only a half-baked product of the Siddha system of medicine. Its one branch of Nine Poisons Medicine [*navapashanam*] was modified and newly formulated by Hahnemann. They were great metallurgists producing rust-free iron and stain-free copper. More significantly they were the pioneers in 'atomic medicine'. They had known how to increase the potency of a remedy to the atomic level that is to increase the potency of a medicine millions of times so that even a tiny amount of it could produce immediate and lasting results. They don't accept any disease as incurable including the major and chronic diseases of old age and death. They were Masters of Immortality and deal with that subject in many thousands of books. We can go on and on describing their marvelous achievements in all branches of science. Once this hidden tradition of knowledge is looked into and made use of by the western scientists the world will see another period of renaissance and humankind will leap into a higher species.

In the higher science of consciousness, they had reached ten degrees of knowledge. Western philosophers, scientists and psychologists had known only upto the eighth degree called insight. The sixth degree of knowledge is thought, the seventh intuition. Since we have already explained these ten degrees of knowledge fully elsewhere, we need not enter the subject now. But we would like to give a hint of their superior achievement in the cognitive science of consciousness. In the *Mandukya* Upanishad, the *rishi*, for the first time in human history describes the *Turiya* state of consciousness. The Siddha Thirumular elaborated it into three *Turiyas*, *Jiva*, *Para* and Siva *Turiyas*. In the nineteenth century, Vallalar developed his consciousness still further and tells us about the fourth and final level of Suddha Siva*Turiyadita* and describes his own experience of it. All in all, he describes forty three alternate states of consciousness. No western psychologists including Freud, Jung and Ken Wilber could have ever heard of it. My plea to humanity, particularly to the scientific community is this: This treasure of scientific knowledge remains untapped. It contains more treasure than one can imagine. When compared with the science of the Siddhas, modern science is child's play.

~~~ ~~~ ~~~

25. SCIENCE OF CONSCIOUSNESS

Is consciousness a product of matter or the mother and source of it? According to the materialists, and the evolutionary scientists, 'in the beginning was matter'. And matter evolved into various forms of gases. By accident, one of these permutations and combinations produced nitrogen. Out of nitrogen was produced amino acids and protein. They in turn produced organic matter and life. Life evolved from one-celledamoeba to multicellular organisms like plants. Later plants evolved into aquatic animals like molluscs and fish which later evolved into animals and birds. Finally, they evolved into apes and from one branch of apes, the homo sapiens evolved. And they were endowed with the highly developed nervous system. The acme of this human evolution is the brain. The brain is constantly churning out thoughts. Thought alone can think about itself. Thought is consciousness that is conscious of its own existence and functioning. This unique characteristic of man's thinking faculty is variously called as the reflective consciousness, self-awareness, self-remembering, the witnessing consciousness etc., by various philosophers and psychologists and spiritualists. The universe was produced by the Big Bang about 13.7 billion years ago. It kept on expanding as matter for some 10.2 billions of years. And then a miracle, by accident, according to the scientists, happened: Life was born. For the past 3.5 billion years it was life or the embodiment of consciousness that evolved. So consciousness was a product of life and life itself was a product of matter. The basic law of consciousness is memory or the recognition of pattern. Pattern alone gives a thing its unique characteristics. Every atom of every element has its own unique number of electrons, protons and other subatomic particles. This is the story and explanation of evolution by the ancient materialists and modern scientists.

On the contrary, the idealistic philosophers, religionists and the spiritualists raise some questions which cannot be brushed aside as nonsense or illogical. They offer the notion of teleology or a purpose to nature. No random accident can create a Shakespeare or Plato or a Darwin who embodied and exhibited to the world by their masterworks, their own forms of high intelligence and order. So, right from the beginning of the origin of the world by the Big Bang there was a purpose behind every action of nature. In other words, this purpose was to transform the immense chaotic energy into order, into orderly planets that rotated in their own orbits and beings who led some kind of orderly lives by eating food, procreating and growing etc, all such actions born of intelligence whether instinctual, intellectual or critical. So the universe and all beings in it are from the beginning only manifestations of a purpose or intelligence. This intelligence or consciousness only evolves into higher and more complex forms of it. The bodies are only various manifestations or currencies and consciousness is the original seal or design of them. This is the argument of the idealists and spiritualists.

Science and technology have proved one thing for humans to see and follow: the simple, prudent and wise rule is this: Follow what works and further it. Go, proceed and advance in that direction. And be bold enough to discard and forget what did not work in the past. If we apply this basic rule of wisdom, what do we get? History has taught us a lesson: Religion, Philosophy, utopian systems of politics and economies have all failed to give results since they all are based on and stop with theory and speculation. When it comes to practical life, they are almost useless except as old comic books for childish minds. It is useless and waste of time to revive and applaud old and worn-out notions of void, illusion, maya, ideal reality and so on. They are mere words. One cannot eat the word bread and pacify one's hunger. Throw away all these nostalgic nonsenses and first come to face reality as it is.

The second lesson history has taught us is that these speculative visions, philosophical, spiritual or mystical or otherwise are meant for only a few advanced souls, say for a Buddha, a Christ or a Plato. But science aims at reaching and teaching all humans through what limited sense and mental capacities they have now. Unfortunately, these common people have not developed their higher forms of consciousness such as intuition, insight, spiritual eyes or divine eyes. Science wants to replace these higher faculties with gadgets like electron microscopes to investigate the subatomic world and huge telescopes to see far into the Milky Way. The more their powers are increased, the more capable they are beyond the capacity of human sensory apparatus thus conquering their limitations they are born with. This way of expanding one's sensory and mental world is possible for all, for even illiterates whereas the other way of developing one's inner senses was not possible even for great minds like Aristotle in the ancient world and Bertrand Russell in the modern world. Their spiritual eyes were not opened. Russell openly confesses in his classic 'The History of Western Philosophy' that he does not understand Bergson's philosophy of intuition and all mysticism. But he was able to understand Einstein's almost mystical theory of Relativity both special and general with his mathematical knowledge. He even wrote a book explaining the abstruse theory of Relativity to the layman entitled 'ABC of Relativity'.

What is the right path to follow now at this critical juncture, at this transitional period? After the advent of Quantum Physics and the proving of the uncertainty Principle many charlatans have entered into the so-called New Age Movement. They were all traditionalists. A traditionalist is always looking backwards either towards the Garden of Eden or *sunyata* or Maya or ancient gods. His very temperament is very old and anti-scientific and anti-progressive. They care more for maintaining the status quo than to take mankind to its next stage in evolution. They are always walking backwards. Their unconscious aim and methodology is to halt or minimize the speed of science and technology. Nothing fruitful will ever come out of these traditionalists. One has to first of all identify these enemies of science in the garb of spiritualists and avoid them like the plague. One's first task is to clear one's mind of all cobwebs, all trash of such nonsensical, superstitious misbeliefs however noble their source may be. Detox your mind first as you detox your body. And then detox your soul by purging it of all religions and all small boundaries that enlarge only your ego-consciousness but never allow you to get away from it and be free. But then what is one to do? How to discern the truth from the false? How to identify the charlatans from the real scientists who will take humanity into the future?

There is a simple way: See whether he was a recognized scientist like Fritzof Capra or Arthur Eddington or Albert Einstein before he started talking about New Age Science. And then see his motive, whether he wants to advance science, scientific temper and method into spiritual domain or wants to amass wealth and go after reputation and personal recognition. For instance, invention and development of the cyberspace was one real step in the advancement of science towards spirituality. Cognitive science is another. Cloning, microbiology, nanotechnology, genetic engineering, robotics, gerontology and anti-aging medicine are some more symptoms of the true development of scientifying spirituality, not spiritualizing science which is going backwards. Always look to the future. That is the right way to look at life. Some of the new age gurus recommend and emphasize the dictum: Always live in the present moment. It is true but only partially true. You can live life fully only in the present. Again true but again it is only half true. Dilthey rightly pointed out: mere self-knowledge and living in the present will not give you all the knowledge you need for your survival, let alone your development. Read history and learn its lessons. Otherwise, your future will be spoiled. You cannot understand the ways of life, you will be half-blind. You are not alone. You live in a society and that society is always changing. In which direction it will change? No one can predict perfectly. But one can learn something about it from the indications one can get from the history of its past activities. That was why the wise old Bacon said, 'History makes men wise'. In our case, be very careful and watchful of the tiger of religion. If it is quiet now and lying low, it means it is waiting for the right moment to pounce upon humanity and eat it. Never trust the tigers that proclaim to have become cows and walking in the garb of scientists. Authority and its offspring power are the aim and motive of these traditionalists, the power to oppress and suppress the rights hardly fought out and dearly won. By principle authority is dead against science, the major obstacle and enemy of science that impeded and stopped its progress for nearly two millennia.

Was there not the science of consciousness in the teachings of Christ? How can there not be? If Christ had truly cured people of the so-called incurable diseases like leprosy and lameness, blindness and death he must have known and applied some kind of superior knowledge or higher form of science. If these miracles upon which rest the foundation and success of Christianity were historical facts as the gospels and apostles proclaim they must have come out with the detailed explanations of such a science of miracle-making. They should have made it available to one and all. If they had revealed this secret science, if there is any such science, in fact humanity, in the past two millennia would have evolved into a higher species. Instead of one Christ of the gospels, the world would have seen millions of Christs. But the church did not do so. They closed the door on all humans. The possibility was denied for all. Instead the secret was sealed in a box, ever so tightly and thrown into the sea. People ever since have been searching for this hidden box containing the secret but no one had found it. The church gave out an alternative answer, a pseudo-remedy in the notion of 'Faith'. Just have faith in Christ and you will be saved after your death. Can one have all the superhuman powers of a Christ like raising the dead and resurrection? No. They were reserved only for Christ. Why? Because he was the only son of God. A new mythology was created around the figure of Christ and this myth has been ruling and subordinating the minds of billions of people and dwarfing them. Was it the intention of Christ? With Dostoevsky, I too don't think so. He was too compassionate a person to do that. But the church and the churchmen formed themselves into a separate priestly class, the counterparts of the Brahmin priests of India whose only job was to preserve and propagate the superior significance of God's word or the Vedas and reap the seats of social and political power and prestige and lead a comfortable and in some cases of luxurious lives. In short, power once again replaced and occupied the seat of love and compassion. Instead of producing Christs, they produced millions of Christians. Instead of producing spiritual beings, they produced zealots and fundamentalists and fanatics in the name of the lovable compassionate Christ. Not only Christianity, every other religion has adopted the same method. Every religion has been turned into an organisation and the aim of the religionists was and is to strengthen the power of the organisation by adding more and more numbers to it. For this strength gives and determines power, social, political and economical. Every religion is acting like a political party. And every spiritual system of salvation discovered and delivered by its prophet has become something similar to a political and utopian ideology. Even political ideologies were no exception to the historical rule. In the name of Marx who wanted to build a Heaven on earth with every inhabitant on it fully realizing his or her potential and become a creative being, the communist parties have transformed its adherents into Marxists instead of making them into Marxs with his high intelligence and oceanic compassion. Only the letter is remembered and reiterated while the spirit is forgotten. The historical rule of power has never been changed: Few versus All.

But then what is this secret science of transforming human head and heart into those of a prophet, a Christ or a Marx? What are the steps to be taken by humanity so that the whole of it will leap forward and upward in the course of evolution, and everyone will be a Christ or Marx both in knowledge and compassion and power? Some attempts have been made at the solution but so far nothing substantial has been achieved. Transpersonal psychology, Humanistic psychology, Human Potential Movement, New Age science, Theosophical Movement are some of the mass movements besides political and economic movements that have taken place in the erstwhile USSR and China.

Whether the universe started with matter or idea, what we are witnessing now at present is that we have unleashed to a vast extent the power of matter in the form of electricity, electronics, computers and atomic energy etc.,. We have also started exploring the possibility of the existence and power of spiritual matter starting from the twentieth century. Quantum physics digging for the treasure in the quanta instead has raised this ghost of the science of consciousness by declaring and proving ever since, by so many experiments that at the deep quantum level human consciousness has the power to manipulate matter. This fact ushers in a new era of science and the possibilities are immense and the potential unimaginable. Whether the scientists who are staunch materialists like Stephen

Hawking or Richard Dawkins acknowledge it or not, a global shift in the collective consciousness of humanity has already taken place. A new paradigm shift has already taken place and gaining momentum. Day by day the number of scientists accepting this new fact of a spiritual science or cognitive science is increasing. Many well-known names in the field of academic science are seen on the internet coming out with their own theories of the science of consciousness. No one, however great his reputation be, can either halt or slow down this new tsunami. The questions before us now are: how to make the most of it? How to avoid the old traps of religions and pseudo-science? And how not to enter into bylanes and blind alleys? We need proper and almost infallible guidelines something similar to those offered us by Francis Bacon and Descartes to go beyond these ancestors of ours. Let me repeat once again the first warning and guideline: Do not spiritualize science; rather scienticize spirituality. See whether the ideas of spirituality and the idealistic philosophy withstand the strict experimental tests of science.

Is there an exact science of consciousness? Can it be logically and experimentally demonstrated and proved? Yes. Sir Isaac Newton declared that the cosmos was made up of matter which had according to him atoms or energy or motion and extension. His contemporary and rival Leibniz also said the same thing adding Monadology. He did not confine himself to atoms. He went beyond them and said that in the beginning were monads, individual particles which produced atoms of matter as well as atoms of consciousness. Both matter and consciousness were inseparable or at least were born as twins from the same mother: The Monad. Matter is condensed, solidified, consciousness and consciousness is rarified, minute matter. Both are different forms of energy and motion only.

According to Indian spirituality or ancient science, the world and all the things and beings in it are made up of two components: knowledge [Sivam] and energy [Shakthi]. In modern scientific terminology, they are called Information and Motion. Of late even Stephen Hawking who first denied it, has now confessed his error and agrees to the fact that data or information can be retrieved even from black holes.

So the apparent cosmos consists of polarity or two opposing forces each operating always against the other. At one time one predominates and subdues the other but never destroys it. For they need one another for the development and the very survival. Take for instance, electricity. It is produced only when two opposing currents, positive and negative confront each other and unite. Out of the synthesis of these two antithetical forces is born electricity.

This process of polarity or dichotomy has been known to humans from time immemorial. In ancient China, they were called Yin [the feminine force] and Yang [the masculine force]. They are called in our own age of information as binary [0, 1]. The ancient Siddhas called them with the letters 'A' and 'U'. When they are united together, they produce the sound 'O' which produces or gives birth to a new genesis of a new being or state of consciousness called 'M'. 'M', the letter denotes silence in consciousness, ambrosia or nectar in the body or in the laboratory. In human life when 'A' represented by a male and 'U' represented by a female join together a new being, a child is born. Thus 'OM' [A+U+M] becomes and operates not only as the primordial sound, but also as the basic law of nature which was called by Plato as the law of Dialectics. The Siddhas, like Pythagoras, conceived another notion or law of nature that Mathematics or Numbers rule nature. Everything or every being can be denoted by an exact number by identifying its combination of matter or motion or body depending upon its condition of organic level or inorganic, and its level of life or vital power. The organic level was called, 'the letter representing the life principle [*uyir*] or vowel and the matter level was conceived and called as 'body principle' or form [Mei] or consonant. When they combine together, they make beings like humans alive and active, the soul activating the body. And these wholes are called soul-body complexes or Uyirmei or the combination of vowel and consonant. For instance, in the word, 'Ka', K is a consonant and A is a vowel.

And the Siddhas discovered the ultimate secret of nature. What is the exact relationship between number and letter? It was developed into an exact science. And out of this exact science were coined words like god, man, female, etc.,. Each word exactly referred to a number. For example, the notion of God or the Absolute was noted by the letter 'A' and the number '8'. The soul was denoted by the letter 'U' and the number 2. The conjoining of these two letters or numbers [A+U] produced OM and the number 10, the state of Perfection or Salvation or Enlightenment. The jiva or individual soul (2) by constantly being in association with the Absolute or Siva [8] is transformed into or ascends and evolves to the highest level possible both in consciousness and body.

- The entire creation or cosmos is ruled by this basic law of 8 and 2. All beings and all material things consist of these two numbers representing the positive or male force and negative or female force. Unfortunately, they are found in nature in a raw and corrupt condition; say like with rust in iron and the green stain in copper. It is the task of the human to separate both 8 and 2 and purify them. How to purify everything in nature and every being? These scientific processes were discovered one by one and added together, classified and given as an exact and complete science in the book form by the Siddhas, the ancient scientists. This science was called 'The Science of Purification' [*Suddhilyal*]. Even now it is available in the form of books.

According to this ancient science of the Siddhas every edible food or every medicine must first be cleansed and purified and the poison must be removed. Rice or wheat as food gives us warmth and energy. But, with their natural inherent poison corrupt our body and mind. And hence our diseases of body and mind. The right way of cooking or producing a medical remedy is to know the exact agent by which the poison in the food or remedy can be removed and only the purified food or remedy containing only nectar or ambrosia must be given to the patient. Then only the disease will be completely cured. Otherwise only temporary relief can result. This is the error and mistake with almost all systems of medicine available now in the world.

We are living in the so-called new age. Roughly one can say, that it started after 1960s in the west. It brought in a new paradigm shift, a shift of focus of the scientists as well as the laymen from matter to consciousness. Many factors contributed to this 'Aquarius Conspiracy'. Two of the major factors were the discovery of the Quantum Physics with its notorious uncertain principle declaring there operates no causal law in the subatomic world and the revolutionary notion that man's thought could influence matter at the micro level. All through history philosophers such as the Buddha, the *Upanishadic rishis*, Christ, the idealistic philosophers like Plato, Leibniz and Berkeley and particularly the Tamil Siddhas were voicing the opinion that thought is only subtle matter and matter condensed thought. And quantum physics demonstrated this ancient esoteric truth by telling the world that matter is condensed light and light is the bridge to and a lower form of consciousness. The process of densification of light led to matter and the process of rarification led to consciousness. This scientific fact of the relationship among consciousness, light and matter and their various permutations and combinations was revealed to the world half a century before the birth of the new science of quantum physics by Vallalar.

Absolute pure consciousness is God, announced the Upanishad. Absolute compassion is the mother of all kinds of causal, subtle and physical forms of light, declared Vallalar. He defined god as 'Light within light within light', referring to the first light as that of consciousness, into which is embedded the second light of Atman which gave birth to the first and which in turn was given birth to by the innermost light called Absolute Consciousness or God or Arul Perum Jothi, the Infinite Light of Absolute Consciousness.

'In the beginning was the word; the word was with God; the word was God'. Saint John described the genesis of the world through the power of the word. The German epic poet Goethe rephrased it: In the beginning was Action. He had his own reason for changing the word into action or motion. Swami Vallalar, a contemporary of the German poet changed the wording of St John's famous sentence: In the beginning was Compassion [Absolute]; Compassion was with God; Compassion was God.

There are a few advantages, greater advantages with this change than the former two forms namely word and action. In the case of the word, history provides ample demonstrations of this fact – every religion claimed that its own word or revelation through its prophet was the very word of God and the words of scriptures of other religions and their prophets were not the original words of God. Some religions went so far as accusing the word or scripture of other religions as the voice of Satan. This conflict led to eternal conflict, feuds and even to wars slaughtering millions of fellow-beings.

In the case of Action of Goethe, the same kind of trouble brewed. Action by whom? What kind of action? Was the action moral or beyond good and evil? All these questions remained unanswered and led only to more confusion.

No such problems arise when we say 'In the beginning was [the energy of] compassion. Compassion, by its very nature is the highest form of light, energy and goodness. By its very definition and nature, compassion needs the other [person] to give its energy to, to share its abundance with. Hence its necessity to keep on creating beings and the worlds for them to live in happily with all the necessary atmosphere and circumstances. And absolute compassion needs no personal gods though it has the capacity to manifest itself into one and many. Absolute compassion is the final law of nature and transcendent to it or that which created nature itself. It divided itself into the universe and beings. The strange but unique and true law of compassion is that the more one gives to others, the more one will be given. According to this para-natural or to use the forbidden word, the Divine Law, this basic fund of energy of compassion keeps on growing bigger and bigger, larger and larger. It never diminishes. It cannot. The modern-day astronomers announce that the universe is ever expanding. Billions and billions of galaxies are being born in the vast sky every second. This ever-expanding law was called by Vallalar as the eternal Law of Total Compassion. And this Law of compassion of Causal Light is the mother or unifying force of all the four fundamental forces of nature like gravitation, electromagnetism, the strong nuclear force and the weak nuclear force. This was the first law of the nature, the unifying field for which Einstein was searching all through his life but failed to discover. This basic law was discovered and announced to the world by Vallalar the master Scientist Siddha, almost a century before the advent of Einstein.

Most of the western philosophers ask one question and try to answer it, everyone in his own way: Why science did not develop in ancient Greece though they had discovered all the seeds of it? Euclid had discovered and written a textbook on geometry; Pythagoras had discovered many truths about geometry and the harmony of music based upon the numbers. Archimedes had discovered the law of density, the mechanism of lever, fulcrum and pulley etc., and so on. Almost all the branches of science had their origin in Greece in the west. With all these preparations,

Greece did not produce a Newton, a Galileo or Einstein. But instead it produced intellectual giants in arts and humanities such as Socrates, Plato and Aristotle in philosophy, Homer and Demosthenes in literature, the Master architect who built Parthenon, Pericles and democratic form in politics and so on.

Historians try to answerthis question in two ways: 1. Though the seeds of sciences were sown in the land of Greece, they were not given enough time to develop and grow into full trees. Greece was conquered by Rome and its citadels of learning like Academy of Plato and the Lyceum of Aristotle were destroyed by the Roman legions, as they destroyed the citadels of the Jewish culture like the Temple at Jerusalem. This has always been the way of treatment of all conquerors of their colonies. Destroy the foundations of the culture of the enemy and your conquest will be complete only then. Culture is the unifying force and strength that could stimulate rebellion against oppression and slavery. Make the slave accept his fate. Never allow him time or energy to think. This is the strategy of all conquerors. Military invasion and physical conquest of the land is only the first stage in capturing a nation. Cultural invasion fulfils and completes that job of subduing a people. Make the slaves voluntarily give consent to the victorious. This psychological warfare started long before Alexander. And Greece fell a prey to this perilous law of history. And science was a stillborn child there.

It could not develop fully. It had to wait for the right condition for another two thousand years. Another major enemy of science was religion. In the west, it was the uprising and firm establishment of Christianity all over Europe for the next sixteen centuries till the Renaissance.

If these two arguments are true, why did not science arise and develop into its full stature as at present in the east, particularly in China and India? China had already discovered paper, the printing machine, gun powder, the magnetic compass etc. Similarly in India, mathematics including calculus had been developed fully. In arithmetic, zero and the Arabic numerals were known. Medical systems like Ayurveda and Siddha including surgery were very popular. And the Siddha system had known the secret of transforming even metals into edible medicines. Again foreign invasions starting from the Greek Alexander, through the Huns, the Muslims to the British could be cited as historical forces that curbed the development of science in India.

But in my opinion, these are only minor external causes. The basic internal cause is a different one. It is a law of life, life of an individual or a people or a civilization. It can be formulated in three different ways, but the underlying truth is the same. According to an individual or a people, what is the best way of life in their estimation? What do they consider as the true way or method of arriving at truth about life, the world and God? What is their topmost priority or value in life? In other words, what is their highest single interest in which they focus and concentrate all their energies and time? The answers for these questions determine the direction, quality, duration, decline and fall of an individual or a race.

The simple acronym I ascribe for this system of mine is ILI. I stands for interest; L for levels or rungs of the ladder and the second I for intensity or heat with which the interest is pursued by the people or person.

The ideal pursued not only by the Greek people but the Indian, Jewish, Persian, Egyptian, Arabic and Chinese people was the contemplative life. The most perfect and the noblest way of living conceived by people all over the world was in the famous words of Aristotle 'The contemplative Life'. So the historians have termed this ancient period starting from the 8th century BC to 2nd century AD as the 'Axial Age' of philosophy. Man was defined by Aristotle 'The philosopher' as 'a thinking, rational animal'. This ideal in all its stages was the target put before all societies in all countries in that millennium: by their respective prophets: by Zoroaster in Persia, by Pythagoras, Socrates, Plato, Aristotle, and the stoics in Greece, by the Buddha, Mahavira, the Upanishadic rishis and the sage Thiruvalluvar in India, by Confucius and Laotsu in china, by Jesus in Palestine and so on. Only philosophy and religion were accorded the foremost place in human life. Science was not given the first value. For those ancient people did not consider nor believe in science as a methodology to arrive at truth. So it did not become a way of life with them.

The basic fact of life that determined this course of life was the limitations and aberrations of the human faculties. How to combat and overcome these limitations? This fundamental question was answered by religion in mythological stories, other worlds of heaven, incarnation or supermen as saviors etc. Imaginations, hope and escapism played major roles in these solutions offered by religions. But most of the terrestrial problems like hunger, disease, old age and death still remained the same demons haunting humans. The age of mythology and religion lost its momentum and slowly came to a halt.

Next came on the world scene philosophy. Instead of believing and having faith in gods, and saviors, these philosophers attempted to solve the problems of humans created by their limitations of body and mind, at the human level itself, by man's own effort, both physical and mental. Austerity, renunciation, tapas, fasting, *hatha yoga* were the physical measures offered by them. Devotion, karma yoga, raja yoga or control of mind and thoughts, philosophical inquiry, dialectics, logic, classification and analysis of knowledge were some of the mental measures recommended by these philosophers.

These measures appealed to some as a way of escape, as a way to forget one's problems for some time. In the famous words of Karl Marx these measures offered by both religion and philosophy were the opium of the people. Instead of providing food for the hungry stomach, they made the people forget their hunger for some hours. Again unfortunately hunger awakened them from their illusory dreams and sleep. These measures failed.

At last arrived the science in the form of technology or gadgets. What religions, spiritual teachers and speculative philosophers could not do, these gadgets did. They simply and directly showed reality – not only to some great, initiatives but to all and every human, the truth in all its stark nakedness. The first such gadget, the most effective one was 'the telescope' invented by Galileo Galilee. Before this gadget was invented, along dispute had taken place concerning the central planet around which all the other planets revolved – earth or the sun? According to Ptolemy and Bible and most of the philosopher's earth – since man lived upon it – was the centre around which all the other six planets revolved. Astronomy proper, as a science was not yet born. It was a part of astrology, the pseudo–science. Galileo's gadget the telescope showed the skies as it was, to one and all. Sun was the centre around which all the other planets revolved. Seeing is real believing. Science is the only true way to truth and reality. Science got momentum and that momentum never slackened and it never will. For as long as human limitations are there, science and technology will be there. Now all peoples all over the world have seen which is true, which gives real food, imaginative speculation or practical technology. They would not turn back to fictitious dinners, airy nothings. They are tasting real food. Heaven is not far away beyond the boundaries of the universe. Science and technology are building heaven here itself upon earth. It is not a dream or utopia but the real thing. Humans, all of them are equipped by science and technology to become day by day omniscient and omnipotent. And science arms them, equip them. Science has become the way of life for the whole of humanity. Science has become the number one value in their lives. Science has replaced philosophy and has become the religion of humankind. Hereafter one can leave behind him all philosophies and religions. But one can never survive without science and technology. Science is the new God. For it provides all the necessary things to all. It works and works wonders, in the real sense of the word.

~~~ ~~~ ~~~

26. SCIENCE OF FOOD AND COMPASSION

All beings live on food. Without food, they will die. Starvation deaths and famine have been everyday occurrences throughout history. In fact hunger is what drives or motivates all beings to act in life, to go in search of their food. Food is the fuel that propels the engine or the machine of the body-mind complex of any being. All these facts are obvious and known to all. But what is not known are the facts about the relationship between food and compassion, and the answers to questions Vallalar asks us such as 'how much of food a man needs every day? And how much of energy is derived from what one eats? How much of food is digested and absorbed and how much of it excreted out of the body through its nine orifices? How much of waste, excretory matter stays in the body? What happens to them? How is the body's health affected by them? How to increase the efficiency of the digestive system? Finally, can human bodies create their own food as the plants do and become self-sufficient as far as the food problem is concerned? Can humans solve the problem of hunger and famine and eradicate them from the face of the earth once for all? Can there be alternative sources of energy or fuel for the human body? How the Siddhas and Vallalar tackled their problem of food? Can the world learn anything from their lives and the methods they adopted?

Let us try to answer these questions one by one.

What is the relationship between food and compassion? Food is needed to pacify the hunger of man. The quantity of food depends upon the intensity of hunger. Hunger is supposed to be inevitable. For it is an instinct. And an instinct is a channel through which nature controls the human body and its laws enslave it. Nature is the master and man is the slave now. This slavery to nature must be conquered and the relationship reversed. That has been the aim of all teachers of spirituality and founders of religions. They learnt and preached their own ways of doing it.

For instance, Christ is reported to have gone to the desert and fasted for forty days and prayed to God. Here, one fact about the physiological functioning of the human body is to be noted and acted upon. Fasting and praying should always go together. Fasting without prayer will produce ulcers. For the gastric juices like hydrochloric acid produced by the body during the time of hunger which, in fact, cause the hunger, need something to act upon, to feed upon. If there is no food, they will prey upon the intestine and damage it causing ulcers. Prayers prevent this process of damage from occurring. During prayer, the gastric juices are not produced. Rather they are reversed at the source and sublimated into spiritual energy and saved in the centre of the brain, in the *ajna chakra*.

When this energy accumulates into a six faceted crystal – like solid, it is transformed into divine energy. Only with this divine energy, one acquires the capacity or qualification to see God or the ultimate dimension or all dimensions.[7,8] The same process takes place with sexual juices or semen also. We shall consider about it in the later chapter. One more noteworthy scientific fact or use of fasting is that it enables the humanbody to produce its own food as a plant does. Again we shall treat it later.

Mind or thought is the manager and supervisor of the body. They act like twins. Modern medical science acknowledges this fact when it talks about psychosomatic medicine. According to it, each acts upon the other. For example, stress or depression can cause diabetes, high blood pressure even cancer. Equally any physiological disease like amputation of a limb can cause much depression even insanity.

So thought is the key to the functions of the body like hunger. When thought, during prayer, is directed towards God, the gastric juices are sublimated at the source itself, in the brain and mixes with the blood and boosts up the immune system, energy and health or sublimated and stored up for spiritual work.

And let us remember that according to the SuddhaSanmarga system of Vallalar, God is defined and known as light of absolute compassion. When thought, a fragment of consciousness is transformed into compassion, a complete, holistic state of consciousness, one merges with God, one attains the state of Godhead. At that stage, nectar or ambrosia will be produced in the body. One will not need any external food. Another nutritional fact about compassion is that it can transform anything even poison into ambrosia.[9] So the whole intake of food will be transformed. No waste material or excretory matter will be produced in the body.[10] When no waste matter is produced in the body it will be transformed into a pure body. This is the first body in the process of transmutation of the natural, impure body into a divine body. This pure body is a disease free, old age free body. It can last for hundreds of thousands of years, according to Vallalar.[11] Hunger will be conquered. There will be no more of its functioning. One will be, for the first time, free from hunger or debility for want of food. Hunger, thirst, fatigue, sleep and other instincts of the body like sex and fear of death will be conquered totally and eradicated from the system of body permanently.

When one's thought is replaced by compassion, one goes beyond the silent state of yogic Samadhi and enters Sahaja Samadhi, the domain of karma yoga or contemplation in action. When one is always in meditation, Vallalar reveals, one's body, its needs, its powers of taste and digestion and absorption, all are transformed.[12] Very little food is required by a yogi; either the excretory, waste matter is not produced or if at all it is produced, it will be fragrant like a flower. And the efficiency of the digestive system will be increased a thousandfold. The energy derived from the food and absorbed by the body will increase accordingly.

If this is the effect of a meditative state of a yogi, what would be the super condition of a divine person who is always in a state of compassion? The powers of taste, digestion and absorption will increase a millionfold. His body will be capable of producing the higher forms of nectar. And the saint lists out a lot of different forms of nectar produced in the body and the locations in which they are produced such as mind, psyche, spirit and the centre of divinity or total compassion. A whole science of ambrosia is formed, developed and described in all their details by the Swami. The very first symptom of such a transformation will be the change in taste of one's sweat; it will turn sweet from being salty.[13]

A complete system of yoga of food and science of nutrition was discovered and displayed by the Swami in his body and described in his books, a fact and a feat unparalleled in the history of man. Other spiritual masters at the most, stopped with sattwic, vegetarian food. But Vallalar goes beyond them. He leads us through to staying with just boiled distilled water, calcined metals and minerals to a condition where no external food is necessary for man. For one's own body will start producing the required food as the plants do.

This yoga of food and science of nutrition is given by Vallalar in 5 stages:

1. Common foods available in the markets are classified as life-giving foods and death-

producing foods. This classification is based upon 5 principles of the science of nutrition:

a] the food should be easily digestible so that the gastric juices will not be wasted.

b] it should not produce constipation in the body, thereby clogging the cells with waste material.

c] it should produce large amounts of heat in the body, with a minimum quantity, such as 18 *kaya siddhi* herbs recommended by the Swami.

d] it should not decay. Foods that decay will start decaying inside the body and will produce corruption and finally disease, old age and death of the body. Some of the non-decaying foods recommended by Vallalar are 1. Country sugar or jaggery 2. Sugar-candy of the palm tree, 3. Honey and 4. calcined metals of iron and copper and other metals such as zinc, magnesium, silver, gold etc.,

e] a food item is selected for its nectar quotient. How much of nectar is contained in it? That determines its superiority, not only its caloric value. How much of light it contains? That is why all roots growing in darkness under the ground are to be avoided. Don't add darkness to the already dark body. The aim is to enlighten the body. Light is life, health and longevity and immortality. Darkness is disease, old age and death.

The process of transition from food-dependence to independence of it must take place in a very gradual manner. One should not hurry the process. Otherwise, new diseases both physical and mental might manifest and harm us. For we are going against nature, we are swimming upstream, against the current of nature. Slow and steady is the prudent way to win in this important but dangerous way of transformation of the natural body into a pure body.

What are the 5 stages in the yoga of food recommended by vallalar?

1. Take only life - giving foodstuffs available in the market. Avoid death – producing ones.
2. Along with them, eat daily atleast 5 of the 18 kaya siddhi herbs recommended by the swami. They are: 1)Eclipta Alba 2)Solanum Trilobatum 3)Mukiascabrella 4)CentellaAsiatica 5) Oxalis Corniculata.
3. Reduce gradually the intake of the above two categories of food and add gradually the non – decaying foods.
4. Stay only with the herbs and non – decaying foods.

5. Stop all of them and stay with boiled rainwater only. Continue this till the body produces ambrosia in the tongue, throat and the brain.

~~~ ~~~ ~~~

27. SCIENCE OF BREATH AND COMPASSION

According to the Siddhas, the quality or purity of one's mind is determined by the foods one eats. If one takes *sattvic* foods like sweets and fruits and vegetables and other vegetarian foods, one's thoughts will be of sympathy, empathy, friendship, brotherhood, equanimity, love, cooperative tendency and compassion. One will be a good human being or a good citizen, spiritually inclined and care for the welfare of other beings and so on.

If one takes spicy, hot, sour foodstuffs and non-vegetarian diet, his mind will always be disturbed, chaotic, ambitious, avaricious, greedy, self-centered, egoistic, dominating, oppressive and other qualities of ferocious animals like the lions, tigers, wolves and foxes. When such a person becomes the leader of a nation, not only his nation but the whole world will face violence, aggression, wars, occupations, suppressions of human rights, oppressions of all kinds and the ever-suffering lot of humanity will have to undergo unimaginable amounts and kinds of sufferings. Dante's vivid portraiture of hell will manifest upon earth itself. The world has witnessed and experienced such reigns of terror under the regimes of conquerors like Genkiskhan, Hitler, Attila and other dictators.

If such a person becomes the leader of a religion, the sufferings will go deeper. There will be not only physical tortures, but agonies of the mind also. Even the saints might undergo subtle tortures. For fear of hell, it is reported in medical texts, thousands of Christians went mad, and millions of them got depression and other mental disorders. Guilt based upon the original sin haunted the minds of people.

Finally when one takes in *tamasic* foods, one becomes lazy, lethargic, and inactive and feels always sleepy. The slave mentality and alienation will set in and one will be like an automaton or a plant. Instead of living one's life with zest and vitality, one will stagnate and vegetate.

This connection between foods and mind must be always remembered and realized in life. This is an obvious fact for most of the people. What is not obvious but subtle is the yogic fact of the relationship between mind and breath. This fact is commonly ignored by most of the spiritual schools and more significantly by the western medical system of allopathy. But the Siddhas put it in the form of a yogic rule: The quality of mind is determined by the quality of one's breath and in turn the quality of breath is determined by one's thoughts.

What does it mean? Let us explain it. When one is calm and peaceful, one's breath is also calm, peaceful, natural and rhythmic. *Pranic*energy is not wasted much. According to the Siddhas and Vallalar, one should not exert one's body or mind too much. For overexertion will lead to the additional waste of breath and the *pranic* energy along with it. To put it in modern medical terms *pranic* energy can be arguably and approximately equated with ATP energy of the body.

According to this dictum of the Siddhas, with every act of inhalation, one takes in 8 units of *prana* along with the oxygen. The air is only the vehicle, a lorry. The real goods it carries is the *prana*. And *prana* is the cosmic energy that is the prime mover, the ultimate cause of all sorts of motion of animate and organic and inanimate and inorganic bodies including the planets and galaxies as well as the subatomic particles. Every outgoing breath or exhalation, takes with it from the body 12 units of *prana*. So with every breath, one loses 4 units of *prana*. One's bank balance of *pranic* energy is constantly depleted and overdrawn. When the bank balance reaches the zero point, one dies. Before that, with less and less of *pranic* energy and along with it the weakness of one's immune system, one falls sick and all sorts of diseases physical and mental, chronic and acute attack him.

To stop this loss of prana is the aim and purpose of *pranayama*. *Yama* means control. *Pranayama* means the control of *prana* and conservation and preservation and saving of prana inside the body by preventing the loss of it during breathing. To realize this in actuality one is taught in the course on pranayama by the guru to change the ratio of inhalation, retention and expulsion of breath. One is asked to alter them very gradually. For one is going against nature. It is a very dangerous practice, as the Russian mage Gurdjieff rightly pointed out. One can even go mad. The side effects of doing pranayama in excess or in the wrong way are many. One's nervous system could be wrecked. Diseases of the spine which cannot be diagnosed by modern methods of CT scan and other systems, one might be afflicted with.

That is why it is always stressed that one should practice it under the guidance of an expert, one who himself has undergone all the steps and experiences of the different processes.

The ratio advised to overcome the loss of prana by the Master Yogi Thirumular is 16:64:32, i.e, 16 counts of breathing in through the left nostril, [ida kala puraka], holding the breath for 64 counts [kumbaka] and slowly letting it out through the right nostril [resaka through the pingala] for 32 counts. But this is the final stage. The beginning stage should have only half of it. 8:32:16. This ratio should be practiced daily, morning and evening with an empty stomach for only five minutes. Gradually the duration might be increased. If one finds any disturbance in the physiological functions of the body except more of well being, one should stop the practice immediately and consult the teacher.

After two or three years, one should go after the final ratio of 16:64:32. This should be continued all through life until it replaces natural breathing and becomes the very rhythm of body's breathing. As in learning cycling, this altered ratio of breathing must become automatic and done unconsciously.

But then, what will be the result? When this new form of breathing is established forever, the very anatomy and physiology of the body will undergo a lot of changes. Overall health of the body will be improved. Increased vitality, more joy in living, power of miracle making, longevity will be some of the results. Finally, Thirumular affirms even death will be conquered.[14]

The gist of the matter is this: one should not waste one's breath. For breath is prana. Vallalar forbids fast walking, running, loud speaking or chanting or singing and all sorts of sports and games except yogic postures and whisper-like slow chanting and singing. Sports and games are called the western yoga. But this is not accepted by the Siddhas. For with them one loses a lot of breath and thereby pranic energy. And this loss of prana will lead one quickly to the graveyard. Those who want to increase their longevity should avoid all these overexertions of body and mind. That is why the Siddhas always sit in Samadhi, stop their thoughts, and retain their breath as long as possible. They take very little food, say one small meal a day and save their gastric juices that are wasted in digesting the food. They also save their reproductive juices and save all of these downward-going energies and send them upwards by pranayama towards the centre of their head, towards the

Pineal Gland. There these energies are stored up and the pineal gland is activated which is slumbering now. When it is activated, all kinds of paranormal powers such as telepathy, telekinesis etc., will manifest spontaneously.

So the saving of prana by saving of breath is the way to better health, increased longevity, and even to immortality. Coming back to our point, breath is linked to mind and its thoughts. This we saw earlier. So controlling the mind is also a way to control your breath. Only prana manifests as both thought and breath. This fact can be easily verified. Look at an angry man or a dog. The breathing will be fast and agitated. During the agitated condition of sexual act also one's mind and its counterpart are running fast and wasting a lot of prana.

And we also saw that *rajasic* food also makes one violent, disturbed and competitive and over ambitious and a cancer cell in the body of a society. So food, mind and breath are all interlinked.

When one enters meditation, one's mind is free from thoughts, peaceful, joyous, silent. His breath is slowed down and his pranic energy is saved. Finally when one has learnt to be always in a meditative state or Samadhi called *Turiyadita*, one's breath stops completely. Another form of inner breathing takes over the command of body. This inner breath is called by various names in various esoteric systems and religions. It is called Inspiration by the poets, *Mukya prana* in the Upanishads, God's breath or Holy breath in Christianity, Rhua in Judaism and Rhu in Islam, Vaasi, Pari, Ceer, Ceerkazhi, Maanadi in the Tamil wisdom tradition. When one has attained this penultimate state, it is called in yogic parlance as Sahaja Samadhi or Karma Yoga. This is a superior form of Samadhi. One need not sit in a place. One can do anything but one's state of Samadhi will not be disturbed. No thoughts will arise in the mind. No external breathing of oxygen will take place. This cosmic prana will activate the body-mind machine. Instead of human, individual mind, the cosmic mind will act through it. The individual person becomes a divine, cosmic person. All sorts of siddhis or miraculous powers one attains. He/she goes beyond the laws of nature and commands nature. And nature obeys him/ her like a slave.

This is the boon of stopping one's thoughts and attaining yogic Samadhi. But Vallalar says there is yet another way of attaining Sahaja Samadhi and attaining all sorts of siddhis divine. It is in fact a short cut. It is the way of compassion. When one is in a compassionate state towards all beings one transcends human nature. Again, when one's state of compassion becomes stabilized, fixed and permanent, his very body-mind complex is totally transformed. He is transmuted into a divine person. He will start leading a divine life in a divine body. Both will be infinite in quality, quantity, in all of its attributes.

So when the no-mind or beyond mind state of absolute compassion is attained by one, his thought is transformed into a supra-mental divine thought which can create anything even galaxies just by willing. For in the state of compassion of a divine person, all the three powers of desire [itchasakthi], will [kriya sakthi] and knowledge [gnanasakthi] are fused together into a unified force, the power of God.

That is why Vallalar considers the attainment of compassion as a superior way or yoga to other forms of meditation, tapas or austerity, prayer, yoga and other sadhanas. When you are in compassion, you are godly. When you act in compassion you are doing the job of God. This is the way to become like our Father in Heaven. This is the way to become perfect like our Father in Heaven. This is the only qualification needed to become his chosen son or daughter and sit by his side on his throne. To understand the science of godhead and attain it was the final aim and destination in the path of vallalar'sSuddhaSanmarga. And this is possible only by attaining the state of all – compassion.

When one is in a state of compassion, nectar is produced in one's body. When it gets accumulated, one's immune system is boosted. One gets health, longevity, immortality. Gradually one becomes free from hunger, disease, old age and death. All the other thoughts except compassion produce poison in the body. When it gets accumulated, one falls sick, grows old quickly and dies prematurely. Compassion is the best food, thought and medicine.

~~~ ~~~ ~~~

28. SCIENCE OF EYES [OPHTHALMOLOGY] AND COMPASSION

Eyes are the light of the body. They perceive light and bring it into the brain and the body. Eyes are more powerful in bringing salvation or enlightenment of consciousness and body. The transformation of consciousness from a relative, human, egocentric state to an absolute condition or non-condition is the process called Enlightenment. And the eyes play a supreme role in this process. For they are the instruments that wield the power of light, the bows that shoot the arrows of light. Eyes are the windows to the soul. Look at one's eyes, they reveal the condition and intelligence of the soul. Even the seventh degree of knowledge called intuition is known through and attained by practising the art of seeing and Thiruvalluvar explains the education of it in two chapters in his immortal secular scripture Thirukkural.[15]

How does a person look at other beings? What is the condition or quality of one's sight? Is it peaceful or disturbed? Is it serene or angry? Is it greedy and lustful? Or is it loving and compassionate? When the eyes are filled with tears out of devotion, it is an indication that the centreof awareness is sublimated to the psychic depth. When the eyes are filled with tears out of compassion for the sufferings of other beings, it shows that the awareness has reached atman or spirit. And when it stays like that forever, when it becomes permanent the person is transformed both mentally and physically into a cosmic person. Vallalar is reported to have constantly cried out of devotion to God in every being. There had formed two channels of tears or river-beds on his cheeks.

The way to see God, as practiced and recommended by Saint Manickavasagar and Vallalar was to ask God, 'Oh my Beloved! When can I see your glorified body face to face?' and cry for his darshan. When the flood of tears overflows and finally stops out of dearth of stock the Lord will appear before you. He has to. He is duty bound to do so.

The way to attain God and live like him as recommended by Vallalar is to constantly see God literally in every being and serve it with devotion as it is shown to a deity in a temple. Every being is a walking temple. So you are always with God, surrounded by innumerable incarnations of God. It is a literal fact. But unfortunately, one's mind neither acknowledges the fact, nor act upon it. When one acts upon it, and it becomes a way of life, it becomes the life of the spirit and one attains all the four forms of eyes in one's own body.

Yes, Vallalar, like a scientist of ophthalmology declares that man is blessed with four types of eyes: (1). The physical eyes one is born with. Even the animals and birds are born with them. (2). The mental eyes or eyes of imagination.

When you calculate a sum mentally, you are working with it. Or when you imagine something your mental eyes function. With education particularly of mathematics and geometry, one can develop the mental eyesight. Reading and writing fiction is another way. (3). The third form of eyesight is rarely cultivated though everyone is endowed with it. Only a few yogis and seers develop it and even among them a handful only attain perfection. This is the eye of the spirit. It has to be initiated by one who had already got his third eye opened. One becomes a god with this opening of the third eye. One can see almost all the dimensions of reality. With the combined sight of the two eyes, one is able to see three dimensions. With the combined and holistic sight of three eyes, one can see all the dimensions of reality. Vallalar claims that he is able to see into infinite dimensions of reality, far into the galaxies at the macro- level and deep into the quantum field, at the micro-level.

His biographers narrate some incidents in his life that show that he had developed highly advanced capacities in telepathy and clairvoyance.

Once he was conversing with a sanyasin. Suddenly there were tears in his eyes. The sanyasin was alarmed. What is the matter, my friend? Did I say something that hurt your feelings?, he asked. Vallalar replied,'nothing of that sort. On the highway a pregnant she goat was run over by a bullock cart. It is struggling for its life. It is experiencing intolerable pain'. The sanyasin had already heard about the paranormal and supernal powers of Vallalar. But he had not seen them. Now he had an opportunity to verify it. The highway was a furlong away from his ashram where the conversation took place. Immediately he ran towards the highway. The scene in front of him was exactly as the swami had described. The she goat was in a mass of blood and in extreme agony. He got confirmation of the supernal powers of the swami. He ran back to his house and asked his friend, 'how did you get your miraculous powers?' But the swami did not answer his question. His interest was different. He instead asked the sanyasin another question: you had run all the way to the road. Why didn't you bring the goat? We could have healed it. On hearing this, the sanyasin realized his mistake. He ran back to the road, and brought back the wounded animal. Vallalar applied some herbs on the wounds, bandaged it and it was subsequently healed. And according to the report, after the incident Vallalar took it with him and it always remained with him, to its last. In the old paintings of Vallalar, one could see it lying in a corner. By the way, Vallalar was photographed eight times by a noted photographer one Mr. Masilamani who was brought from Chennai for this very purpose. But in all the eight photographs only his dress was seen, his body was not seen. Light rays travelled through his body. By the practice of total compassion, he had transformed his body into a light, transparent one.

In another incident, one Chidambara Swami a vedantin came to visit Vallalar. He debated with him whether physical immortality was possible. The debate lasted for two days. And as usual Vallalar won the debate. When the sanyasin took leave of him, there were tears in Vallalar's eyes. A disciple asked him why he cried. Swami replied, my friend, the vedantin has got only six more months to live'. With his eye of the spirit opened, Vallalar was able to see deep into the soul of other beings and was able to ascertain how many more years it would remain in the body.

Finally, when the eye of compassion of the supreme God is opened in you by Himself, you can see the whole cosmos in a second, or in a timeless moment as God sees it; all that ever occurred in the past, all the galaxies and all the beings in them, their anatomies and physiologies, all that are happening now in the present and all that are going to happen in the future. Once Vallalar wanted to see the far end of the universe and know what sort of beings were living there. Immediately, he tells us in a verse, God blessed him with the eye of all-seeing light of absolute compassion and with it, enabled him to see at once all the billions of galaxies in the universe and all the beings living in them.[16]

Ophthalmology of modern medicine knows about and discusses only the physical eye. Psychology deals with the mental eye, to a little extent. The two higher eyes are yet to be known, let alone be explored as Vallalar did attain and used them. Modern science has a long way to go. First, it has to overcome its superstitious boundaries it has imposed upon itself. It has to make itself free from the shackles it has inherited. There are no limitations for humans. As the sage of Boston rightly put it, 'Limitation is the only sin'. All humans including the scientists must have faith in the unlimited power of the human mind, which is only a replica of the cosmic mind and particularly in the infinite potentialities and possibilities of the human body which is nothing but a miniature cosmos. We, living in the 21st century have not tapped even one-millionth of its potentials. Vallalar saw and realized all of it. He has also shown us everything about it. Only, we have to take heed of it.

The thrice-great Hermes said long back, 'As above, so below'; it holds true even now. As the macrocosm is, so is the microcosm. This human body is a miniature cosmos. It contains everything there is in the universe. It is not only figuratively true, but also literally true. To realize it fully is the task of man in his lifetime. And Vallalar did it thoroughly, one hundred percent. That is the way for the future evolution of humankind.

How did he do it? What were the changes in his evolved body? He gives a long list of changes that occurred in every limb of his body at the initial stage of transformation of the physical body into a pure body.[17]

His eyes had attained the status and power of the sun and the moon, his right eye had become the sun and his left eye the moon. The radiance and power of his right eye was so immense that people were not able to bear it. Once, by chance, when a strong wind removed the cloth with which Vallalar always covered his body and head including his right eye a little, a disciple saw his right eye and at once swooned and fell. He recovered after a day.

Vallalar himself says that God had blessed his eyes with the divine power, that he was enabled to perform miracles just by seeing. We can cite an incidence by way of example. In 1872, he built a temple for worshipping the Lord of Light of Infinite compassion at Vadalur near Pondicherry in South India. He named it as 'The Hall of Wisdom' [Jnana Saba]. The land, measuring about 106 acres was donated by the people of the village. But the enormous sum of about Rupees 75,000 which is equal to 75 million in today's value was very difficult to procure. Every villager could donate one or two rupees only. Finally, it was donated by God, according to the register in which the names of contributors and amounts donated by them were recorded.

It happened like this. One day Vallalar asked his disciples to bring a very large utensil from the kitchen. He asked them to pour water into it and fill it. Then he looked at the water and it was transformed into solid gold. It was broken into pieces and they were taken to Bombay and sold. With the sale proceeds, the temple was built. The chief disciple of Vallalar, professor Velayudham of Tholuvur ascertained this fact in his declaration he gave to the then management of the Theosophical society at Adayar, Chennai, in which he says, 'my guru was a successful alchemist'.

On hearing this miracle, the then collector of South Arcot visited the place to make enquiries. He held a walking stick made of cane in his hands. Vallalar touched it and it changed immediately into gold. It became unbearably hot. The tahsildar who took it in his hands got burnt. Once again Vallalar touched it and it became a cane stick. Vallalar is reported to have said that such miracles were possible only by those who had no desire at all. And the collector with his team went back in peace and wonder.

Not only his eyes and hands, but every part or limb of his body was transformed into an organ of compassion by constantly doing compassionate service to all beings with it. His whole body was transformed into a body of light of compassion. 'Now you have got a body of compassion' said the Lord to him, according to the Agaval poem.[18] He had attained the last and ultimate form of transformation in the process of becoming God and leading a life of His own. Like the heroine of the Hollywood film 'Lucy' who says at the climactic end 'I am everywhere', Vallalar is now everywhere. Not as the story-writer of the film thought, that humans could achieve such an all pervading body by making 100% of the brain cells to function, but by attaining 100% compassion in the body, brain and mind complex, it is possible.

The stature of godhead and the title of the Son or Daughter of God cannot be conferred upon anyone with less than the absolute degree of compassion. It will be a contradiction in terms and against the very nature of godhead.

~~~ ~~~ ~~~

29. SCIENCE OF INFORMATION AND COMPASSION

MODERN science after the advent of quantum physics and its technology quantum mechanics has come to a stage where it believes that the universe of matter consists of only two things – information and energy. The former is amply demonstrated in the silicon chips, algorithm and the computer revolution and also in genetic engineering. The latter, energy was equated with matter in the famous equation $E = mc^2$ of Einstein a century ago. Information technology and atomic science have literally been ruling science in the twentieth century as well as our lives. Our very way of living has been radically transformed in the last thirty years. Our very identity has changed into a new one of scientific man which was unthinkable for the past two millennia, even by thinkers of the first order like Aristotle, Newton and Darwin.

Aristotle defined man as a thinking, rational animal. Religious teachers all along history have portrayed man as a slave to God obeying his orders for fear of punishment by ignoring them. During the Renaissance period this so-called fallen state of man was rejected by rational and progressive thinkers such as the philosophers of the revolutionary Franch. 'Liberty, equality and fraternity' - was the slogan voiced by the revolutionary masses all over the world. Man was liberated from the oppressive claws of the tyranny of monarchy and religion. Rousseau defined man as a political animal. Politics occupied the central focus of humans. Liberty was seated upon the throne in the United States by its historical 'Rights of Man' in its constitution. Equality formed the basis of the Russian revolution and the Communist countries. This image of equality through political agenda and transformation of society was shattered when a new form of inequality and oppression appeared between the ruling party members, officials and ordinary citizens. Confronting these new issues and social problems of power, the Italian thinker, Gramsci, during his prison life changed once again the definition of man as a cultural animal. According to him, culture is not a secondary influence in society, not a product or super structure in the edifice of society as Marx and Engels thought but the very infrastructure or foundation of the society.

But all these definitions failed with the decline and fall of the Soviet Empire and the communist regimes in the Eastern Europe and China with the rise of information technology. The underdeveloped communist China was transformed into a developed nation in a miraculous way in a very short span of two or three decades by science and industrial technology particularly by the information technology. What European countries and America were able to achieve in about two centuries, Japan, Korea and China achieved in two decades. This amazing feat was made possible by the information technology. Every process, event, technology was accelerated a hundredfold, a thousand times. Time and distance, the basic limitations of humans were conquered with the help of mass and telecommunication technologies. Television and internet made possible any fact or data to reach the far corners of the globe instantly. The life of every human was instantly transformed. When this radical change and its subsequent result of ambition for a higher standard of life by everyone in all these poor countries was kindled, a new, collective revolution took place in both the physical and mental conditions of humanity. For the first time in human history, the drudgery of manual labour, sufferings due to poverty, illiteracy, slavery to the more powerful authorities were all swept away. Science became the way of living for humans at the end of the twentieth century. Unlike religion and philosophy, science proved its efficacy and gave immediate results and technology got firmly established as the only way of life. Now it is accepted by all humans living on earth including the fundamentalists of religions who cannot survive without the gadgets of instant telecommunications and the latest military weapons. At last, the definition of man has been altered to 'the scientific man'. This new label, I think, will stick to him for a very long time, until all peoples on earth enjoy the fruits of science and technology.

But we see already signs and symptoms of change in this definition of man. People in the developed countries, who have already reaped the benefits of technology have also experienced the dark side of it such as life-threatening tendencies of pollution of air, water and sound, global warming, erratic weather conditions, increasing number of natural catastrophes like tsunamis and earthquakes and the breakdown of atomic reactors causing terrible diseases of radioactivity for millions of people. Consequently, new movements such as green movement, blue cross society, anti-nuclear movement, sustainable technology, vegetarianism and veganism arose to rectify the ill effects of technology. A part of humanity is looking for an alternative view of life, for a new definition of man, for a new way of living which would give them only the fruits of technology but at the same time would curb and curtail the side effects of it or at least would minimize the damage.

The answer to all these scorching problems was provided by the scientist saint and progressive thinker of the nineteenth century, Swami Ramalinga Vallalar who foresaw that all these evil things would take place in the future. He goes to the root cause of all the problems of man in his self -centeredness and herd instinct and traditional walls of superstitions and segregations that separate humankind into various opposing groups. He also discovered the only answer for all the eternally haunting problems of humanity in one word: compassion. Compassion as a total way of life alone can save the individuals and humankind as a species. Without this radical and total change, no half-measures or changes in ideologies or technologies will do. No permanent and lasting change can come. As J Krishnamurti rightly pointed out, all these evil phenomena are the results of thought. Thought is man's number one enemy. Thought is at once a boon and a curse to humans. We, living in the twenty first century have witnessed the truth of this statement. Vallalar wants to replace thought with compassion. whatever thought can do, compassion also can do. And it can do it better a thousandfold, a millionfold. For it is the highest form of knowledge as well as the highest power whereas thought is only a fragment of consciousness. If thought can be compared to a coin of one dollar, compassion can be called a million-dollar cheque. Only thing we have to do is to fill up the blank cheque and encash it. The seed of compassion is already there in each of us. It has to be given a chance to grow into a fully developed tree. It should become a way of life. Compassion, as Vallalar stressed, is the only criterion in all actions of our life, whether individual or national. In his own words, if any act has compassion, it is just; without compassion, any act is evil. It is as simple as that. This simple statement has all morality, all philosophy and strangely but truly all science in it. It will help man in the sciences of evolution, nutrition, space travel, cognitive science, nuclear physics, new material science, anatomy and physiology, nano-technology, medicine, gerontology, chemistry and what not. It will empower man into all the knowledge and powers of a Siddha or superman. All the future visions, physics of the future and physics of the impossible of cutting-edge scientists like Michio Kaku and Ray Kurzweil will be made possible. All the political, social and economic and scientific ideologies and utopias of

Rousseau, Thomas Jefferson, Marx and Bacon will be realized. The superman of Nietsche, Dostoevsky, Teilhard de Chardin and Sri Aurobindo will have a chance of materialization and realization is possible only with compassion. The other ways of will and power, centralization of power, religious affiliations and economic power can only lead to disaster and extermination of homo sapiens as a species. Science and technology with a human heart is possible with compassion. Globalization not only of economy and natural resources but spiritual globalization and universal brotherhood of mankind will be made possible only with compassion as a yoga, a philosophy and a science.

Finally this series of labels on and definitions of man will end, according to Vallalar, in 'the compassionate man'. This new brand of man will be a 'man-god in potential'. He/ she will develop into a true god with all his divine powers and attributes by learning and mastering the ultimate science of compassion. This will be the end, the highest point of evolution. There can be no higher stage to evolve.   God or the most compassionate intelligence created all the worlds and things and beings and finally descended into inorganic matter and stayed inside every nanoparticle immanently. Now, with human evolution, the action is reversed. The ascent of man into godhead fulfils and completes the circle. Compassion descended and degraded itself into dark matter. Once again, through the same compassion, beings and matter will be transformed and evolved into the light of absolute compassion. Man is only an agent for this final evolution and transformation. This agency is the task of man entrusted to him by god or nature or that Omnipotent and omniscient collective cosmic intelligence.

But then, how does compassion become a science? According to the second law of thermodynamics called entropy, all things and beings are constantly losing heat or their energy and decaying and decomposing. Even the sun with its enormous amount of heat is fast losing its heat and one day, in future will have exhausted its fuel and collapse into a dark hole. Whole galaxies and the universe itself will run down and collapse into nothing in distant future. Nothing or no one is an exception to the law of entropy.

In fact, man is subjected to disease, decay, old age and finally death because of entropy. Everyone when he grows into adolescence and adulthood fights against this inherent law but finally succumbs to it in death. This is what we witness in the world everyday.

But there is a loophole in this law of entropy. It can operate only in closed systems, not in open systems. The reason is that the waste produced in the system must be thrown out. When there is no outlet for chaos or waste material, the functioning slows down and finally breaks down totally.

Vallalar utilizes this loophole. He solves the problem of entropy in two stages: [1] by cutting down on the waste produced in the system of the human body and the world and [2] finally stop producing the waste and excretory matter in the body. The body is now producing waste and throws it out through the nine orifices. Vallalar, in his science of food and nutrition wants us to take in only those foods that never decay and change into foul-smelling excretory matter. He recommends and gives out a list of such foods. Secondly, with a constant state of compassion in one's mind he announces a new scientific fact that all matter nutritional or poisonous will be transformed into ambrosia or nectar. And the body will make use of the whole material as food; one hundred percent of food will be converted into energy. The body will then act like an atomic reactor totally transforming the uranium into atomic energy without leaving out any radioactive atomic waste.[19]This happened, he affirms, in his own body.

What is the reason for aging? At the age about twenty the human body stops growing and starts decaying. Because, according to Vallalar, the system of the human mind till that time was an open system. But corruption had already started in the form of ego-centric consciousness closing the boundary of mind constantly. One day when the closing is completed and when one feels totally individualistic and alien from all other beings and things of nature, the mind becomes a completely closed system and the law of entropy starts functioning rapidly. Old age sets in and thereafter there is no escape from it. It triumphs in the death of the body.

But with compassion towards all beings remaining constant in one's mind, it is not allowed to close but always expand into larger and larger circles. When it encompasses the whole world and all the beings in it, it keeps on opening its boundaries farther and farther. There is no end to this process of opening one's mind and enhancing its territory. Entropy is not even given a chance to open its account, let alone grow more and more as it does with common men and women. In the case of cancer patients, it works overtime. Cancer is another name for Himalayan egoistic and egotistical mind. It is only an outer, physical manifestation of inner alienation and total self-centeredness. Compassion is its very opposite force that always heals, gives life, health and longevity. Finally the ever growing mind of compassion conquers entropy and its offspring death.[20]

In short, the egocentric mind is the culprit who creates darkness in the body-mind complex, invites entropy, all sorts of diseases, old age and death. First purify your mind with love and compassion. And keep on purifying it. This is the real meaning of the word enlightenment. Enlightenment of what? Whatever that is dark, not only mind or consciousness but the body also. Body is composed of dark matter. And by food, air and impure bad impressions and negative thoughts, we are darkening it still more. This process goes on every moment of our lives. But the opposite must take place every second: The enlightening of the body mind complex by pure food or nectar, by pure air or god's breath or holy breath and by pure and positive vibrations, impressions and thoughts of love and empathy and compassion. By constantly darkening our mind body machine, we end up in death. By enlightening it with the invisible, subtle light of love and the causal light of compassion we will attain eternity of pure consciousness and immortality of the body.

Vallalar's science of enlightenment and immortality identifies four stages in these processes: 1) Enlightenment of consciousness called Mukthi or salvation. Most of the religions and philosophies and yoga systems of the world stop with this stage. They consider it to be the ultimate stage attainable by man. They refuse to think about immortality of the body, let alone construct a process for attaining it. But Vallalar makes an elaborate science of it. 2) To transform this waste producing impure body into a pure body that secretes its own food in the various forms of nectar. He names them all and the organs in the body where each sort of nectar will be produced. The lifetime or duration of such a pure body is more than four million years. It will be golden in colour. Like the physical body it can be seen and touched. The body will grow younger and look like that of a twelve-year-old. Grey hair, wrinkles, disease, old age, motion, urine, perspiration, food, sleep, thirst and shadow will not be manifested in this pure, golden body. Hair on the skin will always remain in the same condition never growing or shrinking. The person with such a golden body will be a karma Siddha. He will be able to transform his body into an immortal one that can last for eons [kalpa]. He will be an immortal being, but will live on this earth only. He will be able to raise the dead within the time frame of 3 ¾ years from the time of death. The duration of his lifespan will be about four million three hundred and twenty-three years. This person will be like a performing and always action –oriented angel. Like gravitational force he or she will be a force field, an effect only caused by higher beings. But his feeling, knowledge and power will be transcendental.

This pure body has to be transformed into a pranava body. It is also called a sound body, omkara body and space body. This is the third form of birth humans are expected to give birth to themselves.

The first birth is the natural one from the womb of the mother caused by the union of a sperm from the father's body and the ovum of the mother.

The second birth is that of the pure body by one's own effort by cleansing and totally purifying all the cells of the body and all the tissues and all the eight systems of the body. For example, all the intakes such as food, water, air, impressions must be of utmost purity. And finally, all the thoughts arising from the mind must be of love and compassion only, with the result that in due course of time, wrong actions, wrong habits and wrong manifestations of the impure, natural body will be slowly transformed into those of a pure body. Mutation will take place in the physical body, mind and soul. A new, higher form of species will be born. The anatomy will be the same as that of a human but all the physiological functions will be totally different. It will produce its own food in the form of different varieties of nectar, in the tongue, above the uvula, and at the centre of the brain and so on. This new branch of a higher science of ambrosia is described by Vallalar elaborately in all its details. [for further details, see the author's book on science of Vallalar]

The transformation of the respiratory system will take place in two stages: 1) the atmospheric air with all its constituents of oxygen, carbon-di-oxide, nitrogen, hydrogen and all other gases will be totally made use of by the body without producing any waste matter in the form of carbon-di-oxide to be exhaled. One breath will be enough to sustain the body for a longer period, say, for hours and days. 2) In the next stage, instead of gases like oxygen or carbon-di-oxide, the Siddha will be directly drawing the pranic energy which is everywhere in the universe and will live on it. He will be like an amphibian who will be able to live at once with the atmospheric air and without it. This has been already proved in front of the scientists by Indian yogis such as Swami Rama in the experiment conducted by the Green foundation of America and Swami Madhusudhana Saraswathi who played tabla for half an hour in vacuum.

As for consciousness, it will be a cosmic consciousness caring for the welfare of all beings in all the worlds.

This second birth is a conscious rebirth by oneself where male or female by uniting both the male and female parts of one's body and transforming it into a whole androgynous body like the one described by Plato in his Symposium or like the Saivite God ArthanariEswara, a form of Siva whose body is manifested as half male and half female. If one wants to remain a male or female, the transformation in the body may not take place, but the consciousness will be a holistic one like that of a hermaphrodite.

The third form of birth is also a conscious one by one's own effort. The process of giving birth to this pranava body or sound body or mantra body or space body is the penultimate one. It is described in the Hindu mythology in the story of Lord Subramania meaning swaya Brahman i.e. being born as god by one's own effort. All souls or jivas are only manifestations of Siva and Siva, in this mythological story, gives birth to Subramania. Siva Himself is transformed into Subramania who is supposed to conquer all forms of darkness or the mythological beings called asuras, the dark forces of the universe.

In the myth, this truth of transformation of humans into god is hidden and it is only hinted at with the twilight languages of signs and symbols. But Vallalar, being a scientist and a being of absolute compassion, explains and describes the process to the world in all its scientific details.

In fact the flag of his system of SuddhaSanmarga denotes only this third form of birth. After hoisting the flag, he explains its form and colour in a scientific way. He publishes for the benefit of all humankind the process that takes place in the anatomy and physiology of the human body. He says: In the human body, a subtle channel (nadi) runs upwards from the belly button upto the third eye region of the head. At the end, there is a membrane. The lower part of it is white in colour and the upper part is yellow.[21] The white colour denotes the male reproductive juice called semen or vindhu or bindu meaning at once light and seed. The yellow colour means the female reproductive juice called nada or sronitham or sound. These are now in the form of liquids. These liquids containing the essences of light and sound must be sent upwards through the central channel by heating them with pure heat produced by tapas [austerity], meditation, prayer and compassion. The bindu is to be transformed into para bindu or transcendental form of light energy. When this is accumulated in the region of forehead, paranada or the divine transcendental energy of sound will descend from above. The union of these two energies {A+U} will produce a new, divine child {M}. This is the way of the birth of a human with a pure body into a god.

Vallalar describes the form, qualities and powers of this pranava body as follows: It can be seen but one cannot touch it or feel it. Its form will be like that of a boy of 5-8 years old. It has the powers of travelling to the far corners of the universe in no time and can also live in this world. Its consciousness, knowledge and powers are both human and divine. It has all the powers of god such as the five powers of creation, providence, destruction, veiling and grace. It is also golden in colour. Its carrot value is approximately from 32 to 216. Its form is causal effectual, at once acting for the ultimate godhead and commanding all the forces of nature and angelic, higher beings.

Finally, the last and fourth form of birth is called the gnanadeha or cosmic body of causal light of compassion. But here, there is a snag, a paradoxical situation for the aspirant. By one's own effort, no one can attain this ultimate stage of god. One can only qualify oneself fully with being always compassionate towards all beings without any discrimination. One can yearn for it, and apply for it. But to accept the petition or reject it is the power of god ArutPerum Jothi only, the most supreme and highest power of causal light of absolute compassion or wisdom light.

The description of this final cosmic body of godhead, as it was described by Vallalar is as follows: It's form is causal. It is the causeless cause of all worlds, things and beings in the cosmos. It pervades everywhere. It is inside everything. Its consciousness and knowledge is eternal. In no time it knows all and does all. It is omniscient and omnipotent. Its carrot value is infinite. It is both visible and invisible. If it wants to appear before anyone, one can see it. The choice is its. Only by vibration or sound it can be known. Its power is infinite. Its freedom is infinite. It is beyond time. Its ultimate stage is both form and formlessness, being and nothing, beyond attributes and all good and super attributes. It is beginningless and endless.

But this last destination in the journey of the soul is possible for all humans. It is proved by the historical fact that Vallalar who was born like any one of humans from the womb of a woman attained this supreme state of the Causal Light of Infinite Compassion in 1874 at Siddhi Valagam near Neyveli in South India.

This is the road map given to humankind by Vallalar for their future evolution when Sir Charles Darwin the discoverer and founder of the evolutionary theory of nature wrote in a letter to Professor Chancy Wright of America that he did not know how the homo sapiens as a species will evolve in future. Vallalar, in the same year, demonstrated to the world in his own body how the future evolution of our species will take place.

The scientific community has a duty towards humanity at least to be aware of this scientist – saint's claims and verify it for its truth or fiction. This is the realistic alternative model before us and a better one than what the science fiction writers, futurist scientists and Hollywood films portray as visions of our future: Not to transform this god-given natural body with infinite potential into a cyborg, half human and half robot being, but to change and transform this very natural human body with all its limitations caused by its ego centeredness into an infinite, limitless, divine body of Light of Compassion.

The path is laid for our future by someone who has already travelled on it and reached the correct destination of godhead. And it is not any myth or fiction but a science spread out before us with all its steps, stages and details of them with minute accuracy starting with the right kind of food and ending with compassion as a way of living.

This is not a philosophy meant only for a small number of elite and highly gifted with speculative minds; not a yoga for a select few with extraordinary will power and concentration but is meant for all humans, easy to understand and easy to follow.

And there seems to be no alternative to this sensible and scientific plan that can safely take our species to its final destination of a divine life in a divine body.

According to quantum physics, the universe is composed of two things only: Information and energy. Law of entropy, the second law of thermodynamics, operates both at the macro level of the world and at the micro level of the subatomic world of matter and inside the DNA of the human body.

The loss of information in the DNA causes aging. It forgets how it developed the limbs of a baby when it was inside the womb of its mother. The miraculous limbs like the brain and the heart, kidney and liver are grown by it with the impure and odd materials eaten by the mother. When the same baby grows into a child or adult and loses a limb or two in an accident or surgery, the same DNA is not able to regrow those parts. For it has forgotten its own technique due to the loss of memory, due to the loss of information by eating wrong foods, by cultivating wrong, egocentric mental habits. Darkness in the forms of these wrong foods and habits engulf it. And Vallalar affirms that this recently acquired habit of loss of information is not irremediable. It can be overcome by right mind and body. The veils grown may be set aside or destroyed and the memory recovered fully. And humans also can regrow their lost limbs.[22]

In the course of evolution it is a recent phenomenon only. For even now some of the animals such as some lobsters, flounders, sturgeons, sharks and alligators and some lizards never grow old. These animals are called 'animals that are immortal' by Dr Michio Kaku. They never age biologically but killed by accidents, starvation and other causes, he adds. The mechanism of regrowing lost limbs and lost cells indefinitely can be recalled. There need not be any loss of information in the DNA.

At the macro level, black holes were supposed to be pits of destruction by the astrophysicist Hawking. He assured the world that not even information could escape its extraordinary gravity. Later when another scientist pointed out that information could come out of them, he confessed frankly he was wrong.

And the law of compassion suggests another hypothesis about black holes. When a sun undergoing the bad effects of entropy and finally collapses into a black hole, losing all of its heat, it becomes a pit of total darkness. But it cannot be, according to the law of compassion. For the sun is the origin of all energy and life-giver for all beings on earth. With the help of sunlight, the plants create starch out of the process of photosynthesis. This starch is stored in the grains, fruits, leaves and roots of the plants. The animals eat the plants and humans eat both the plants and animals. So the sun's compassionate act makes all life possible in the world. This kindly action cannot go unrewarded. For every action there is an equal and opposite reaction. The sun's act of life-giving and sustaining life by giving energy must have a reaction upon itself. It cannot turn into a void. My suggestion or hypothesis is this: The sun could turn and evolve into a subtle and invisible sun. Out of visible, solid matter of brain is born the invisible mind and its thoughts. In the same way, the physical, hot sun might evolve into a subtle, invisible sun of mental matter. For the great yogi Thirumular says in his immortal classic, Thirumanthiram that there are five suns, namely i) the physical sun in the sky [andadhithan], ii) the subtle sun in the human body [pindadhithan], iii) the mental sun in the mind [manadhithan], iv) the Gnostic sun in the spirit and v) the divine sun [sivadhithan]. He could have seen all these suns in his yogic meditation. But, just because it was said a long time ago by a yogi and not by a scientist, we cannot rule out the possibility. For instance, modern scientists see through their telescopes the planet Mars and confirm that it is red in colour. But for thousands of years, the yogis and rishis of India have called Mars the red planet (Sevvoy). How did they know or see its red colour? So this possibility cannot be ruled out or dismissed as nonsense. The scientists must take a note of this fact and explore the possibility of evolution of the visible, physical sun into an invisible subtle sun. According to the Gaia principle, which is now almost accepted as true by all the scientific world, why can not the sun also be a living organism, with all its intelligence?

The very word 'INFORMATION' informs or means that it is or forms the inner layer of a thing. The material, outer covering by matter is only an ex-pression of gross matter or energy. So according to quantum physics everything is composed of information and energy.

But according to the science of Vallalar, everything consists of four layers; i) the outermost, ii) the outer, iii) the inner-outer and iv) the innermost. Quantum physics has discovered only the first two layers, the physical [outermost] and the mental or information [the outer]. The third layer called the inner outer is known by its use and purpose or science and technology of it. The fourth layer called the innermost is known by its uniqueness and mainly by its relationship to the cosmic intelligence or oversoul. The third layer can be known and uncovered by the faculty of intuition when it is highly developed. It is also called in yogic parlance as the psychic centre. The fourth or the innermost layer is like an arc of a circle. The circle can have any number of arcs but only one centre. The innumerable points in the outermost boundary of the circumference are connected to the centre from various angles and perspectives. This centre is the cosmic intelligence. The arc is the relationship between it and the object or being. This analogy holds good for each point of the circumference also. For each object has four layers. But the centre or Oversoul is the transcendental (and immanent) fifth layer with no dimensions or with infinite dimensions.

The fourth layer of a thing or being or an idea or information can be known by the direct contact of the spirit of a human with the core of the thing for there is no intervention by the senses, mind and the individual psyche. This faculty is known in yogic terminology as 'insight' of Atman.

The fifth layer or oversoul can be known, touched and seen only by total compassion. The identity as an individual is completely lost; a new identity as a cosmic person emerges. And this cosmic person will be endowed with cosmic intelligence and all knowledge or omniscience. Total, absolute knowledge of all things, past, present and future will be always known to him.

Unfortunately, modern science stops with the first two layers. But the scientists with their highly developed faculty of intuition discover the laws of nature and invent gadgets, though some of them might refuse to admit the notion of intuition, since it is used as the major weapon against science by the religionists. So the scientists have to attack everything or idea individually, analyse each part of it thoroughly before coming to its usage part or utility centre or technology of it. This process might go on endlessly, forever.

But, with compassion in its absolute condition, its capacity reaches beyond the grasp of information technology and enables the human to attain omniscience and omnitechnology. Humans will be transformed by compassion into gods. Every drop in the ocean will first feel the oceanic sense and bliss and later literally expand into a new ocean by itself. This process of expansion will go on indefinitely and everlastingly. That is why the astronomers say that the universe is ever - expanding and this is no longer universe but multiverse.

With the discovery of computer science and the technological inventions like chip manufacturing, robots and 3D printing of drones, etc., physics became a part of information technology. With the discovery of genome and subsequent advances in its technologies like cloning, genetic engineering and so on, biology has become a part of information technology. Like these, every field of science is engulfed by information technology.

It is true that it is an advancement made everyday. But how long it will take for humankind to know and master all of nature one by one? The dream can never be fulfilled and realized by this method of bits and bytes. We, humans are breaking a coconut into pieces and then eat it bit by bit. But an elephant swallows with its big mouth an entire coconut. With compassion a person's inner mouth of knowledge expands, grows bigger and bigger and takes in the world of knowledge and information in one gulp. The greater the degree of compassion is in one's mind, the larger will be the light of intelligence. With more light, more of darkness, of ignorance veiling the mind will be destroyed and wisdom or knowledge will appear in the mind's eye. Compassion is more than information. It is the ultimate power that created the universe and is still maintaining it and it will ever protect it. On the contrary, lack or deprivation of compassion will bring on us not only violence and sufferings, it can also, as some futurists fear, bring in the 'sixth extinction' of all life on earth.

The path of compassion alone as a way of living on the part of all humans can save the homo sapiens. The information technology can only be a part of it but cannot be nor act antagonistic to it.

'Knowledge is our destiny', said Carlsagan the astro-physicist. And he was one hundred percent right. Some four centuries before, Francis Bacon had already discovered the fact that 'knowledge is power' and with that power almost all the ills and problems of humankind could be solved and their lot ameliorated. He had also stressed the truth that this scientific way was the only road to progress, not speculative philosophy, nor imaginative other worldly salvations. His utopia, 'The New Atlantis' ascribed the highest seats of power in his imaginary society of the future to a team of scientists; 'He had simply replaced the Platonian idea of 'The philosopher king in 'The Republic' with the new notion of scientist – rulers. Later after thoroughly studying history, the modern historian Lord Acton diagnosed the power of the concept of power and declared the positive as well as the negative aspects of it when he said, 'power corrupts and absolute power corrupts absolutely'. Not only political power-mongers like Hitler and Gengiskhan but scientists employed in the field of manufacturing arms and ammunitions, nuclear bombs and biological weapons could also be corrupted by the form of power of knowledge. In the twentieth century the concept of power in almost all of its perspectives was analysed by two philosophers: Bertrand Russell in his classic, 'Power; A social analysis' and Michael Foucalt in many of his books diagnosed the ills of power in its macro as well as micro levels. Today ethics of cloning, ethics of engineering, particularly genetic engineering and ethics of science and scientists in general has become one of the hotly debated issues among the elites and intellectuals of the world.

What is the remedy or antidote to this poison of power? Socrates and Plato offered goodness and wisdom as a way out. Evil was equated rightly with ignorance by Plato and wisdom with goodness. They were wise men, very. But their wisdom allowed and even recommended the noxious institution of slavery in the Greek society. Equality among all was not a notion in their dictionary of wisdom. Their concept or equation of wisdom = goodness was not complete and they themselves did not realize it in their own lives. One other manifestation of the shortcoming or limitation of it was the antagonism of Plato to democracy as a political form which alone with all its disadvantages can give humanity a greater form of equality than any other form of government. History proves it and its evidences are legion.

Even the great, compassionate Buddha finally allowed his wandering monks with their begging bowls to eat non-vegetarian food. His compassion stopped at humanism. It did not encompass the welfare of animals or plants or beings other than humans. The fulfillment and completeness of compassion was not realized. It went halfway and stopped. Ahimsa and non-killing was not given the first priority. It was given to personal salvation or Nirvana through wisdom or MahaPrajna. Of course, he stressed both Mahakaruna [total compassion] and MahaPrajna [super consciousness], according to Buddhist scriptures. But it is reported in his biography, he himself took flesh of animals. According to one version, his death was caused by eating diseased pork.[23] His compassion did not attain perfection. Hence, it did not become a science and transform his physical body into a disease free, age-free, death-free pure body as it happened in the case of Vallalar.

Buddha preferred MahaPrajna to Maha karuna, wisdom to compassion. Hence his forgetfulness of the social and economic fact that was pointed out by the universal sage Thiruvalluvar in his famous couplet; "If no one eats flesh, no butcher will slaughter any animal".

Here Vallalar being a scientist, differs from the Buddha. Whereas for Buddha compassion was a moral code, a subordinate one to wisdom and personal salvation, for Vallalar, it was a science, that can bring in not only individual mutation but a collective one for the whole species, and that new species will have a different form ofpure body, mind and soul and can produce its own food of nectar, cosmic consciousness instead of the present relativistic, egoistic consciousness. Imagine an internet in built in the body from the inception and conception and birth. It will be the birth of a superman and finally of a man-god with all the powers of god.

Here a question arises: will not all these super powers corrupt the person? No. Certainly not. For the primary cause of all these powers and bodily mental and spiritual transformations is not knowledge but total, absolute compassion toward all beings without any sort of difference or discrimination such as gender, colour, language, race, nationality, species etc. Like God, this new human will be all Providence toward all beings, goodness perfect.

That is why Vallalar says in his Agaval poem, the scientific scripture for the scientific age that the superior form of intelligence is born of love and the highest form or level of superconsciousness, the divine all knowing intelligence is born of Absolute Compassion. In short, the degree of compassion in a person determines the degree or level of one's knowledge, health, longevity, powers, bliss etc.,. So mahaprajna is only secondary, it is subordinated to maha karuna. The highest wisdom is born only from the most perfect compassion. They are not two but one. The very thought of dichotomy between wisdom and compassion breeds all kinds of ills and sufferings, conflicts and wars among humanity. This error has to be reflected upon, seen in the march of the Zeitgeist, in the terminology of Hegel and remedied. Of course, knowledge is our destiny but it is knowledge, as Vallalar modified it and corrected its error and defects, born out of total and all compassion that always thinks for all. It is democracy for the welfare of all beings, not only humans. All beings are treated as cells in the great body of god.

How is this highest form of knowledge produced by love and compassion? Vallalar explains it in a scientific manner, with a scientific analogy. An electric bulb, when electricity is passed through the tungsten filament, gets heated up and emits light, fluorescence. In a similar way, the human body is the bulb. The life spirit or soul is the tungsten filament. When the electricity of love is passed through it, subtle heat, not the physical heat, is produced and out of that subtle heat, subtle light is emitted. This invisible, subtle light is a new, higher form of intelligence,[24] as against the intelligence of the computer which is nothing but computing or adding or subtracting one by one though done with electronic speed.

This higher form of intelligence is not thought but pure consciousness or insight, the eighth degree of consciousness. With insight fully developed, one can learn all knowledge of a thing or concept or being just by seeing it or meditating upon it.[25] It is beyond intuition, the seventh degree of knowledge. When one's intuitive faculty is developed child prodigies in mathematics like Ramanujan and Sakunthala Devi demonstrate it in their lives and child prodigies like Mozart outshine all the othermerely skilled persons. With the mathematics of Ramanujan, they say, one can imagine and see with one's inner eye some eleven dimensions. With this superior intelligence born of the subtle light of love one can see still more dimensions of reality, the parallel universes of quantum physics.

When this love develops into compassion encompassing not only devotion to god but covering all beings and fruitions into the causal heat which gives out causal light, one attains godhead and achieves omniscience. Then one can see, master, control everything in the universe. This causal light is the divine energy that creates the universe and sustains it with all its beings. This is the ultimate power of all, the unifying force of all the four major physical forces of gravitation, electromagnetism, strong nuclear force and the weak nuclear force. This is the one unifying field for which Einstein was searching for all his life but failed. This is the real force that binds together all the worlds, things and beings in the universe with the so-called super strings. Light is supposed to bea product of electromagnetic force by modern science but subtle light and finally the causal light of absolute compassion are yet to be explored by scientists. Then only they will come to understand the higher sciences discovered by Vallalar.

Some experiments have already been conducted in this direction. In one experiment a bowl of water was placed on a table. A man was asked to look at it with anger, and its molecular structure was analysed. There was some change in its structure. Later after some time the same man was asked to look at it with love and affection. When the molecular structure was analysed, this time there was a drastic change in it. So human emotions affect the very structure of molecules of matter at the quantum level. In future, better and more powerful gadgets might be invented to measure and photograph the higher forms of subtle light of love and causal light of compassion. Then, humans will be really Siddhas or Suddhasanmarghis, in other words, scientist creators and masters of reality physical and mental spiritual and divine.

Perhaps Immanuel Kant was right when he intuited that humans perceive the truth of arithmetic through intuition. We also perceive time and space through our faculty of intuition. Though we are born with the faculty, our everyday lives our circumstances and our systems of education do not allow us to develop it. Only a few mathematicians, some logicians, and a small number of inventors in science develop it more fully either consciously or unconsciously. Da Vinci and Goethe consciously developed it and had mastered the art and science of intuition to a rare level. We could add the name of Ramanujan to the list. Others, both artists and scientists were only allowed glimpses into the region of intuition. Even Einstein the great had a few glimpses like the photo electric effect for which he was awarded the Nobel Prize and the Relativity Theory in which he refuted the idea of absoluteness of space and time of Newton and coined the word space-time.

Somehow the Italian epic poet Dante of the Divine Comedy had intuited the notion that angelic intelligence was superior to all forms of other intelligences and it was born of love. Again, he mentions the strange truth about love that the higher angels were chosen for their greater love and they grow younger and younger with more love. Buddha, Christ, Socrates, Plato, Dante and other great saints and poets had known the power of love but they had not developed it into a complete form of science. The world had to wait for a long time, for a Vallalar to do it. With all due respect and reverence for these great souls, we must take into consideration the fact that humanity was not ripe for the science of compassion. For in their times science as a separate discipline was not known. It had not ascertained its superiority over other channels of arriving at truth. Now is the time for it; for homo sapiens as a species is at a transition phase now. They are about to evolve collectively into a higher species. And the agent of transmutation is compassion only. No other option will do it – not wisdom, nor will to power, nor organizational power, nor utopias of ideologies, nor religions, nor any new age with its childish techniques and alternative therapies. These are all distortions and dissipations of the collective energy needed for the transmutation and transformation of the human species.

~~~ ~~~ ~~~

30. SCIENCE OF AWARENESS AND COMPASSION

The ancient, enlightened masters such as the Buddha and Socrates had taught humankind the yoga of self-awareness. Buddha called his yoga and meditation 'Vipassana'. What did he mean by this? To be consciously aware of the functions of all physiological actions of the body starting from watching one's breath and bringing it under one's control. For when breath is controlled, mind will be controlled. Another method of controlling one's mind is to watch its own responses and reactions to the stimuli it receives from the external world and from its own body like hunger, thirst, sex etc. When this witnessing consciousness is stabilized and stays for all the twenty-four hours of a day and three and sixty five days of an year, one has earned for himself or herself the fourth artificial degree and form of consciousness called 'Turiya consciousness'. It means one has earned the admission into the superhuman region beyond the normal human modes of consciousness of wakefulness, dream and sleep. Now the human condition and limitation of sleep, fatigue and being bound by time is crossed over and conquered forever. Before attaining this fourth level of consciousness of Turiya, no amount of reading the scriptures, talking or writing about spirituality or practicing yoga or meditation or prayer will get one beyond the human level. All these are only to get this ticket of admission into para human dimension. Vaasi yoga or breath control, meditation or thought control, prayer or emotion-control, austerity or instinct-control etc., are all only ways to enter into this first level of super consciousness or Samadhi in yogic terminology.

Socrates talked about philosophical inquiry as a method of attaining this higher consciousness. His purpose was not, as the western philosophers including Aristotle misunderstood, to find out the definition of concepts moral, ontological or metaphysical or political, but to reach the limits of thought. When thought realizes its own limitation and grows tired, accepts its failure and falls asleep, a miracle happens in the human consciousness. It leaps into a new and higher level of consciousness called intuition and insight. These new faculties take one into the domain of Turiya. This state takes one into the heart and core of things and concepts.[26]

Not the definitions or philosophical discussions are important but these higher states of intuition and insight. Philosophical inquiry is one way of reaching the state of Turiya. Observe every Platonic dialogue. Throughout the dialogue, Socrates will be questioning others ahead and taking the inquiry or the capacity of thought step by step like extending a rubber band. At its extreme level it will snap and break. Thought will stop. Intuition will take over the command. And finally at this stage of the dialogue, Socrates will come out with his own monologue and mostly with his myths like 'the myth of cave in the Republic' and the myth of the 'whole man in symposium'. For it is too difficult to express in a rational way what truths one discovers through intuition in a flash. The great scientist Einstein confessed that he got his theory of relativity all in a flash, in a moment but had to wait and struggle for years to put it mathematically in order to express it in a convincing way to other scientists. Unfortunately, Socrates was not an advanced genius in mathematics like Einstein. So he had to resort to myths. His disciple Plato had somehow intuited this truth and hence his emphasis on mathematics.

Socrates might have learned this way of philosophical inquiry into truth from the upanishadic rishis through traders from India. Dr.S.Radhakrishnan alludes to such an encounter of Socrates with an Indian philosopher in his book, 'Eastern Religions and western philosophy'. In recent times this method of philosophical inquiry was adopted by the Indian born spiritual philosopher J.Krishnamurti. In all his talks and dialogues with others, one can discern his method of seeing a problem or analyzing a concept from all possible angles and perspectives for a long time with his thinking. Finally all of a sudden he will come out with a solution of his own to the problem. Most of the time, it will be different and unique from the solutions known to man so far. He learns it from his highly developed faculty of intuition and insight. From awareness through self-awareness to objective consciousness is the way of philosophical inquiry into truth.

This method in yogic terminology is called 'Sat Vichara' or enquiry into truth or jnana yoga. It is based on awareness and thought but develops and goes beyond them into the domain of higher levels of consciousness.

The scientist Saint Vallalar calls this method of philosophical inquiry into truth as 'Bothantha' or perfecting of knowledge. This is one among the six anthas or perfections or methods of attaining truth or god. They are i) Vedanta, ii) siddhanta, iii) yoganta, iv) bothanta, v) nadanta and vi) kalanta.

Since this methodology of philosophy as the other five systems of inquiry is based upon mere awareness or thought or knowledge which is only a fragment or lower level of consciousness, Vallalar though he acknowledges and accepts their truths and efficacy, and synthesizes them into an eclectic system of knowledge and called it 'SadantaSuddhaSanmarga' is convinced that they are inadequate in transforming relative human consciousness into absolute, divine consciousness, searches for a complete form of consciousness and discovers it in absolute compassion. And he confesses and claims that this revelation was made to him by God Himself. As a result, he was revealed into all the secret dimensions and powers of compassion for the first time in human history. And he recorded all that god revealed to him into a gospel, a whole book and called it 'The yoga and Science of Compassion'.[27] In fact, he wrote it in seven parts. Unfortunately, only three parts of it are available now. And the third part remains only a fragment. Let us hope and pray that the remaining four parts also will be revealed to us in the future. The book is written in the form of a Socratic dialogue, in the form of question and answer. In it, he argues for compassion like an able and an expert logician refuting all the objections that could be raised against compassion and explains all the benefits, moral, yogic, spiritual, social and evolutionary of the way of compassion in all the scientific details.

In a way, this book can be called the latest revelation of God to humankind to save it from doom and extinction. Vallalar was the scientist philosopher chosen by God to reveal this ultimate science of compassion to the world. And we are blessed at last with a scientific gospel for the scientific age, about the ultimate science of love and compassion in a scientific manner. As far as I know, who has to some extent gone through almost all the scriptures of the world such as The Sacred Books of the East edited by Max Muller, 'The great books of the western world' edited by Mortimer J Adler and 'The classics of western spirituality' etc, without the ultimate wisdom contained in this small but precious book, the knowledge of humankind will not be complete. I don't mean to offend the feelings and convictions of any person. I only plead you to look into the book once and then decide for yourself whether what I say is true or a tall claim. Just give it a chance, nay, give yourself a chance; give other homo sapiens as a species a chance and a rare one at that.

Almost all the new age gurus emphasize awareness as the ultimate yoga or sadhana for the salvation and enlightenment of man and everyone teaches his or her own way or technique to enhance one's awareness. Every spiritual teacher tries to dilute or simplify the technique to suit more number of people so as to reach more number of people. Some do out of compassion and some for commercial purpose. In the west, this technique of awareness has made a lot of impact. Zen, yoga, awareness, spirituality all have had their heyday after the advent of quantum physics which ushered in, in the words of Michio Kaku, the physicist 'solipsism' or subjective idealism once again into science through the back door'. In simpler terms human perception or thought can influence matter at the subatomic level.

The scientist spiritualist Vallalar had known and declared about the subatomic world some half a century before electron was discovered by J.J.Thomson in 1897. He had given a complete atomic science much earlier in 1850s and given details and various names of the subatomic particles including the Higgs Boson. He called it 'Paramanu' meaning the 'god particle'. But he denies it is the ultimate particle.[28] He lists out other particles much smaller than this.[29]But this is not the place to divulge completely the atomic science of Vallalar. Suffice it to say that Vallalar affirms that love is also an atom that contains enormous beneficent light inside it.[30]When man comes to know how to split the atom of love, a higher kind of atomic energy would be available for humankind. And finally, 'Compassion' is literally and really the ultimate atom, the ultimate power, the ultimate particle/wave that literally produces all worlds and beings and Vallalar equates it with god himself or herself or itself. The complete system of science of compassion is elaborated by Vallalar in his Agaval poem in more than 40 lines and in the whole of the book on 'Yoga and science of compassion' [Jeeva karunyaozhukkam] in prose.

In short Vallalar gives us the entire science of creation in two short and simple formulae: 1) Love = individual soul and 2) Absolute compassion = god. Modern science of heat and light are supplemented and complemented by him with two more higher sciences of heat and light. Now modern science knows only about physical heat and its product physical light. And its velocity of about 3,00,000 kilo meters per second is known and proved as a constant in nature. On the contrary Vallalar says, there are infinite varieties of heat and love but basically of three types: 1) physical heat and physical love, 2) subtle heat of love and its product of subtle light and 3) causal heat of compassion and its light. Modern science is yet to explore the two later fields of higher forms of heat and light. When they realize the truth of these higher forms of heat and light they will come to know the truth about life spirit as love and god as all compassionate energy and light. Then only science will be complete. Instead of stagnating with the knowledge of matter only, it will also come to know and deal with the knowledge of soul and the oversoul. Then only scientists all over the world would come to realize the real and supreme science of the master scientist Vallalar and about his ultimate science of love and compassion.

Coming back to the difference in quality between awareness and compassion, awareness is a lower form and power of consciousness though fundamental. But the highest and most complete and comprehensive form of consciousness and power is absolute compassion. God himself is a name for it or an embodiment of it, according to Vallalar.

He openly declares in his Agaval poem that "those who do not realize compassion in themselves do not know themselves; they do not have self-knowledge and they can never know God".[31] And he says this knowledge was revealed to him by God himself.

Some two thousand years before, the same truth was revealed to humankind by Saint Thirumular in his immortal verse:

Those who consider Love and Siva as two are fools;

Only love develops into Siva, no one knows;

Those who realize only love becomes Siva,

They sit on the throne of Siva as Love incarnate.

-Thirumanthiram

Here a question is raised by some orthodox people: love and compassion are not something new. They have all along been preached by all saints of all countries. True, but partially true.

Compassion has been taught as one virtue among many. But Vallalar affirms repeatedly that it is the supreme virtue and the flawless one. All the other virtues are only fragmentary and incomplete. All the other virtues at the maximum transform the brutal tendencies of humans into peaceful and lovable human beings. But compassion turns him and transforms him into a Divine Being, into God. All the other virtues may give him some physical and mental powers, but compassion gives him all sorts of divine powers such as creation of worlds and things. The science of miracle making is only a by-product of the science of compassion. With the power issuing out and emanating from the state of total compassion, one can do anything. He will be literally a god among humans. Even the lord of death will run away from him.[32] A human will have and lead a divine life in a divine body. He will attain all the eight attributes of godhead such as 1) omniscience 2) omnipotence, 3) self-sufficiency, 4) having a pure, divine body of light of compassion, 5) total bliss, 6) freedom from all bondage, 7) infinite grace and 8) all pervadingness or Immanence.

31. COMPASSION AS THE UNIFYING FORCE

The Hindus in India conduct a ceremony after one dies. His or her body is cremated and ashes are taken to a place where three rivers meet and conjoin into a bigger river and dissolved. What is the meaning implied in this ritual? It points out the mistake committed by the departed soul and advises it to remember this fact in its future incarnations: There are three forces functioning in any life, human or divine. They are desire, will and knowledge. Unifying them into a single force has the power and capacity to manifest anything physical or intellectual, spiritual or divine. This fourth force determines the success of an individual in life and spirituality. The degree to which one attains it in one's life determines the degree or level of one's success. When it is abundant, all forms of abundance and even miracle making powers called siddhis are acquired by these witnesses. When it reaches its fulfillment of 100% or absolute compassion, even the cruel fact of death is conquered. This is the secret process of manifestation of anything. God became divine by mastering this law of unification by compassion.

We, humans are endowed with these three powers [itcha or desire, kriya or will, gnana or wisdom] but they act separately and are antagonistic to each other. Each develops itself separately according to the circumstances and depending upon one's efforts and their direction. For instance, householders and worldly-minded common men and women develop their desires in a thousand ways thereby dissipating their energies. None of them is given concentration enough to develop itself, mature and manifest in things. They are born as eggs and immediately broken. They are not given sufficient attention and concentration to grow into fish let alone into a whale. Most of the humans remain small people living small and petty lives and die like dogs on the street.

The yogis particularly the Raja yogis with their immense efforts of will in controlling their bodily instincts and mental urges develop their will power to an enormous extent. For example, Gurdjieff the Russian spiritual philosopher was reported to have the power to kill a yak that was twenty miles away. Yogi Sri Aurobindo is reported to have said in 1930s that the independence of India had already been attained whereas in reality it happened in future on August, 15th, 1947. In the early 1920s he was a leader in the struggle for Indian independence. He was imprisoned and placed in solitary confinement for a year. During that period of solitude, he practiced yoga and developed his power of will enormously. When he was released, he announced his renunciation of politics saying there was a better method of obtaining independence for his nation through yogic will power which was a more powerful means and irresistible weapon.

The scientists develop their faculty of reason and increase their knowledge. They are able to reason out any concept with their exact mathematical calculations and arrive at the core knowledge of any concept or thing. Once they come to have the core knowledge of a thing and the laws of nature, they are able to manipulate nature itself as they wish. This knowledge is turned into gadgets like smart phones and televisions by using which even illiterate people get the benefits of esoteric knowledge of science like quantum mechanics they could never understand in their lives.

Let us not forget now the fact that all these three sorts of people die at last for want of knowledge of this law of unification of all the three forces and due to failure of acting upon it. And Vallalar gives us the solution to this problem of separate forces each developing separately. The harmonious development of the three forces is possible only when the fourth component of compassion is added to it. And what is compassion? How does it become supreme force?

Normally a person acts out his desires. For instance, if one wants to build a house, one must have a desire to possess a house. This desire must grow into an ambition. One must constantly and millions of times must dream and visualize his dream house. Finally the power to act or will is born as a new faculty. This new faculty must be developed against all odds and obstacles. Most people lose hope at this juncture. Thirdly even if the will is fully developed, one must have the required knowledge of building a house. So he goes out searching for the knowledge of an architect or civil engineer who could build it for him.

Human lives exhibit various levels of success and failure because they are various proportions or permutations and combinations of these three forms of energies of desire, will and knowledge. But then, why do they fail in their endeavors? For the simple reason that they are motivated by their small egoist and egotistical subjective consciousness. When everyone acts out with this limited, self-centered force, millions of such narrow, self-centered forces clash with each other. The result is competition, strife, violence, survival of the fittest; success becomes accidental and for a few and failure for most of the contenders. On the contrary the tender compassionate force has no competitor to combat with, no friction whatsoever. It is objective, all –encompassing, all embracing, large, force of will of light. Instead of subjective will, narrow, egoistic, violent, one has and applies objective, all-loving ego-free will. The power of will is there acting to create things but free from its stains and corruptions, shortcomings and limitations.

There are three steps in the development of will : 1) the narrow, self-centered, subjective will that is developed at the cost of others and their own wills, 2) the large, compassionate, objective and self-giving, ego-free will of a mother or a philanthropist or a member of a service organisation, an NGO, and finally 3) the divine will which always is motivated by care for the welfare of all beings without any discrimination whatsoever, like rain that showers its benefits on all beings, like the sun shining and giving light and energy for all.

This divine power of will is an all compassionate one. Hence its omnipotent, unlimited, illimitable, infinite power to create the vast universe or multiverse with all its billions and billions of galaxies and beings in them. This divine will or god has at once the powers of desire and required knowledge to create these worlds because all the three powers are fused together and act as one power. Hence its omniscience, omnipotence, immanence and transcendence and infiniteness of attributes and immortality and eternity. For it is an incarnation of absolute compassion. The scientific temperament might question this personal god or the prospect of incarnation. Not necessary. Just consider it as a natural law, like the law of the super-strings, or unified field theory. For those with a religious or spiritual temperament, the notion of a personal god is permitted. For they need to pray, get solace, and have direct relationship of love and devotion. They need a Father figure for their own comfort. For a power that could create billions of galaxies and beings, it is not difficult to appear in the form of a person. The quantum theory with its own brand of quantum consciousness and the hypothesis of Schrodinger's cat will not, I suppose, object to such a proposition.

Unfortunately a human is still a non-entity, a minuscule, with negligible knowledge and very little power. This is because of his narrow, ego-consciousness. It is his own creation or miscreation. He has confined himself into a prison which he built for himself.

The moment the humans were blessed with the concept or hypothesis of god, they were blessed with the possibility of becoming godlike, with the deliverance from his suffocating human condition of limitations and mortality. Scientists like Stephen Hawking and Richard Dawkins might object to this concept of god. They might argue with all their arsenal of immense scientific knowledge that the universe does not need a god for its survival and functioning. Moreover this idea of god was the cause inthepast history of man, for belittlement and degradation of mankind. True all true. But Vallalar wants us to know both the advantages and shortcomings of the problem and shows us the solution. He accepts all of your accusations against the idea of god and its manipulation by religions against mankind. His question in the words of Nietsche is this: not whether there is a god or is he beneficial to man or is he listening to men's prayer etc, but 'Are you a god? Why is not every human a god endowed with divine knowledge and powers? How to do it ? How to increase the limited, relative knowledge of man and enhance his happiness into divine, eternal bliss?' That is the question raised by Vallalar and answered positively and scientifically. His answer is the development of compassion for all beings as against the aggressive, violent, egoistic 'will to power' of Nietsche. Lord Acton rightly answered Nietsche when he said, power corrupts and absolute power corrupts absolutely. But Acton was speaking about political, economical and institutional power of man. God being omnipotent is beyond corruption. For his very motive is total compassion. And his omnipotent power is a by product of his benevolent divine nature. Those who go after power for power's sake are bound to fall like Lucifer.

Light is life, health, longevity and immortality and eternity. And compassion is the ultimate light, the causal light from which are born all the other forms of light like that of sun, the moon and fire and so on.

So far in human history, all the other forms and ways of salvation such as prayer, contemplation, philosophical inquiry, yoga, art, mythology and finally science and political utopia and economic ones in the twentieth century were given a chance and tried. All of them failed for they were inherently inadequate means.

The only fully qualified and complete one is compassion. Though it has been known to mankind and sown as a seed in their minds, its full dimensions and power were not revealed so far. At last Vallalar came and did it for us: To turn and transform all humans into divine beings through the power of compassion. And what is the process he recommends to do it?

Now compassion lies in the human mind as only a thought, an idea, as equality was an idea in Greek democracy, particularly in Plato's mind that gave equality of status to all men and women and abolished private property. But it was not developed into a mass movement. It had to wait for some twenty two centuries for the advent of Marx and Lenin to found a society based upon equality. But then that too failed. Why? The third step in the science of ideas was not taken. What are the three steps in the science of ideas? 1. The mere idea or thought in the books of thinkers, 2. A mass movement based on the idea which means the idea has gathered momentum and turned into a force, 3. The force must be developed still further and sublimated into a field, an eternal, ever-operating field like gravitation, electromagnetic, nuclear or quantum field. Compassion as a force and then into a field has to be built up. It is already there always operating from the time of the big bang or even before it. That is why there is order in the cosmos. Compassion is the agent that brings in order where chaos reigns.

This lesson from nature, man must learn. Chaos in human society can be conquered only by compassion. It must cover the whole of humanity and its collective mind as a cloud of light and then only the showers of benevolence humanity can feel and enjoy. 1.

In nature and in human lives, we find evil powers on the one side and good, benevolent powers on the other side. They are eternal companions, two sides of a coin. They are like harmony in music and disharmony. To rectify disharmony and convert it into harmony is the task of the artist. To do that, he has to fine-tune the instrument properly. In the same way, humans have to fine tune their minds properly with the tendency of compassion. It must become a way of life as against violence, aggression and competition.

If compassion becomes a way of life there will be progressive changes, miraculous ones at that will occur in the human body,Vallalar asserts. Its present condition of decay, disease and death caused by waste matter will be gone. And a new body, a pure one that will be producing its own food of ambrosia will be born and replace this shit-body. It will be blessed with four forms of eyes, namely 1] the present physical ones, 2] the mental eye, 3] the eye of the spirit and 4] the eye of compassion or the divine all seeing eye. It will have cosmic consciousness and immortality.

When the human society is made up of such super humans, homo sapiens will be entering into their next higher level in evolution. Unlike the violent mutants shown in Hollywood films, the mutation through compassion will transform humans only into Christ and Vallalar, incapable of evil or violence. They cannot harm any soul but only help them in all ways and alleviate their sufferings and lead them towards their higher evolution.

Finally, the very atmosphere of nature will be transformed. All the basic five elements of earth, water, fire, air and space that are now impure in their nature, will be purified by the love and compassion of these divine beings and upgraded into pure elements. First this transformation or purification takes place in the five elements of their bodies. When such bodies multiply into millions and billions the same transformation or purification will take place in external nature and its five elements also. For we already saw, that whatever takes place in the human body will take place in nature also. They are interlinked. Vallalar called both the body of nature and man with one word, the outermost layer [purappuram].[33]

At the final stage which was attained by Vallalar the whole cosmos becomes the body of such divine beings. Their bodies will have the forms of god called Satchidananta.[34] Each of them will have a cosmic body, a cosmic mind and cosmic intelligence. Their motive for action will be the welfare of all beings in the cosmos and improvement of the condition of cosmos. All lower forms of life will be born as humans and evolve into higher beings and finally into divine beings with divine bodies. Evolution will go on till all beings are transformed into god from whom all these beings came or who became and descended into these lower beings during involution.[35]This could be the cause of population explosion.

~~~ ~~~ ~~~

32. THE ULTIMATE SCIENCE OF LOVE AND COMPASSION

Can love be an object of science? This may sound ridiculous and superstitious for the scientifically oriented minds. It may be recognized as a study for psychology. Even psychology has not been so far accepted as a branch of science, inspite of the immense efforts on the part of its great pioneers such as Sigmund Freud, C G Jung, Alfred Adler etc. Once it was acknowledged as a department of humanities. Of late some kind of a little recognition or attention has been given to it after the discovery of new cognitive science, since it is based upon the affinity and connection between mental ailments and the structure, physiology and functioning of the brain, particularly so after the advent of the neuro cognitive scientist Vilayanur Ramachandran and his famous discourses in the field.

Even though cognitive science or neuro-psychology is acknowledged to some extent as a new branch of science by academic scientific world it may take a long time for it either to acknowledge or recognize love as a science. The antagonism of the scientists towards the notion of love arises from two sources. One objection arises from the accepted definition of science as an objective study, as an experimental method where there is no place for any subjective emotion whatsoever. The second reason is historical. The ultimate weapon of all religions that have always acted aginst the interests and advancement of science has always been this concept of love. Only in the name of love almost all the persecutions of scientists by religion have taken place. The famous example in history was the torture of Giordano Bruno and Galileo and thousands of others including Darwin. Bruno was imprisoned for eight years and tortured and finally burnt at the stake. Whole books have been written on such persecutions of scientists and their counterparts in philosophy by the rationalists. We need not dwell upon this well-known fact and amplify it.

Like a cat that burned its tongue with too hot milk, scientists even today are afraid of religion and are not ready even to take into consideration any idea or concept from the religious side let alone love. But seen objectively, it is politics, not pure science. It is high time all these past grievances were forgotten and enter a new paradigm shift in the history of science.

Let us now try to answer the first objection that love is a subjective emotion. No, love is not a subjective emotion only. Love is not a thought only. Love is not a feeling only or a sensation only either of the body or a thought or feeling of the mind. Love is more than all these subjective attributes. It is the highest form of objective energy like electricity, like gravitation, atomic energy or any other physical energy. In fact, love is the ultimate unifying energy of the latest super string theory that unites all the four basic laws of energy fields that govern the universe, namely the gravitational force, the electromagnetic force, the strong nuclear force and the weak nuclear force. The super strings are made up of love energy, in its ultimate and highest form called compassion absolute, the causal light of infinite compassion.

In the beginning was compassion. From compassion proceeded the act of creation, the creation and beings and worlds in which they could live. Why did creation take place? For, by its definition and its very nature, compassion needs the other or other beings to act upon, to give, to showerits love. So creation became an inevitable act. It divided itself into two. The two became three, three into four and so on into infinite varieties of beings and planets and things.

As a second stage when love manifested itself into unique beings, they were called gods such a Siva, Vishnu, Brahma and by other names in various nations in various periods of history. This scientific fact was declared by the Tamil Siddha – Siddha means scientist – Thirumular, that love when it accumulated into an immense quantity was called Siva.[36]Love became Siva, not the other way round. Lovecreated all the personal gods and their feuds among themselves that became history, godly and human. As Dr Samuel Huntington pointed out in his classic book on globalization, what is taking place now in the world is not the clash of civilizations, but their corresponding gods.

This clash, this strife, this violence of global proportions can be solved and peace returned only when this scientific fact of love and compassion understood by all the members of humanity. That love-energy existed even prior to gods and the gods were either invented later or were created later by it. Only by understanding the science of love-energy properly a secular, scientific spirituality will arise in the world and peace will reign upon earth. That was why Ramalinga Vallalar had to write a whole book of revelation called 'Compassion as the way to salvation'.

It was not only by the Siddhas of the Tamil tradition that stressed this science of love and compassion but they had their counterparts in the west also such as Empedocles, Jesus, Teilhard de Chardin and some of the western mystics like Jacob Boehme and Meister Eckhart. The reason why they failed was their half-hearted endeavors. They all thought only about their own salvation or lastly the salvation of humanity through love as a last step. Their love did not become all consuming compassion. It did not extend beyond humanity to all the other beings like plants, animals and birds. But they forgot one terrestrial fact: they were the real owners of this earth first. Homo sapiens were very late comers and their great –great- great- great - grandsons and granddaughters, according to the theory of evolution. We might boast now of being the crown of creation or of having been created in the image of god himself. But this was all realized later. Without the seed or foetus, the well grown-up body of a man is not possible.

Without the vegetable kingdom, without animal kingdom, the human kingdom could not have been born at all, let alone rule them as kings of the earth. This was the basic error committed on the part of religions and their so-called scriptures: lack of compassion towards our ancient forebears and our ingratitude to those innocent beings. This was the error of man we learn today from scientists that one species is dying every day. And still it doesn't affect us in the least. And we go on destroying them and butchering them out of our unlimited greed of consumption.

Compassion is total, absolute and causal light. Love is subtle light, a little lower in gradation. Physical light is the lowest degree of light deprived of almost all of love. It contains only very litte love, a negligible amount.

Love is light. And lack of light is darkness and dark matter coming out of dark energy. Deprivation of love in mind is strife, hatred and violence. Deprivation of light is darkness, ignorance, matter and death.

This fact about love and its opposite strife was known to the Greek thinker Heraclitus. He said love and strife and the dialectical conflict between them created the world and life on it. Christ admonished all humans to love god and to love their neighbors. The first part of the teaching was given more weight by the organized institutions of the religions and sowed the seeds of strife among human societies and neglected the second portion of the teaching.

Prayer to god or love of god got the upper hand and destroyed the love of the neighbour along with the neighbours in millions. The world became a large slaughterhouse. That was why Vallalar, the scientist of love and compassion changed the order and said: Compassion towards all beings is more important and diviner than prayer. In fact for all people of sense, compassion is the only form of worship or prayer to god.

Love thy neighbour as thyself. No, go further. Love thy neighbour as god himself. Not only your neighbour, love all the beings, vegetable and animal as thy neighbours, as thy god. Worship the walking god, instead of the god in the temple. The walking god was created by god himself but the god in the temple was man-made. The former is the living, alive god whereas the latter is of matter with form or formless. In the name of the latter, the lesser, you are killing the real god created in his own image, created by the original god: when you are destroying the body of a human or any other being whether for the reason of food or for any other reason you are killing your father in heaven, your co-creation upon earth. You are destroying the most sacred temple of the living god, in the name of god. You don't in reality know what you are doing. Killing any being is the real sin for which there can be no redemption at all. For every action, there is an equal and opposite reaction. It is the law of motion discovered by the great scientist Sir Isaac Newton. According to that law, if you kill, you will be killed. If you eat the body of another being, your body will be eaten. There is no exception to this rule. That was why Vallalar wrote an inscription on the doorstep to his temple called 'Hall of wisdom':'Only those who haven't killed any being and who haven't eaten any flesh are allowed'. Which means wisdom cannot be attained by these two acts of violence. For they are against love, the very foundation of the universe and god himself.

The cosmos is on a journey from chaos and strife towards love and compassion, from darkness to absolute light. It is the course of the history of the universe. It is also the course of history of humankind.

Every moment we are creating our bodies afresh. That is what metabolism means. Every second or nano second millions of cells are destroyed by the functioning of the body. All energy spent means the loss of millions of cells. To replace them, to recuperate the loss of energy, fresh fuel is needed by the body and we provide it in the form of food, water, air, thought, impression and knowledge from the external world. And the body converts them all into a biochemical called ATP which is the source of all our energy. It is the bank of energy in the body. When there is no reserve in that bank deposit we get depression in the mind and chronic fatigue syndrome in the body.

This economy of bioenergy in the body is known as metabolism, comprising anabolism and katabolism. We know these basic facts of the economy of the body from high school textbooks of biology. But what is not taught there by modern science is another fact of higher moral science taught by Vallalar.

Every moment we are creating our body. That is an established fact. It is taking place at the quantum level. But the question is, are we creating or destroying the body? For instance, upto the age of about twenty, the body grows tall and develops all the eight systems of it. After that, at a point, it starts declining and decaying. The old age sets in. Why? What is the reason? Science tries to answer it in many ways. We are offered many theories of aging and none of them is convincing nor gives results. The very sad fact that the scientists and doctors who propound such theories of stopping the clock of aging and attaining ageless bodies have aged, grown old, their black hair turning visibly grey, which means those theories don't work.

In his own case, Vallalar who lived in his physical body for 51 years says that the symptoms of old age set in but he fought against it successfully and grew back younger.[37] And he declares categorically that by following the system of SuddhaSanmarga as preached by him, and practiced in his body anyone can reverse the aging process.[38] And what is the method of attaining youthfulness? He answers that the process of decaying of cells must be stopped. Why do they decay? By corruption. Corruption of the body with wrong foods and wrong eating habits and wrong thoughts and wrong thinking habits. We corrupt and destroy our body mind complex in both ways.

The discipline and regimen concerning food and eating habits, we dealt with under the title 'yoga of food'. Here we are going to see what Vallalar says about the corruption of the mind and how it destroys the human body and subsequently the world.

First, about the corruption of the mind and body. Human body is like a computer that runs according to a program. Its various functions are only various permutations and combinations of the input or program. If you want to change the program first you have to remove it from the system or decondition it and then recondition it or introduce a new program. The same thing applies and upholds in the human mind also. In it, the core belief and the belief system operate as the program in a computer.

Unfortunately, our core belief has always been one of the inevitability of death. We have been taught and indoctrinated in schools, books, the scriptures and in all possible ways by the society including the scientific community that death is the inevitable and indestructible fact. Even atheists and agnostics materialists and communists who deny god, have no qualms about accepting the lord of death as the most realistic and scientific fact. They forget the implication of their submission. The moment one acknowledges and accepts the inevitability of death it begins its operations. It starts killing you. You begin to die. Instead of growing, you start declining and decaying. You begin to have diseases. Sickness becomes the order of your life. Death is the mother whose offsprings are diseases and old age. The first corruption that leads to and gives birth to all sorts of mental and physical corruption is the core belief of death. Unless it is eradicated totally and removed from the unconscious and life-spirit, no system of rejuvenation or regeneration will work. All the efforts towards realizing such endeavors will be of waste. That is why so far, no one has succeeded in conquering diseases, old age and death. Even the great Buddha who started his quest rightly saying he wanted to find out ways to eradicate these evils, finally was misled like all philosophers and saints since he accepted the fact of inevitability of death. He found solace in philosophical solutions like not being born again. Once you are born these evils are unavoidable, and inevitable. In this case, Christ was much better. Atleast he identified death as man's last enemy and it can be conquered. But unfortunately his apostles and the church put a brake there, a bar in between Christ and ordinary humans saying resurrection on earth was possible only for Christ because he was the only begotten son of God and others like us were children of the fallen Adam, the sinner.

Vallalar calls death as 'a chronic disease' a contagious disease and the contagion takes place through thought. That is what makes it most dangerous. The enemy, the virus enters the body through the mind and its thoughts. Not only through belief but as function also, it corrupts the body. Vallalar says that every moment we are creating either light and immortality or darkness and death in the body. For love and compassion are made up of light and thought is dark and death. Every moment poison is produced in the body by any and every thought other than love and compassion. It may bring billions of dollars, name and fame but qualitatively it is poison and corrupts the body. When this poison accumulates in the body, it results in disease, old age, and death. On the contrary love and compassion brings forms of subtle light and causal light and forms of ambrosia, they produce ambrosia in the body. When this light and nectar accumulates in the body, it produces health, strength, youthfulness, longevity and immortality. And when it reaches the state of total absolute compassion for all beings without any discrimination whatsoever, it reaches a boiling point of 100^0C where the body mind complex is permanently transformed into a permanent state, an unchanging state of divinity.

How do greed and thought other than love affect the external world and nature? What are the effects of them on humankind? Let us first understand the unique relationship of humans and nature. Both the human body with its five senses and circumstances in the external world are denoted by Vallalar in one word 'Purappuram', meaning the outermost layer of man. Both man and nature are made of the five basic elements. Man is not confined within his body of, say, six feet. He is a part of the world and in turn all nature forms part of him and inclusive in his body mind complex and its awareness. That is why he is able to beaware of it, understand it and even manipulate it. There is a one-to-one correspondence between man the microcosm and the universe the macrocosm. Almost all the traditions of the world accept this equation, this eternal relationship between man and the cosmos.

And Vallalar extends this correspondence between the microcosm and macrocosm into four exact layers or levels: The body and the five senses in man correspond to the external nature and both are called 'the outermost'. Whatever happens to the one will affect the other in a similar manner. Recent disorders of the ecosystem of the world such as global warming, more number of earthquakes, unpredictable climate changes are all the results of human excess and greed, overexploitation and violence.

And one of the most significant events of man's greed and violent thought is the cause of war. We saw above how thoughts of love and compassion produce nectar in the body and thoughts other than love produce poison in the body. When this poison is produced in most of the human bodies in a region and gets accumulated to a critical mass, like the critical mass of accumulated atoms, acts likewise and release poison into the atmosphere. And we have wars.

As Teilhard de Chardin says and proves in his book, 'The Phenomenon of Man', there is a thought-sphere called 'Noosphere' above our atmosphere where the collective thoughts of all humans get accumulated each and every moment. And this process of our thoughts ascending to the atmosphere and noosphere is increasing nowadays a billionfold after the advent of telecommunication, satellite-information-sharing and the cell phone age. The cause and effect chain acts almost instantly.

When thoughts other than love and compassion are bombarded into the atmosphere and noosphere they are polluted to some extent. When violent thoughts are produced by the mass media and television and broadcast repeatedly all over the world, violent thought clouds are formed in the noosphere and they in turn affect the mind of man and nature, the end result producing wars, famine, economic depressions and all sorts of strife. And all sorts of natural disorders like volcanoes erupting suddenly, tsunamis and epidemics like aids are all results and consequences of such violent thought clouds created in the noosphere by man's preoccupation with violence and all sorts of perversions.

The only remedy for all such maleficent happenings is to sow the seeds of love and compassion, sympathy and harmony, in the minds of people, especially in the minds of children and young people whose thoughts are more peaceful and more powerful. This will help in producing peaceful minds in later generations resulting in peaceful atmosphere and reduced levels of stress in the lives of people though not totally stress-free conditions.

The fundamental notion of science is reason or thought; that of pure spirituality is compassion. And the basic idea upon which religion is apparently built is love, but its real foundational strength is faith or belief and organizational power. Both science and spirituality when organized large scale, may degenerate and deteriorate into power structure wielding instruments of authority and suppressing and oppressing freedom and love. Authority and love can never go together. And authority and freedom are always antagonistic to each other. Only compassion can bring to a halt all these confrontations and struggles between power and freedom in individuals as in institutions. But ego consciousness, the root of all power mongering and authority makes people forget this fundamental wisdom of life and causes all sorts of strife. To remedy this all pervasive power play and authoritative attitude, there is only one way: To spread the gospel of compassion, compassion as a way of life, to make it into a mass movement, to take the message of compassion to every nook and corner of the world, to every human born on the earth, and to found small groups of people who believe in this new gospel where prayer itself is to do compassionate service to the needy and the hungry.[39]

To fight institutional power and authority, another theory was advanced by some thinkers: Anarchy. This idea was tried by Socrates, Jesus, Buddha through Bakunin and Peter Kropotkin to J. krishnamurti and Noam Chomsky. This can cause some ripples in society and even make some waves, but the salt of the sea is too much or too large to be transformed into sugar. A large society needs organizations to regulate and govern it. The moment an organisation is born, authority and power are born with it. That was why Plato suggested Philosopher-kings to occupy the seats of power. But philosophy only strengthens one's reasoning faculty thereby boosting one's own ego on account of his superior knowledge. And philosophy is built on thought. Thought can never solve man's problems because thought itself is the cause of most of the problems. Going after thought is a never-ending process. It is like allopathic medicine that cures the disease but also creates deadly side effects. To remedy the side effects, one has to prescribe more drugs which in turn will create some other side effects and so on.

The world, history tells us, has tried all the methods and ideas and ideologies except the right one to solve its problems, the way of god himself, the way of compassion, the way of caring for the welfare of all, all beings, vegetative, animalistic and human. Only when humans work on the lines of god, only when they function like god, that is , in an all-compassionate way they can call themselves as children of god. This is pure spirituality beyond religions,affiliations and sectarianism. When Bertrand Russell the scientist, rationalist and anti religious propagandist says, 'one of the three ruling passions of my life is unbearable pity for the suffering of mankind', he was only preaching this gospel of compassion. In the west, today, we find many champions of compassion as a way of living such as Ramdas, Karen Armstrong who published her 'Charter of compassion'. Without the charter of compassion, the charter of human rights cannot take place. Long back, in the eighteenth century, Rousseau gave us a motto that called for 'Liberty, equality and fraternity'. Without the last the first two become meaningless. They can never realize themselves in actuality. The history of America proves the unsuccessful attempt at liberty without fraternity. The history of the decline and fall of the mighty Soviet empire proves the unsuccessful attempt at establishing equality of all humans without fraternity in heart of its people. Mere ideology based on thought, however powerfully indoctrinated into the minds of the people can never succeed without love in the system, without inculcating compassion for other beings. Unfortunately, fraternity or compassion cannot be enforced by law. People volunteer themselves for compassionate service. And every human being has such a soft corner in him or in her. It must be touched and activated. That it is possible on a large scale is evidenced in the birth and development of mass movements like Red Cross movement, Blue cross movement and Veganism. This tendency has to be tapped and extended far into every branch of life. All the so-called issues political and economic have failed only because they were not based on compassion which alone can save humankind and make it evolve further.

~~~ ~~~ ~~~

33. TRANSMUTATIONS IN THE FUTURE 'PURE BODY' OF HUMANS

We saw in the last chapter how every limb of the body will be transformed ultimately into an organ of compassion-matter or divine matter. Vallalar explains the process of this transformation in three major stages. He calls them as i) pure body, 2) sound body or pranava body and 3) light body of compassion or divine body. And he also gives us all the details of transmutations at every stage, the details of new anatomy and physiology of the evolved higher body.

First let us see what transmutations occurred in his own body when it was changed into a pure body as he describes it in the Agaval poem [from lines 1449 -1494]:

i) Skin becomes thinner tender soft subtle and mellow. [Astronauts experience the thinning of their skin while travelling in space. Vallalar's skin and soles became so subtle and thin, he used canvas shoes unlike the sanyasins who wear hard wooden chappals]

ii) Nervous system functions intermittently not allowing constant bombardment of stimuli from the external world. It functions only when love and compassion are taken in and given out. All the other times it takes rest.

iii)   Bones become soft, tender and pliable like those in a baby's body. They grow younger, they become denser but pliable like rubber. Stiffness hardness and osteoporosis of bones are overcome.

iv)   Muscles in the body also get softened and loose like those of a baby.

v)   All the blood in the body coagulates and congeals inside the blood vessels. There is no more need for the circulation of the blood. An alternative system of nectar supplies food and prana (air) to all the cells in the body. This is described in the following lines.

vi)   Semen condenses itself into a single crystal-like mass in the region of the forehead. (In another place in his oral teachings, he refers to this crystal as having six facets or six sides).

vii)   The brain [which is now like an unripe bud] blossoms fully and all its petals or parts blossom and stretch and grow fully. And it starts secreting its honey or real nectar or ambrosia or elixir of life. It flows all over the body and drenches it. Like a spring, the brain is producing the nectar and like a lake the whole body is always filled up with it. This elixir hereafter does the work of blood, running all over the body and supplying food and prana to all the cells. In another verse Vallalar refers to this blossoming of brain as golden flower with divine fragrance,[40] giving its honey.

viii) Forehead glows and becomes bright and is soaked with sweet sweat. (In his prose works, Vallalar points out that the salty perspiration of the impure physical body will be changed into sweet nectar in the pure body. He calls it 'the outermost nectar or ambrosia' springing in the human body).[41]

ix) Breath becomes cool and peaceful and silent. Its heat, agitation and violence are gone forever. (In another verse, he describes this cool breath as 'divine fragrant air blowing softly on the platform of the forehead').[42]

x) Smile appears even on the faces of the inner bodies. Bliss is felt from the innermost core of one's being and spreads from inside out.

xi) Hairs on the skin all over the body stand erect. [another meaning for this line is that hairs are burnt into sacred ash].

xii) Eyes produce rivers of blissful tears and they run down towards the legs.

xiii) The lips vibrate and the mouth lets out sounds of joy.

xiv) The harmonious music of the spheres is heard by the twin ears and also in the inner third ear.

xv) Body becomes cool all over.

xvi) Chest becomes soft and undulating and rocking with divine inner rhythm.

xvii)   Both the hands join together and always remain in the position of saluting the Lord.

xviii)   Both the legs revolve automatically as though in a dervish dance. [Another meaning for this line is that all the ten pranic airs circulate properly in the body including pari or the inner breath]

xix)   The unripe mind melts and ripens fully, into a fruit and gives out honey of its own kind, the outer nectar.

xx)   The bulb of the intellect is infused with the electricity of compassion. It grows white hot with wisdom and throws out brilliant light. Or the ever-changing intellect of the moon becomes full moon of wisdom and gives out bright light of superior intelligence.

xxi)   Thought that gets naturally shaped with its company is now in the company of God, gets transformed into bliss.

xxii)   The energizing part of I –consciousness is activating the parts of the body wherever and whenever it is necessary. The body is ruled properly by the natural instinct and not directed by egoistic consciousness.

xxiii)   The heart or pure intelligence, now that the doors of senses and mind are cleansed, wants to commune directly and harmoniously with the universe and enjoy life blissfully.

xxiv)   All the mental faculties inside and all that are seen outside become only forms of bliss.

xxv) All the five senses discard their parasite of the egoistic consciousness and become the channels of the spirit directly without the intervention of the artificial, fictitious mind.

xxvi) All the 36 tattwas or basic elements of reality are totally destroyed.

xxvii) Only the pure sattwa is retained.

xxviii) The world of illusion with all its attractions vanishes.

xxix) Only the longing for infinite compassion springs and overflows the heart.

xxx) Oh! my divine love! You have arisen in my heart and keep growing so that you could influence all souls into blossoming through me!

xxxi) Oh! my unique love! You have arisen in my heart and keeps growing so that I can see your golden feet and taste the ultimate ambrosia of compassion arising out of it!

xxxii) Oh! my unique beloved! Thou hast given thyself to me entirely and hast alchemically transmuted and transformed me into thy own stature by thy divine light of absolute compassion!

xxxiii) Oh! my unique beloved! You became a bud in me, then blossomed in me and enlarged your fragrance in me so that the process of transmutation would be complete!

xxxiv) Oh! my unique beloved! Thy divine flower transformed itself into a fruit, mellowed and matured and then fully ripened into a juicy one!

xxxv) Oh! my unique beloved! Thou, that hast completely enveloped me, body, soul and spirit hast blessed me with all the qualities and grades of perfection and self-sufficiency.

xxxvi) Oh! my unique beloved! Thou hast destroyed all the parts and faculties in my body that contributed to my sufferings and transformed them into a new creation of a body of bliss!

xxxvii) Oh! my unique beloved! Thou hast entered my heart and merged into it so that I could attain a golden body!

xxxviii) Oh! my unique beloved! Thy transcendent Self overflowed and entered me, transforming my limited self into an infinite one like yours, has now transcended me and passed beyond!

xxxix) Oh! my unique beloved! Thou, that hast always created unlimited food of ambrosia of compassion hast now started the eternal spring of it in me also!

In the above canto of his Agaval poem, Vallalar has told us all the anatomical and physiological changes that took place in his body and mind complex when it evolved and attained the state of pure body. As far as I know, no one either before or after Vallalar, has come out with such an exact, elaborate and scientific way all the details of transmutation in one's own body. Let the scientific community read all these, verify for themselves and then come to a conclusion as to its veracity. To close the issue without even considering it will not be an act of objective scientific one. They owe it to humanity.

~~~ ~~~ ~~~

34. TRANSMUTATIONS IN THE "PRANAVA BODY"

A silkworm knows by instinct how to be reborn as a beautiful butterfly that flies in a vast sky, which act it could not do in its past body of a worm. It could only crawl on earth very slowly like a snail. With its new body, its capacity to move faster and cover a larger area is multiplied more than a thousand times. But a human is not able to fly without the technological gift of an aeroplane. His instincts are forgotten though they lie deep in the unconscious.

Humans were originally designed to give birth to higher forms four times. Only the first birth is natural from the womb of a mother. All the other three must be created by his own efforts and knowledge. In the last chapter, we saw the process of the birth of a pure body. It must be transformed further into a Pranava Body and finally into a Gnostic- light Body. The last one cannot be attained by human efforts alone. It has to get the sanction of god also. One must earn the qualification of attaining 100% compassion, not even an iota of dislike or hatred towards any one or anything must be in one's self.

But the final fruit of human efforts is the boon of a Pranava Body. It is variously called by Vallalar as 'Omkara Body' 'space-body''sound body' 'mantra body' etc. It is the body of a god, a god higher than the trinity of the Saivite religion, namely Lord Subramania. Subramani literally means a gem of self-created Brahman or supreme godhead. He was known as commander-in-chief of gods who was created by Lord Siva with the sole purpose of destroying all the demonic, dark forces. He was all light. In fact according to the mythology, as it was described by the Sanskrit epic poet Kalidasa in his immortal epic 'Kumara Sambhava', Siva himself gave birth to Kumara or Subramania. "Su' means 'Swayambu' or self-created. Brahman means the ultimate godhead. Thus, in the description of the process of creation of Lord Subramania was given the process of a human transforming himself or herself into god. Kumara means eternally young. But unfortunately the scientific facts were hidden and veiled by signs, symbols and twilight language of mythology. And no one came forward to decode it and explain the process in simple scientific terms for two millennia until Vallalar appeared in the nineteenth century.

Another legend tells us that when Adi Sankara wanted to interpret 'Brahma Sutra' of Badarayana his guru advised him to read the portion on the creation of Kumara in 'Skanda Purana'. Sankara, it is reported, read it eighteen times so that he could understand and digest all the details thoroughly. Then only he started writing his own commentary on Brahmasutra. The significance and implication of this legend are that it is the supreme and ultimate secret of life: The process of transformation of a human into Brahman or godhead.

According to Kalidasa's epic and Skanda Purana the womb or place in which this process takes place is the 'Third Eye' of Siva, the region in the face of a human body in between and behind the eyebrows. In Chinese Taoist literature, this place is called as Saced square inch. This place is known in saivite literature as 'Chitrambalam' or 'Citakasa' or 'Chidambaram' meaning the divine sky or the dwelling of god. The ultimate education of immortality that is taught here by god to the initiates is known as 'The Education of Chitrambalam'.[43]

Vallalar was born in 'the century of progress', when science at last triumphed over religions and attained the supreme status as the only way to truth. I mean the nineteenth century. Vallalar was born on 5th October 1823. He got his physical body transformed into a body of light on 30.1.1874.

On 15-11-1872 Vallalar hoisted his SuddhaSanmargha flag in front of his dwelling place called 'Siddhivalagam'. It means the citadel of supernal powers. After unfurling the flag Swami delivered a speech usually called "The greater oration or the greater teaching".[44]In it he explained the structure of the flag and its meaning. He said: 'this is the age of sanmarga. As an indication it has hoisted its flag. What it means is this: In our body, there is a nadi, a subtle channel that runs from the belly button up to the centre of the brows. At its apex, it has a membrane. Its upper portion is yellow in colour, its lower portion is white. At the bottom of the membrane, there is a nerve that runs up and down. This flag can be experienced in our meditation'.

What does he mean by the above statement? The yellow colour denotes 'Paranada'. The white colour symbolizes"Parabindu". Nada means sound like thunder. 'Bindu' means 'light' like lightning. When both nada (A) and bindu (U) join together, a new genesis (M) takes place. This is the explanation and meaning of AUM or OM. A+U constitute O and M is the newborn baby or silent super consciousness, depending upon the event or place or thing or being. The whole cosmos is made up of A and U and various permutations and combinations of their union. Man or woman is no exception. Even god is no exception.

Now, coming back to our point, bindu in man means 'semen' the reproductive secretion in the lower muladhara. When it joins the nada or sronitham or reproductive secretion in woman and combines and merges with its egg, conception takes place in the womb of a woman in her abdomen. The result is seen in the form of a human child after ten months.

But a similar process takes place in the body of a yogi or Siddha, in the forehead region of his face, in the third eye region of Chitrambalam to be exact. Even a man can give birth to such a divine child like 'Kumara' as Siva gave birth to. In fact every man and woman is entitled to do so. It is their birth right as a human. But we are not aware of this potentiality. The fact was shrouded in mythology.

The semen or bindu is white in colour and in liquid form. It has to be boiled and heated up to 100^0C so that the liquid is converted into a vapour and sent up or sublimated through the subtle channel to the third eye region where it is stored up. When it is accumulated to a critical mass this 'para bindu' or transcendental or divine white light is absorbed into Paranada or divine sound or vibration of god. This is denoted by the yellow colour meaning the golden body of Nataraja. When white and yellow are mixed together, the result is the red colour. That was why Kumara or Subramania was given the colour red and called 'Sevvel' meaning 'the Red Lord'. Now the new divine body of light in red colour is born in the upper womb of the agna chakra or forehead. This fact in the mythology, was denoted by the statement that Kumara was born in the third eye of Lord Siva. In fact every jiva is a potential Siva. Only we have to qualify ourselves by replacing our ego centered consciousness with a totally compassionate absolute consciousness like that of a Siva. Some two thousand years ago, the great yogi Thirumular declared in his encyclopaedic work on yoga called 'Thirumantram' that 'Jiva and Siva are not two. Jiva is Siva. Jiva is not aware of Siva. When jiva is aware of Siva as Love complete, jiva will become Siva'.

So, every human has the potential to give birth to a 'Pranava Body' like that of Kumara. It can travel all over the universe in no time. It can destroy all darkness and dark and evil forces. It can live for eons and eons. It is almost omniscient and omnipotent. It will have all the five supernal powers of god such as creation of worlds and beings, sustaining them, destruction or transformation, veiling and grace. One literally becomes a superior god and attains almost all the supernal powers or siddhis of a god. It is the penultimate position, next only to the highest godhead that has a wisdom-light body or a body of light of compassion which is all pervading and ever growing, indestructible and eternal.

This is the process of a human transforming himself/herself into Brahman or god by one's own effort. The coded message of ancient mythology was decoded by the all compassionate Vallalar and given to us in scientific biological terms.

The heat to be generated for transforming the liquid form of semen or sronitham into a vapourous state is attained by prayer, tapas or austerity, yoga, meditation but mainly by compassionate way of living. But chastity or continence called 'Brahmacharya' is a must. The Sanskrit word 'Brahmacharya' means protecting and saving Brahman.Here Brahman is equated with semen. For semen only becomes a human and human only can evolve into Brahman.

Only in a human body this possibility is realized. Not in any other body is it possible. Hence the utmost importance given to the human body by Thirumular and Vallalar.

Thirumular emphasized the significance of the body in unambiguous terms:

"If the body dies the life-spirit dies."

Enlightenment of consciousness will not take place.

I learnt the technique of immortality of the body

I developed my body, I developed my life-spirit

– Thirumantram.

If the milk is spilled and wasted one cannot obtain curd. Only when the curd is churned, one gets butter. Only when the butter is clarified one gets ghee. The milk can last without getting corrupted only for one or two days. It can be turned into curd. The curd is turned into butter which can last for even six months or one year. But ghee can last for even a few years. In the same way, this impure body can last for a hundred years or so. When it is transformed into a pure body its life span increases to 4,32,000 years. When it is again transformed into a pranava body, its duration extends to eons and eons. Finally, when it is transmuted into a body of light of compassion, it can last forever. But the basis, the raw material that can be cooked into finer and finer materials is the impure, physical body. To forget this basic fact would be a fatal mistake. But that was what our ancestors did.

We saw that the practice of continence of sexual energy or brahmacharya was very essential for all these transformations. But how long one is to keep it up? For the house-holders who aim to continue to live in future, after their death, in the form of their children, Vallalar gives a license: The couple can enjoy their sexual congress once in 16 days.[45] Even otherwise the semen will overflow by itself through urine or motion or by nocturnal emissions. But he is very strict in the case of initiates or sadhaks who are really interested in immortality. Not even a single drop of semen should be wasted, he asserts.

But how to do it? It can be done in two ways. i) By not having sexual thoughts. For thought is the spring that turns physical energy into libido. Rather one is always expected to think of one's ideal or on god. ii) By practicing an advanced technique of Kriya yoga called Vasi Yoga by Vallalar. He explains it. The couple during sexual union should neither breathe out or retain their breath inside. The breathing should take place inside one's body itself.[46]

One more advice he gives to the initiates. Reduce your sleep and conquer your sloth. For they are forces and agents of darkness. They are obstacles on the path of the yogi who practices the habit of sublimating and sending up one's semen.[47] When he mentions semen, he also means the sexual energy of the woman (sronithum).

If one keeps up the practice of brahmacharya for 12 years all the cells in one's brain will start functioning one hundred percent. For a normal person only 5% of his brain cells function. For a genius like Einstein, scientists say, 15% of his brain cells are active.

If one can extend the period to twenty four years one can attain the position and pranava body of Rudra.

If one is capable of prolonging it to 48 years one's body will have the effulgence of a 'sun'.[48]

If one has 100% of compassion in his being, mind and body and practices brahmacharya for 48 years, god will appear before him and confer upon him the title of god and bless him with a wisdom body of light of total compassion as He did in the unique case of Vallalar.

Vallalar describes the qualities and characteristics of the Pranava body. They are as follows: Its form is effectual-causal, meant for action. It will have transcendental, spiritual body, transcendental feeling, transcendental knowledge and transcendental and spiritual elements. Its carat value will be from 16 to 108. Its age will be 5 to 8. It will be visible but one cannot touch it. It can do all siddhis. It is omni potent. Its lifetime is prana kalpa or kalpas of gods, thatis, eons and eons. It is both immanent and transcendental. It will have a sound body, a vibrational body.

~~~ ~~~ ~~~

35. THE ULTIMATE BODY OF GOD: THE BODY OF LIGHT OF ABSOLUTE COMPASSION

This is the end product of evolution. At last, the evolutionary force has realized its ideal, its final task is finished through the agent of humans. It gave them a new direction for development, to take their attention inside. They attained self consciousness. They developed it further and attained objective consciousness, shorn of egoistic, subjective and relative aspects of their consciousness. Whereas the subjective, egoistic consciousness was short lived, ever changing, full of doubts and illusions, hallucinations and delusions, the objective consciousness was lasting, steady, unchanging, clear, stable, penetrating to the core of things and beings, had direct contact with the essences of them and received from them revelations of their truths and real substances. Every scientific discovery, in this sense was a product of real, objective knowledge. But even this objective knowledge was discovered by humans like Sir Isaac Newton and Albert Einstein. Hence their limitations. Their theories were partially true and partially false. The ideas of absolute space and absolute time were revised by Einstein. He proved that both time and apace were relative. He also showed they were not two but one and called it 'space time'. In turn some of the ideas of

Einstein were refuted by the discoverers of quantum physics.

But we cannot deny the fact that these scientists had cosmic knowledge at the human level. In fact they had true cosmic knowledge and proved they had it by revealing to the world what they had acquired by it. As a consequence say, for instance, of Einstein's formula of $E=mc^2$, atomic energy was made possible.

These scientists had better cosmic knowledge than some philosophers and religious leaders who claimed they possessed it. They talked in vague, ambiguous terms which could not be translated into action nor into technological gadgets that could help humanity and alleviate its sufferings.

The cosmic consciousness possessed by these scientists were not permanent states of consciousness like the fourth state of consciousness called 'Turiya' by the seer of Mandukya Upanishad. They had only glimpses of it and during those intense moments they received flashes of intuitions and revelations of truth about the laws of nature. Around these flashes of visions, they afterwards fabricated whole systems with the power of their intellects. And this is where errors crept in. For intellect can never fathom the true reality, it is an inadequate instrument.

Vallalar, being a scientist- seer went beyond Turiya state at the human level. He mentions and describes four states and levels of Turiya namely i) turiya at the human level, ii) para turiya or transcendental one, iii) guru turiya or Siva turiya [of Gods of religion] and iv) Pure Siva turiyadita or Suddha Siva turiyadita which is the ultimate state of absolute consciousness possible. Vallalar attained this final state by the grace of the supreme godhead ArutPerum Jothi, he claims in his scripture ThiruArutpa.

A true scientist Vallalar describes his vision of cosmos and gives us its details. For instance, he says there is not one space, but infinite number of spaces and realities. But he enumerates the major divisions among them and describes their levels, locations, properties etc., Starting from our space which he called 'elemental space' he gives out a list of twelve spaces, inside one another:

Particulars	Terms used by the saint
Elemental space	Paguthiveli
Subtle space	Boothaveli
Life [vital] space	Uyirveli
Art [refined] space	Kalaiveli
Pure space	Suddhaveli
Supernal [divine] space	Para veli
Transcendent space	Parampara veli
Divinizing space	Paraparaveli
Middle space	Nadu veli
Self-divine space	Tarparaveli
Grand space	Peru veli
Grand blissful space	Perumsugaveli

Modern science deals only with the first type of space called elemental space where space and time are mixed up with one another. According to Vallalar time has a beginning, it can also be ended. But space is endless. It can exist without time. In fact, it existed long before time arrived on the scene. The ultimate space Perum Suga Veli itself is the penultimate, formless state of god. Inside this space shines the effulgence or causal light of Infinite Compassion [ArutPerumJothi].[49]

The first five levels of space, according to the experience narrated by Vallalar in his book ThiruArutpa can be experienced by the human consciousness in deep meditation.

The sixth level of space can be seen and felt by an enlightened master who has already had her/ his self realisation.

The next four types of spaces can be seen and experienced by higher beings like angels and gods. [arulanubavam-experience of grace].

Tarparaveli and peruveli belong to the divinity [siva experience].

The ultimate space 'Perumsugaveli' can be seen and experienced only by one who is all compassion, who does not see any difference or discrimination between one being and another, even between a dog and god.

Inside and beyond this space is shining Lord ArutPerum Jothi, the uncaused, causal light of infinite compassion or grace.

To see it, enjoy it, merge with it and become it is the aim and purpose of human life. When it is attained, the ocean of suffering is crossed over once for all. One becomes divine. One is divinized by god with all of his/ her/ its attributes and powers.

How to see it? By sharpening one's perception or awareness. What is the sharpener? Compassion only. No other means like yoga, meditation, austerity etc, can refine your consciousness to such a refined and rarified level. It is the smallest of the small space. [Irai, it is called]. It is more than a billion billion times smaller than a nano particle. But it is possible for all humans to see it. The very fact that Vallalar has seen it and describes it proves it.

II

In the XI chapter of the Bhagawat Gita, the epic poet of India Vyasa shows us vividly and graphically with the power of a master poet the cosmic body of Krishna [viswarupa], the universal form of the Lord with all things and beings in all the worlds such as erupting volcanoes, large mountains, oceans, wars, all beautiful, ugly and violent scenarios found in the universe. The disciple – friend of Krishna, Arjuna gets terrified of this universal form and requests his mentor to appear once again in the form of a human whom he knew as a good friend.

According to the historian of Indian philosophy Dr S Radhakrishnan, Krishna was the chieftain of a small state in North India. Later the image was groomed and developed into an incarnation of god Vishnu by Vyasa. Vishnu himself was one among the twenty eight gods of the Rig veda. The chief of them was Lord Indra who was later debunked and belittled by Krishna in the Bhagvad Purana and in another epic Ramayana he is portrayed as a womanizer and cursed for it in the story of Ahalya.

The point is the potential of every human's body that is at once published and hidden in this myth of cosmic form of Krishna. Krishna born as a human developed his power and fully realized his potential and attained the level and stature of godhead. He is shown in the Gita as a role model for all humans to imitate and follow. But how to do it? The answer given in the text of Gita is by expanding one's consciousness to the cosmic level. When one's consciousness develops into a cosmic one, its twin the cosmic body will be naturally produced.

But there is an error in the very first chapter of the book. It tells us that death is an inevitable fact. When Sri Aurobindo's mind evolved beyond Vedanta, he accepted the siddha's stance of personal immortality and expressed in his classic, The Life Divine, that conquest of physical death was possible and the very aim of his integral yoga was to attain an immortal, divine body with which one could lead an everlasting divine life. Earlier during his adherence to Vedanta, he had written an elaborate commentary on the Gita in his 'Essays on the Gita', some 2000 pages.

One disciple questioned him: once you accepted the fact of death as it was portrayed by the author of the Gita. Now you say, it is not inevitable and can be overcome. Are you not contradicting yourself? Sri Aurobindo replied that the God who sent Krishna some thousands of years ago with the message needed by humankind at that time, also sent him (me) now with the message humanity needs now, in the days of evolutionary science.

Whereas the religionists and traditionalists want to maintain that immortality and divinity were the privileges of some or one religious leader, Sri Aurobindo and some fifty years before him Vallalar, living in the age of democracy and evolutionary biology wanted to extend the teaching of Vedanta and include in it the message of evolution, and democratized the notions of immortality and divinity for each and every human. The birth right is there, they pointed out, but to make use of it and enjoy the fruits of it demanded utmost effort and knowledge and compassion on the part of the individuals who wanted to attain them, they pointed out.

The anaha body mentioned and described by Vallalar goes beyond the cosmic body of the Gita. According to modified advaita or visishtatadvaita of Ramanuja, God is also like a human an infinitely vaster one with a soul and body, the body being the universe and all beings in it and his soul the universal consciousness. Abiding by this tenet of the cult of vainavism the text of the Gita describes the cosmic body of Krishna.

But there is a difference between the anaha body of Vallalar and the cosmic body of the Gita. In the omkara body or pranava body itself the physical body of a human is completely transformed into a spiritual one. But it is a limited one though very large with divine powers. But in the transmutation of it into an anaha body the spiritual body is divinized and transformed into a body of light of infinite compassion,[50] the ultimate energy-wisdom-power.

This wisdom light body is the background of the universe, the sea of energy of light of compassion in which bubbles of worlds and beings arise, exist for a short time and disappear. Only some bubbles of beings attain the knowledge of the ocean consciousness of which they are parts. This state was known as the cosmic consciousness which was supposed to be the ultimate attainment possible for any human by all religions and philosophies of the world. Vallalar adds one more truth to it. He affirms that this bubble could also develop itself into a vast, separate ocean, by the grace of god, like a benevolent father allowing with pleasure for his favourite son to open a new branch of his business.

Here a question is raised by some religionists: How the world can have more than one god? This is a silly question arising out of a stupid mind with an egoistic and relative consciousness. When one erases out the ego centered consciousness and replaces it with the absolute consciousness it is a collective consciousness having no meaning of separate numbers. A human body consists of various organs. Each organ like eye or brain has a separate function and its cells function accordingly. But they all function harmoniously as a single person. If a hundred trillion cells could function with a single purpose like an orchestra with an egoistic consciousness, why not at the divine level with the absolute consciousness?

Also when this final body of wisdom light is attained, one becomes divine with the five powers of creation, preservation, destruction, veiling and grace. One can manifest oneself in any one of the three forms of Suddha, Pranava and Wisdom light bodies[51] and in any other form.

Vallalar mentions some unique characteristics of this final wisdom light body: it has the uncaused causal form [and formlessness at once, a property of all compassion].[52] It is both immanent and transcendent. It pervades everything everywhere. It is behind the activity of every subatomic particle and beyond the super strings. It has both the relativistic knowledge about nature and also the transcendental knowledge since it created nature and maintains it. It is both visible and invisible. If it wants to appear before one, it will reveal itself. It is omnipotent. It has absolute freedom. It is eternal and beyond time. For it creates time and eternity. [pp 442 Prose works of Vallalar].

In another verse, Vallalar says our form is the form of Satchitananda.[53] Sat means truth as well as eternal existence. Chit means divine knowledge as well as its force. Ananda means eternal unchanging bliss. So our form is not human, it is only transitional. Our original form is a divine one of satchitananda. This Sanskrit term is translated into Tamil by Vallalar as 'one who naturally exists forever as truth; one who naturally involutes into the universe and all beings and all things in it; and one who is always blissful'. When he says our form he doesn't mean only his form, but that of all humans and other beings as well. He always talks about all beings having all knowledge, all power, all existence, all types of bliss. That is according to him the way of god, and the way of compassion. Compassion is there within all beings even in animals and plants. Only it has to be brought out fully, made into a way of living and manifested in all one's actions and behavior. It is the easiest and most accessible form of yoga. But it is the supreme yoga that can give one not only enlightenment but immortality and divinity. Vallalar was the first saint who divulged to humankind all these secret dimensions and higher science of the yoga of compassion.

Vallalar had an ability and capacity to see deep into any concept, weigh its strong points and shortcomings, and rectify the defects and bring it to completion. As usual, he takes up the idea and experiences it and then adds to it what is lacking in it: compassion. Gnana or knowledge or wisdom is not enough. For the survival and evolution of the individual and the species something more is needed: Compassion. History of humankind proves it. So he modifies the concept of Satchitananda and compliments it with compassion. For compassion is the indestructible matter and force or field. Hence his golden saying: The indestructible form is the unique form of compassion.[54]

So god is defined by Vallalar not only as Satchitananda but as an embodiment of light of infinite compassion. The mahamantra he gave to the world means: Light of infinite compassion! Light of infinite compassion! Oh Vast unique grace! Light of infinite compassion!. 'Praise be unto you! The uniqueness of god of Arul Perum Jothi is His unique boon on humanity on all of his children of equality with him, and the illimitable and unlimited undying divine life through universal soul-love.'

An illustration could throw some light on this important point of difference between mere acquirement of gnosis and compassionate gnosis. Dr. R.M.Bucke in his classic book on 'cosmic consciousness' provided us with his own choice of a long list of cosmic souls in history. From among them, he singles out one person as a unique specimen of cosmic consciousness not only having it but expressing it in his words and deeds also: Walt Whitman.

Whitman was a great American poet who expressed incomparable things incomparably, in the words of his mentor Ralph Waldo Emerson. Emerson was a great transcendental philosopher, a poet, who provided a great gospel to his century and the world. Whitman was a follower of Emerson and made great poetry out of the ideas of Emerson especially his ideas of freedom and democracy and the infinity of the finite individual.

Emerson aimed at gnosis and stopped there. He did not participate in any movement of reformation like the anti-slavery movement that took place before his eyes. It was not his task, he wrote in his famous journal. But Whitman not only wrote about equality among all things but practiced it in his everyday life. During the American civil war, he nursed the wounded soldiers regularly and they waited for his arrival and genuine company, report his biographers. Dr.Bucke was right in choosing Walt as a cosmic person. Both had understood the idea of cosmic consciousness not only at the level of knowledge but at the being level also.

Vallalar was a world class poet like Walt Whitman but at a far higher level. He has written more than 7000 poems including thousands of melodious and mellifluous devotional songs. Like Emerson, he was also a philosopherand a much greater one, to be compared with the first order philosophic minds of the world such as Plato, Aristotle, Kant, Sankara etc. And he was also a great scientist a great reformer and many things. In addition to all these he was one of the most compassionate beings the world ever saw. He could not see the sufferings of any being, not only human, but a plant or animal. When a plant withered for want of water, he suffered along with it.[55]When people got afflicted with diseases it affected him deeply. Especially the poverty and hunger of the people around him hurt him to his core. He prayed to god to bless him with powers with which he could eradicate their poverty and pacify their hunger. In 1867, he started the 'Sathya Dharmasala', a sanctuary for the service of people. The fire he ignited then in that kitchen is still kept up for some 140 years. Millions of poor people were fed there. Now thousands of such dharmasalas with kitchens have mushroomed all over the world in many countries.

He equates gnosis with compassion in his Bible of a book called 'Discipline of Compassion'.

~~~ ~~~ ~~~

36. CONCLUSION

From the dawn of civilization humans aspired toward an undying state of immortality. Almost all the fairy tales and mythologies and religious scriptures of the world, without exception, have dealt with this subject; of course not deeply and entirely or scientifically but as curiosity, as one among a hundred subjects in a vague way, in twilight language or through symbols or stories of immortal gods – not man becoming immortal but being subjugated and helped by them – or by the description of god as eternal, immortal, omniscient and omnipotent and so on. The condition of immortality was conceived by some ancient writers such as the Thrice Great Hermes, the alchemists all over the world, the Siddhas of India and China and the grand epics of India, Ramayana and Mahabaratha in which seven immortals like Anjaneya and Markandeya are portrayed. Tibetian Buddhism talks about 80 immortals, Chinese Taoism about 8 immortals, the Siddhas of South India about 18 immortals. These systems maintained that such a state of immortality was a possibility for select adepts or yogis, alchemists or seers and not for all people as a collective mutation and transformation of the entire species of homo sapiens. Again most of these schools of philosophy and yoga and religion wanted for man only enlightenment of consciousness into absolute consciousness and rejected the possibility of transformation of the physical body with new limbs and faculties.

Only a few schools of thought acknowledged and accepted the notion of the conquest of physical death like Christ and Sri Aurobindo. But they too were not made available for all. The organized religion of Christianity declared that it was possible only for Christ being the only begotten son of god, to rise from the death and reappear on earth with Resurrected Body. This possibility was denied for all, including his followers. But all Christians who had faith in Christ will rise up bodily after death in the future kingdom of god which is supposed to be located beyond the skies.

Sri Aurobindo in his classic, 'The Life Divine' advocates for all humans a divine life upon earth with a divine body free from disease, old age and death. His method of realizing it was a yogic way called the integral yoga. He argues in it for a different, higher form of yoga by which the highest form of absolute consciousness called supramental consciousness of god must be brought down to the earth- atmosphere so that the inorganic matter and along with it the physical matter in the body will be transformed. He puts emphasis on the point that only higher forms of consciousness can bring about their twins or counterparts in physical forms. But here a question arises. So far in history, all the great saints, seers and prophets who had seen and experienced god directly and received higher forms of consciousness and wisdom and gave out revelations or the very word of god to humankind all passed away, all died physically, including Sri Aurobindo and his disciple- collaborator the mother. The mother struggled for three more decades after the demise of Sri Aurobindo to attain an immortal body with her own new brand and unique discovery of the cellular yoga. Finally she also succumbed to the ravages of old age and death. At the end of her life, she is reported to have said that the first superman will be born some three centuries from now, according to Georg Von Wreckem, her biographer.

With all my respect and reverence to these Masters of humankind, I humbly present my suggestion, after five decades of seeking after truth, enlightenment and immortality, that the way of compassion shown by Vallalar some fifty years before Sri Aurobindo is an all encompassing and comprehensive system, a complete one starting with the science of food, going through four higher forms of Turiya consciousness and ending with total compassion for all beings is a more reliable, realistic and scientific one than all the systems humankind have so far witnessed. If the scientists of the world give it a chance and look at the scientific facts and processes, they will feel satisfied of its efficacy. I think, it is the best of all possible solutions for all the ills of the human flesh it is heir to. The infinite potentialities of the human body can be realized only then. For body and mind are always interacting with each other. The change in one can cause change in the other. Vallalar asks us to work, at once on five levels of body, mind, psyche, spirit and the overspirit, in the terminology of the American sage Ralph Waldo Emerson.

Only politics though spiritual can deter us from combining all these systems which do not reject or contradict but complement each other. Vallalar himself confesses that he synthesized hiseclectic system and called it 'ShadanthaSuddhaSathiaSanmarga' meaning the combined essence of the six systems of Vedanta, siddhanta, yoganta, bodanta, nadanta and kalanta. He absorbed only the gist and essence of these systems and discarded the chaff or waste material of them. Finally he added his own system of compassion to them and remodeled the entire new system in a scientific way in scientific terminology to suit our scientific age. His final revelation or gospel of 'ArutPerum Jothi Agaval' poem of 1596 lines contains only science. Not even a single reference concerning any fable or myth is mentioned in it. It is all pure science and technology.

The ancient Chinese writer Li Pong divided the writers of the world into two classes: 1. The advocates of immortality who wanted to conquer the plague of death upon earth, and live forever, and 2. The apologists for death. This division holds true even to the present time. Some scientists like the British biologist Aubrey de Gray is waging a literal war of words against the apologists. Some technocrat scientists like Dr Ray Kurzweil openly and boldly declare that in the near future, say in 2045, science will have found and discovered the technology, ordinary and nano and gadgets and medicine and methods of genetic engineering and robotics to fight cancer, aids and all other degenerative and the so-called incurable diseases, old age and even death. Cutting edge scientists like Michio Kaku are writing books on the possibility of physical immortality and popularizing such theories and technical advances made in these directions. Popular science journalists like Jonathan Weiner are collecting all the latest scientific information on this subject and write books that advocate immortality such as 'Long for this world'. Whole new branches of science dealing with this subject have arisen of late with various names such as 'anti-aging medicine, regenerative medicine, gerontology' etc. The long tradition of human aspiration for biological immortality is still continuing. It runs like an unbroken chain throughout human history. But the needed breakthrough has occurred only now in the twenty first century.

Unfortunately, all these western branches of new sciences and their advocates are speculating on a new kind of human body, half-human and half-robotic like cyborgs or like the filmy versions of terminators. And they also raise apprehensions about war between humans and robots. Many Hollywood films and science fiction novels and short stories are produced dealing with this subject.

When the teachings of Vallalar reach the world all these fears and speculations will vanish. For the scientist saint shows a way out from such tangles transforming the natural human body without the aids or artificial limbs or computers.

All of his prophesies have come true. For example, he announced the spiritual globalization of humanity in the 1850s, some hundred and forty years before the western elites ushered in the economic globalization in the 1990s.[56]

He also prophesized in the same decade that a new species was being born. And the new species will be a Man-god species. Its first child was Vallalar. He was told this prophesy by god and was appointed by him to oversee this new phase in evolution.[57] With the advent of Vallalar a new species higher than homo sapiens has already appeared on earth. It is going on now, in our midst. That the human lifespan has increased to about eighty years and in the United States according to a statistics the fast growing population is of those centenarians, 'robust oldies' who live healthily after hundred years are some of the symptoms and indications of this trend. Sir Julian Huxley the famous biologist declared in the 1960s that a new species which he termed as neo humanism was already here. And the new trends in biologylike intense interest in gerontology, biological immortality, geriatrics are true signs of what is going to happen in future.

Not only in evolution, but in all other walks of human life such as economics and politics, religion and sociology, compassionate way of living only is the solution, for all of their problems. 'Globalization with a heart', sustainable technology, eco-friendly environmentalism, vegetarianism, veganism, blue cross society, a lot of NGOs springing all over the world like mushrooms are certain forms of the rule of compassion. Erratic weather conditions and radical religious terrorism are the topmost priority of the problems confronting humanity, report the journals and newspapers of the world. They arise out of lack of compassion. Greed for one's own welfare and luxurious living and exclusive devotion and extreme piety to one's own god and church make people antagonistic to others and nature. This truth must be made to understand by all humans and the compassionate way of living stressed both for individuals and nations. This is going to be realized soon. All sorts of violence will come to an end. Unless this happens homo sapiens as a species cannot survive let alone evolve into a higher species. But humans cannot stop the march of the 'Zeitgeist' or the evolutionary force. Heaven on earth or the Garden of Eden or the kingdom of god might not have been in the past as the mythologies of the world conceived but at some time in the future created by science proper and vallalar's science of compassion. This is a scientific fact that is going to happen without doubt.

NOTES

1. மண்மனம் எங்குண்டோ வாசி அங்குண்டு வாசி
எங்குண்டோ மண்மனம் அங்குண்டு – சித்தர்பாடல்
2. சிற்றம்பலக் கல்வி
3. ஜீவகாருண்யமே மோட்சவீட்டின் திறவுகோல்
4. அருள் உறின் துரும்பும் ஓர் ஐந்தொழில் புரியும்
5. எனைத்தும் துன்பிலா இயல் எனக்கு அளித்தனை
6. சுத்த, பிரணவ, ஞான ஒளி தேகங்கள் see chapters 33,34, 35
7. சுக்கிலம் உரத்திடை பந்தித்து ஒரு திரள் ஆயிட...
(அகவல்)
8. புருவமத்தியில் 6 பட்டைவடிவத்தில் ஒரு படிமம் உண்டு...
உபதேசம்
9. ஆலம் அமுதாக்கும் அண்ணல் (அருள்பெரும் ஜோதி)
10. நான் இருபொழுது உண்டது யாவும் அமுதம் ஆனது.
11. கல்பதேகி
12. தியான மயமானால் புசிப்பு மாறும்.
13. வியர்வை புறப்புற அமுதம்
14. காற்றைப் பிடிக்கும் கணக்கை அறிவார்க்கு
கூற்றை உதைக்கும் குறியதுவாமே – திருமந்திரம்
15. குறிப்பறிதல்
16. அண்ட கோடி அனைத்தும் காணும் கண்கள் எய்தியே
அறிந்தேன் அங்கைக் கனிபோல் அவற்றில் உள்ள
செய்தியே பிண்ட கோடி முழுதும் காணப் பெற்று
நின்னையே பேசிப் பேசி வியக்கின்றேன்
இப் பிறவி தன்னையே
17. see chapters 33,34, 35
18. அருட்பெரும் ஜோதி ஆயினை நீ (அகவல்)
19. நான் இருபொழுது உண்டது அமுதமானது
20. மரணப் பெரும்பிணி வாரா வகை மிகு
கரணப் பெருந்திரள் காட்டிய மருந்தே.
21. பேருபதேசம்
22. ஞான சரியை. பாடல் 25

23. see'selected sayings of the Buddha'. Oxford world's classics.
24. அன்பெனும் உயிர் ஒளிர் அறிவே.
25. ஓதாது உணர்தல்
26. மெய் உணர்தல்
27. ஜீவ காருண்ய ஒழுக்கம்
28. திருவடி நிலை – ஆறாம் திருமுறை
29. உரைநடைப் பகுதி –அணுக்கள் – சிறிதினும் சிறிது 'இறை'
30. 'அன்பெனும் அணுவுள் அமைந்த பேரொளியே'
31. அருளறியார் தம்மை அறியார் எம்மையும்
பொருளறியார் என்ற சிவமே–அகவல்
32. குறுகப் பயந்து கூற்றும் குலைந்து ஓடிற்றே
33. புறப்புறம்
34. சச்சிதானந்த வடிவம் நம் வடிவம்
35. தானாகி, நானாகி, சகலமுமாகி
36. அன்பே சிவம் ஆவது – திருமந்திரம்
37. திரைந்து உளுத்த என் உடம்பும் மீண்டும்
செழும்பொன் உடம்பாய்த் திகழ்ந்ததே
38. திரைந்து திரைந்து உளுத்தவரும்
மீண்டும் இளமை அடைந்திடலாம்
39. அறிவு விளங்கிய ஜீவர்களுக்கு எல்லாம்
ஜீவகாருண்யமே வழிபாடு
40 மடல் எலாம் மூளைமலர்ந்திட அமுதம்
உடல் எலாம் ஊற்றெடுத்து ஓடி நிரம்பிட (அகவல்)
விரைசேர் பொன் மலரே அதில்
மேவிய செந்தேனே
41. வியர்வை புறப்புற அமுதம்
42. மேடையில் வீசிய மெல்லிய பூங்காற்றே
43. சிற்றம்பலக் கல்வி
44. பேருபதேசம்
45. ஆகாரம் ½, மைதுனம் 1/16, உறக்கம்1/8, பயம் 0 –
உபதேசப் பகுதி
46. சுவாசத்தை வெளியே விடக்கூடாது, உள்ளேயும்
நிறுத்தக் கூடாது.
உள்ளேயே நிகழ வேண்டும் – உபதேசப்பகுதி

47. சுக்கிலத்தை மேலேற்றும் பழக்கத்திற்கு தூக்கமும்
சோம்பலும் தடைகள்

48. தினகரன் போன்ற தேகம் வேண்டும் என்றேன்
விரைந்தளித்தான் எனக்கே.

49. அருட்பெரு வெளியில் ஓங்கும் ஜோதியே

50. ஞான ஒளி தேகம். அருள் பெரும் ஜோதி தேகம்

51. முத்திறல் வடிவம்

52. உருவமும் அருவமும் உபயமும் ஆகி அருள் நிலை
தெரித்த....

53. சச்சிதானந்த வடிவம் நம் வடிவம்

54. அழியா வடிவு அதுவே அருள் வடிவு

55. வாடிய பயிரைக் கண்டபோதெல்லாம் வாடினேன்

56. உலகத் திரளெலாம் மருவிக் கலந்து
வாழ்வதற்கென்றே வாய்த்த தருணம் இதுவென்றே
வாயெ பறையாய் அறைகின்றேன் எந்தாய் கருணை
வலத்தாலே

57. கொலை புரிவார் தவிர மற்ற அனைவரும் நின் குலத்து
மக்களே

நீ என் குலத்து முதல் மகனே. –அருள் விளக்க மாலை

432

Made in the USA
Columbia, SC
08 February 2022